Globalization and Fragmentation

Globalization and Fragmentation

INTERNATIONAL RELATIONS IN
THE TWENTIETH CENTURY

Ian Clark

Oxford University Press

Oxford University Press, Great Clarendon Street, Oxford OX2 6DP

Oxford   New York

Athens Auckland Bangkok Bogotá Buenos Aires Calcutta
Cape Town Chennai Dar es Salaam Delhi Florence Hong Kong Istanbul
Karachi Kuala Lumpur Madrid Melbourne Mexico City Mumbai
Nairobi Paris São Paulo Singapore Taipei Tokyo Toronto Warsaw

and associated companies in
Berlin Ibadan

Oxford is registered trade mark of Oxford University Press

British Library Cataloguing in Publication Data

Data available

Library of Congress Cataloging in Publication Data

Data available

ISBN 0-19-878165-2
ISBN 0-19-878166-0 (Pbk)

Printed in Great Britain
on acid-free paper by
Biddles Ltd, www.biddles.co.uk

This book is dedicated to

Llanarmon Dyffryn Ceiriog

*the non-global village that provided the distance
and idyllic setting which made its writing possible*

CONTENTS

DETAILED CONTENTS

INTRODUCTION

How will the international history of the twentieth century be regarded by future historians? It was certainly an age of stark contrast, and possibly of paradox. It is not surprising that it should have been depicted as an 'age of extremes' (Hobsbawm 1994).

But how will the twentieth century be *remembered*? As soon as the question is posed, the contradictions spill out. It was an age of unprecedented violence, of threatened annihilation, and yet, for part of the time, of very substantial peace and stability in some areas of the world. It was an age that did more than any other to advance the philosophical claims to human rights in an international context, but it also witnessed the most flagrant violations of them in practice. The century saw the creation of hitherto unattainable wealth but ever wider gaps in its distribution. Above all, the century was characterized by the greater interconnectedness of events on a global basis, while simultaneously being subject to political processes of rupture and disintegration: it has been an age of globalization *and* of fragmentation.

Globalization and Fragmentation

Each of these terms refers to diverse processes embracing political, social, economic, technological, and cultural change. They encapsulate the scope of the uniformity of political ideas and practices; the geographical extent of social interaction and reflexivity; the degree of integration of economic activities; the diffusion of technologies (information, communications, transport) which overcome the significance of space; and the extent of the dissemination of cultural symbols and significations. Given this diversity, no simple and straightforward definition can be offered of either. Globalization, however, denotes movements in both the *intensity* and the *extent* of international interactions: in the former sense, globalization overlaps to some degree with related ideas of integration, interdependence, multilateralism, openness, and interpenetration; in the latter, it points to the geographical spread of these tendencies and is cognate with globalism, spatial compression, universalization, and homogeneity. Fragmentation is but shorthand for the opposite tendencies and has the same two dimensions: on the one hand, it suggests disintegration, autarchy, unilateralism, closure, and isolation; on the other, the trend is towards nationalism or regionalism, spatial distension, separatism, and heterogeneity. These processes are not simply *international* but occur at multiple levels, affecting commitments to internationalism, patterns of regionalism, and even the very cohesion of states themselves.

The claim that international history displays a recurrent tension between these integrative and disintegrative tendencies is, by itself, scarcely revealing: it portrays no more than the fundamentals of social existence. But for the historian, there are two points of outstanding interest which emerge from such an analysis. The first is about *explanation* and the need to account for the relative balance between these two forces: are they simply natural outgrowths over which we have no political control or do combinations of more or less self-conscious political choices determine shifts in the balance from one historical period to another? Is there then a secular and unstoppable trend towards globalization or, as others would claim, is globalization itself 'changeable, as well as manipulable' (Barry Jones 1995: 15) by the currents of interstate politics? More broadly, are the interdependence theorists correct in their claim that states now operate in a qualitatively new environment, created by 'uncontrolled' economic and technological forces, or should we accept the realist counter-claim that 'growing interdependence has been a function of political power and political choice, not of exogenous technological change' (Thomson and Krasner 1989: 196)?

Secondly, does any of this matter? This leads on to a discussion of the implicit *values* raised in the analysis of globalization. An understanding of the factors predisposing the movement towards globalization or fragmentation contributes to a set of wider issues:

(1) Is globalization the prime and beneficent source of international economic growth and should it be welcomed for this reason? Alternatively, does the global market itself depend upon the support provided by state policies and international organizational activity (as argued in Murphy 1994: 9)?

(2) Are we to identify globalization with peace and stability in the international system and fragmentation with tendencies towards conflict? Although some periods of fragmentation have been associated with acute international instability, such as during the inter-war years, we must avoid the superficial conclusion that fragmentation is a malign and negative force for instability and that globalization is its benign and positive counterpart. On the contrary, globalization and fragmentation are themselves too closely interrelated for such simplistic judgments to be made. Globalization may 'stimulate forces of opposition' and thereby 'sow the seeds of conflict and tension' (McGrew *et al.* 1992: 23). Fragmentation, on the other hand, may be the only means of obtaining social justice available to the 'relatively disadvantaged' (Cox 1992: 145).

(3) Globalization, conceived as the transmission belt for liberal democratic values, may be regarded as a powerful, and desirable, cause of political development. In turn, this drift to homogeneity may be thought to reinforce international stability and to make international organizations more effective. As against

this, fragmentation may be the resort of parts of the world which feel threatened by what are regarded as 'hegemonic' Western practices and values.

(4) Globalization is sometimes presented as the preferred alternative to rival-rous, and destructive, regionalism. Present-day diagnoses of the world economy are torn between the vision of an increasingly globalized economy and one which is relapsing into regional blocs, based on North America, Europe, and East Asia. In this image, with memories of the 1930s, globalization takes on the role of hero slaying the dragon of competitive regionalism. But such a simplistic opposition does not stand closer scrutiny (Gamble and Payne 1996: esp. 1–2).

Accordingly, a more sensitive understanding of the historical contexts and impacts of globalization and fragmentation can contribute to these vital issues. It is, of course, artificial to reduce the vast complexity of this century's history sim-ply to two principal themes. However, for purposes of exposition and interpretive cohesion, this book will explore the links between the changing nature of the state and its civil society, the trends towards globalization affecting both states and the international system, and the antithetical processes of separatism and fragmenta-tion. It will attempt to capture some of these contrary trends by appealing to a multilayered dialectic, operating at the sub-state, state, and international levels, between the opposing forces of globalization and fragmentation. The state is challenged from both directions: its jurisdiction is questioned in an interdepen-dent world while, from the other end, it faces problems of domestic legitimacy. Less often remarked upon is the fact that international society is itself subject to erosion into a wider world society, while these trends are creating new cultural, ethnic, and civilizational pockets of resistance. Cumulatively, we have the bas-tardized international system of the twentieth century that seeks to extend the civil agenda to the international sphere, while also tolerating both domestic and international uncivility on an unprecedented scale.

This book does not attempt a comprehensive recounting of world history dur-ing the century: because of its focus on the formative activities of the most pow-erful states, it will occasionally be Euro- or Atlantic-centric, but this is for no other reason than that, for most of the century, globalization's epicentre was to be found in that region. The geographical focus follows from the concern with one set of key questions. In sum, has the trend towards global interconnection been a relatively autonomous process which has established the transforming context in which international relations have had to be conducted and to which interna-tional relations have been driven to adapt? Alternatively, although in practice the choice is not so stark, have international relations themselves been a formative force encouraging, or at times holding back, the course of globalization? Either way, this theme points to profound linkages between national, transnational, and international developments, and this study will attempt a historical introduction to these inter-relationships. The issue is important not just for historical under-standing but as a way of comprehending future developments: an insight into this complexity, and an appreciation of the policy choices that can contribute to either integration or disintegration, is surely indispensable for coping with the new century.

Straightforward histories of the events of the twentieth century abound. The justification for this exercise is, then, not that it will duplicate such studies but, instead, that it will look at these familiar events *indirectly* by examining their impact on the twin processes of globalization and fragmentation. Rather than regard either of these as autonomous, continuous, and irreversible processes, unconnected with the ebb and flow of international relations, this book will argue that they are symptoms of wider political and economic policies and themselves often the product of specific state policy choices. In this sense, globalization and fragmentation might be thought of as the shadow play of the century's main events: by studying this shadow play, we will gain a perspective on the century's distinctive influences.

The significance of such an approach is that neither globalization nor fragmentation is likely ever to be the exclusive tendency within any one historical period: both will tend to occur simultaneously and often the international system will reflect the contradictory nature of their occurrence. For instance, the 1990s have displayed marked tendencies in both directions at the same time: if anything, the economic dimensions of globalization have grown vigorously but they coexist with the unforeseen resurgence of ethno-nationalism which has ruptured the international community, as well as some of its constituent states. At other times, one tendency may predominate over the other: in the 1920s the forces of internationalization were seemingly the stronger, whilst in the 1930s the forces of fragmentation proved irresistible.

This much is commonplace. What this book seeks to add to our conventional understanding of these periods is an explicit association between the dominant state policies of the period and these two opposed tendencies. There is an assumption implicit in much of the literature that state policies themselves have been tossed about on the stormy seas of globalization and fragmentation. In contrast, the present work argues for a more nuanced approach and, in some cases, a fundamental reversal of the causal sequence. It is not just that globalization and fragmentation have impacted, contingently and unpredictably, upon the policy of states. In addition, globalization and fragmentation provide clear evidence of the state policy choices that have been made, and thus offer a convenient point of entry for the historian wishing to understand these policies. In short, what this book offers is not an alternative account of the major events of this century, such as the World Wars and the cold war, but simply an alternative set of lenses through which to look at them and thereby locate them in a wider historical context.

What are the benefits of such an approach? There is a danger in the existing literature that artificially sharp discontinuities are becoming the conventional wisdom. Historians are already beginning to present the overall shape of this century in terms of chronic instability in its first half, widespread stability during the cold war, and a predicted reversion to instability from the 1990s onwards. Such generalizations are, in any case, geographically questionable. But they are historically artificial in that they ignore the ongoing interaction between globalization and fragmentation throughout the century as a whole. It is hoped that the thematic structure of the two processes will allow for a more refined interpretation of various periods (e.g. the inter-war years 1919–39, the cold war 1945–90), as well as of particular processes (e.g. decolonization) precisely because these embodied *ambivalent* trends, with elements of both integration and disintegration taking place simultaneously. Rather than advancing an interpretation of the century which stresses a stark dichotomy between two halves, this survey will develop a more variegated perspective which recognizes both continuities and discontinuities within the framework of a recurring dialectic. Moreover, this offers an opportunity to explain as well as to describe by locating these tendencies in the changing nature of states, and of state policies, operating through the international system.

The State, International Relations, and Globalization

Historical understanding is bound up with profound conceptual and theoretical issues. In a similar way, our sense of perspective about the dynamic forces shaping twentieth-century international history as a whole is equally dependent upon analytic choices. One fundamental choice is between viewing the state as a source of international action in its own right or, alternatively, simply viewing it as an effect of deeper economic and social processes. Typically, even those writers who give emphasis to theories of the state disagree on this point. Fred Halliday of the London School of Economics prefers the latter interpretation. 'International Relations,' he proclaims categorically, 'is the study of the relations not between states but between social formations' (Halliday 1994: 60). Harvard's Theda Skocpol disagrees. For her, the activities of social classes may be important, but their impact is mediated through the instrumentality of the state and, accordingly, 'the structures and activities of states profoundly condition such class capacities' (Skocpol 1985: 25): in this version, the state enjoys 'autonomy' from the social forces which underpin it. That said, the vicious circle is completed when we recall that states are themselves shaped by the wider circumstances in which they find themselves:

Analysts must take account of the embeddedness of nations in changing transnational relations, such as wars and interstate alliances or balances of power, market flows and the international economic division of labour, and patterns of intellectual communication or cultural modelling across national boundaries. Since states are intrinsically Janus-faced, standing at the intersections of transnational and domestic processes, their structures, capacity and policy are always influenced by identifiable aspects of the particular world historical circumstances in which they exist. (Evans *et al.* 1985: 350)

The attention paid to state policies, and to traditionally conceived interstate politics, in this book should not be regarded as another reaffirmation of a realist interpretation of international relations. On the contrary, much of the following analysis abjures the neo-realist distaste for 'reductionist' accounts of international politics (Waltz 1979). Indeed, the argument will place considerable emphasis upon the domestic sources of state behaviour. Instead of regarding globalization as something that happens only *between* states, the essence of the following discussion will be that globalization must be understood as something which, in addition, happens *to* and *within* states but which states, in turn, can encourage or resist. Much of the historical analysis will then focus upon changes in the nature of states, responding to the different environments in which they have found themselves, and on their attempts to reconcile often conflicting international and domestic demands. To this extent, the approach is sympathetic to Michael J. Hogan's depiction of corporatism as a tool of political and historical analysis. Hogan describes corporatism in the following terms:

a corporatist analysis takes account of the strategic and geopolitical notions that typify traditional diplomatic history. But it is far more concerned with the globalization of economic, political, and social forces; with the connections between state and society and between national systems and foreign policy; and with the interaction of these systems internationally. (Hogan 1991: 235)

Corporatism is not without its critics who regard it as overly abstract, ignoring ideals and the role of individuals. It has also been criticized for its neglect of the 'geopolitical dimension'.[1] There will be no adherence to a formal corporatist model in the following account, but its general characteristics, as set out above by Hogan, provide an outline framework which accords well with the argument to be developed.

While the book will highlight the impact of state policy upon globalization, it also accepts the reciprocal effect that globalization has upon state policies in that 'globalisation is part of a broad process of restructuring of the state and civil society' (Gill 1995: 405). Any attempt to analyse interstate behaviour wholly outwith such a context is doomed to artificiality, all the more so given that state 'internal' and 'external' agendas are increasingly in a relationship of creative tension with each other. Thus globalization inextricably interweaves problems of state power in both the domestic and the international domains. As has been suggested, internationalized agendas are now ever more intrusive, as international norms 'affect the domestic structures and organisation of states', and 'invest individuals and groups within states with rights and duties' (Hurrell and Woods 1995: 465–6). If globalization means anything, then it assuredly means the end of the view of international relations as a realm governed by its own, and distinct, interstate political logic.

Historical Outlines

In short, any attempt to engage in a thematic discussion of globalization and fragmentation in this century becomes caught up in wider issues about the choice of theoretical perspective. If one's understanding of the pre-1914 period is shaped

---

[1] See Gaddis (1986: 360), and the exchange with Hogan (1986).

simply by a view of states as engaged in a balance of power, and jostling within alliances to do so, and all this reinforced by the competitive nationalism of the age, then we might regard this as a period of unmitigated fragmentation. However, this stark judgement needs to be tempered by the ambivalent effects of imperialism, the geographical extension of the international arena, the dynamic impact of technology on a steadily integrating international economy, and important changes in the social basis of the state itself. Combined, these reveal the complex texture of a period in which both globalization and fragmentation intensified simultaneously. But were the states the hapless victims of exogenous forces that they could not control? Or were these forces, in some sense, stimulated by the political and economic policies being pursued? And did these policies reflect the new social and political tensions of the age of industrialization?

It is only natural to regard a cataclysmic war, such as that of 1914–18, as representing the essence of fragmentation: there can be no more palpable evidence of disintegration than such a monumental collapse of an international system. Even in this case, however, it will be demonstrated that our judgement needs to be more discerning. On the fragmentationist side, the war not only disrupted international patterns of intercourse but directly encouraged the collapse of states and empires; it also gave encouragement to the new credo of self-determination which, potentially, was a disintegrative force without bounds. On the other hand, however, the war integrated some colonial economies more deeply into the international economy, fostered the enunciation of universalist (if antagonistic) ideologies in the shape of Leninism and Wilsonianism, and encouraged the quest for a return to 'normalcy' in the form of a liberal trading and financial regime.

The inter-war period saw two successive phases in each of which one of the two forces appeared to be predominant. Versailles gave birth to a security order that was nominally committed to internationalist principles. On the economic side, substantial efforts were made to restore an open international economy and, for a time, the United States made its first, if abortive, major contribution to the underwriting of such arrangements. At the same time, atavistic elements of the pre-1914 security system survived and engendered competitive and nationalistic policies on the part of the major powers. The international system was also experiencing the fragmentationist effects of a revolutionary Bolshevik state which eventually was compelled to withdraw from normal interstate relations in its search for socialism in one country. Elsewhere, the war had simultaneously given rise to programmes for imperial integration at the same time as it had done much to stimulate the very colonial nationalism which would resist full implementation of such programmes. It needed only the onset of economic autarchy in the 1930s, and the emergence of totalitarian political regimes, to make fragmentation the dominant political force of the age.

As with the Great War, the Second World War had multiple, and often contradictory, consequences. The loss of life, especially amongst civilians, was unprecedented: for millions, the vestiges of any humane social order all but disappeared. But phoenix-like, out of these ashes, arose a revitalized commitment to international organization and a new international agenda of human rights. The state itself, which had all but lost its purpose since it had been unable to defend or protect its citizens, found a new lease of life in the social and economic compacts of welfarism and Keynesianism. Thus was globalization invigorated by the rhetoric of universalism, whilst, at the same time, and against all expectations, the modern state not only survived but emerged resiliently strengthened by its new-found forms of economic, social, and scientific managerial controls.

The post-war period witnessed the most dramatic harnessing of state policy to wider processes of globalization. Seldom in history has there been such a close association between national power and the temper of international politics. The key issue for the international historian is to investigate the relationship between the momentous integrative trends of the period and the play of national power in the cold war. What was cause and what effect? American cold-war policy certainly was the mainspring of much economic and cultural transnationalism, and a prime mover of European integration in particular. However, if less obviously, it also rescued the nation-state after the calamities of the 1930s (and at that level was fragmentationist against transnational trends), but also encouraged a revival of nationalism in reaction to the predominance of bloc solidarity.

The same period also experienced the convulsions of decolonization. This is a powerful example of ambiguous effects. Imperialism and Westernization had themselves been the most potent instruments of integration and globalization. Set against such a perception, it is easy to depict decolonization as a fragmentationist development. However, on further analysis, it is equally true that decolonization institutionally extended Western state practice to post-colonial countries and encouraged a degree of Third World solidarity in forums such as the United Nations. At yet another remove, the judgement changes again as we contemplate the prospective fragmentation of the cultural consensus which the age of imperialism and Westernization had perhaps artificially induced.

The slackening of the cold war by the late 1960s is associated with the decline of bloc solidarity, the embryonic revival of a multipolar power distribution, and the disruption of the liberal economic order that had been developed in conjunction with American hegemony. Again, however, the historian is faced with difficult problems in distinguishing causes and effects. Did the diminution of the cold war allow the emergence of other international agendas? Or did the diffusion of power, and the salience of new international problems, force the cold war into the background of state concerns? Is the final supercession of the cold-war order likely to issue in a more fragmented international system as the integrative policies of the cold war lose their potency? Alternatively, do globalizing forces now have their own self-sustaining dynamic such that, whatever may initially have brought them into being, they can survive into the different world left behind after the cold war's end?

Before we can begin to answer such teasing questions, and to unravel the mixed record of the twentieth century, we need to look more closely at the periodization of the century to see how the two themes of globalization and fragmentation fit into its wider contours.

How Long was the Twentieth Century?

This section attempts to do two things: to assess what have been the distinctive traits of the twentieth century; and to devise a periodization of the century, both from within and from without, to see how these traits relate to longer-term processes. Periodization is a means to an end and not an end in itself. The only way in which turning points in the relative sway of globalization and fragmentation can be addressed is by placing them in the context of the other major forces of the century, and the only way of determining what is unique to this era is by examining it in the context of large-scale, and longer-term, historical change.

The choice of the dominant characteristics of the age might otherwise seem arbitrary. What are the salient features of the twentieth century? Most of the judgements to date have been gloomy and have stressed the century's negative side. Hobsbawm (1987: 9) sees the century's mood as having been dominated by the fear of global war and revolution, and records that during the period 'more human beings had been killed or allowed to die by human decision than ever before in history' (Hobsbawm 1994: 12). Even such an optimistic commentator as Francis Fukuyama concedes that the century 'has made all of us into deep historical pessimists' (Fukuyama 1992: 3). This pessimism is pervasive. Joll shares the mood in his verdict that 'war, nationalism, totalitarian dictatorships: these have undoubtedly been characteristic features of the twentieth century' (Joll 1985: 8). Christopher Coker sees the century as the 'apotheosis of the modern era' and as closely identified with war because 'modernity and war were synonymous' (Coker 1994: 23). And so it goes on.

Does the century deserve such a dismal press? Or does this collective judgement tell us more about the mood of historians than about the actual developments of the period? It might seem just as plausible to identify the century with other developments. In economic terms, this has been the most productive century in human history. Mankind's mastery of science and technology has developed further, and faster, than ever before. There have been momentous political developments in terms of governments' social responsibilities and management of national economies, so much so that when an economic historian asks the question 'What was the twentieth century?', his own answer is framed in terms of the novelty of government being 'assigned responsibility for maintaining a continuing level of economic activity' (Maier 1985: 101). Elsewhere, Hobsbawm himself seems to shift his focus of attention when recalling that the century 'can best be understood as a secular struggle by the forces of the old order against social revolution' (Hobsbawm 1994: 56).

How then can we decide how the century 'can best be understood' and on what grounds should we allow the identification of the century with one theme rather than any other? Which developments penetrate closest to the very essence of the century and tell us more about it than the rest?

The first step in answering such questions is the exercise of periodization. If war and suffering are the characteristics of all modern history, they tell us nothing about the distinctive quality of the twentieth century. If all social life since the sixteenth century has been shaped by a capitalist world economy, how can economic life have left a distinctive imprint on this century? If the twentieth century is but the culmination of 'modernity', its story cannot be told in separation from that of the Renaissance and the Enlightenment. And if all international relations is but the repetitive play of power politics, shaped by anarchy and the distribution of power, then there is nothing of interest to be said about the twentieth century as a separate historical period. The essential task of the historian, as a first step, is then to identify the elements of continuity and discontinuity which combine to give the century its characteristic qualities. We need to see how it fits in with, and how it stands out from, what came before, and what is likely to take its place.

It is a truism that it seldom makes sense to think of a century as a meaningful period of history: the various developments taking place seldom coincide with each other, let alone with the symbolic cut-off point of the end of a century. It is for this reason that historians resort to the device of the long and short century in an attempt to follow through key elements of a story to a more natural watershed or point of culmination. How long, then, was the twentieth century? Is the twentieth century, taken as a whole, a meaningful period of international history?

A review of some of the historical judgements already made will help to sketch out the issues involved. It is already commonplace to view the long nineteenth century as running through to 1914. Whether in terms of imperialism, alliance systems, German unification, the compulsions of domestic politics, or the effects of the industrialized capitalism of the age, the events leading to war in 1914 have been viewed by most historians as being an integral part of the story which unfolded from 1870. This would suggest that the twentieth century can be deemed to have commenced properly only from 1914 or 1918. Hobsbawm typifies this approach, claiming that 1914 is one of the 'most undeniable "natural breaks" in history' and therefore 'marks the end of the "long nineteenth century"' (Hobsbawm 1987: 6). At the other end, there is already an incipient consensus that the close of the twentieth century will be marked by the combined events of the period 1989–91, namely the end of the cold war and the overthrow of the Yalta divisions which symbolized it. John L. Gaddis among many subscribes to this interpretation:

We are at one of those rare points of 'punctuation' in history at which the old patterns of stability have broken up and new ones have not yet emerged to take their place. Historians will certainly regard the years 1989–91 as a turning point comparable in importance to the years 1789–94, or 1917–18, or 1945–7. (Gaddis 1992*b*: 22)

If both arguments are accepted, we have indeed a short twentieth century, extending from approximately 1914 to 1990. This is, of course, precisely the interpretation that Hobsbawm has made his own. But we need to examine closely the grounds upon which he bases his claim to a Short Twentieth Century. His central thesis is that the 'world that went to pieces at the end of the 1980s was the world shaped by the impact of the Russian Revolution of 1917' (Hobsbawm 1994: 4). He later elaborates of that Revolution that it was 'an event as central to the history of this century as the French Revolution of 1789 was to the nineteenth. Indeed, it is not an accident that the history of the Short Twentieth Century, as defined in this book, virtually coincides with the lifetime of the state born of the October revolution' (1994: 55).

While legitimate, this is certainly an idiosyncratic point of view and will not be accepted here. This book will by no means argue against the importance of the social, ideological, and international clashes precipitated in the wake of the Great Competition between communism and capitalism. However, it is not self-evident that this gives structural coherence to the century as a whole, nor that it exhausts the possibilities for historical explanation. For instance, one wonders if a preoccupation with the lifetime of the Soviet state really captures the historic shift in Europe's place in the world during the first half of the century. One wonders equally whether such a focus does justice to the dramatic process of decolonization with its manifold, and still to be digested, effects upon international relations. Is the rise and fall of Germany's bid for mastery explicable in terms of the October Revolution when, on the face of it, that revolution appears itself to have been precipitated by German power? Would there have been no Holocaust without Bolshevism? There remains also a question mark against how much such a thesis explains about American behaviour in the twentieth century. The focus upon the ideological clash with communism, or upon the geopolitical clash with Soviet power, perhaps assumes too readily that these were the cause of American policy, and not simply rationalizations for it: alternative claims to the fulfilment of America's manifest destiny need to be taken seriously, even when they relegate the Soviet factor to the role of mere catalyst or pretext. Nor can we so lightly dismiss Wallerstein's contention that during the first half of the century, the main geopolitical protagonist of the United States was Germany *and not the Soviet Union* (Wallerstein 1991: 6).

If there are problems in shortening the twentieth century on the basis of such singularity of theme, there are equally dangers in divorcing the twentieth century from longer-term continuities: coherence is lost if these continuities are dismembered. Thus there are critics who would dissent from the view that the twentieth century, whatever its purported length, tells a self-contained and meaningful story. It is instead part of a longer process of development. Such fundamentalist positions come in two principal varieties, those that emphasize 'modernity' and those that emphasize the continuity of the economic system, although the two may often overlap (since many sociologists accept the capitalist economic system as a defining attribute of 'modernity'). Justin Rosenberg graphically illustrates the former position:

There is something about the last three hundred years which sets them apart from all other epochs in human history. In the field of international relations this is especially obvious since these centuries see for the first time the emergence of a states-system which covers the entire planet. (Rosenberg 1994: 1)

Since the twentieth century is an integral part of that continuing story, any attempt to analyse it in isolation is bound to deceive.

Likewise, world system theorists, while accepting that the system evolves through various phases, tend to give priority to the longer perspective: we understand the present precisely as a phase of an ongoing system and cannot understand it without such a framework. Hence Wallerstein tends to see the present phase of world history as running from 1914 to 2050 and as being a period of structural crisis in the world system (Wallerstein 1991: 42). He does allow a tentative periodization of the interstate system—1450 to 1815, 1815 to 1914, and 1914 to the present (1991: 143)—but since he does not believe that this system has an autonomous existence outside the world system of which it is a part, these chronological divisions cannot be accepted as fundamental historical markers.

This book will take the twentieth century as a whole as its chronological framework, not to divorce it from longer continuities, but because the opening of the new century is associated with powerful forces of both globalization and fragmentation, as indeed is the decade at its end. Its intention is to avoid an 'episodic' history and to present a thematic approach, organized around the twin processes of globalization and fragmentation. This is not, strictly speaking, an alternative to all other approaches. Rather, it is offered in the spirit of being a convenient vehicle for integrating and synthesizing many other interpretations. This integration sheds additional light upon such other diverse thematic trends as: the extension and eclipse of the European system, economic change, the evolution and demise of empire, the rise and fall of the cold war, and other cognate developments. In particular, it will be suggested that such an approach avoids the analytic sterility of viewing the twentieth century, wholly artificially, as falling into two halves—one cursed by war and the other blessed by peace. Unless we can undermine that crude stereotype, any projections into the future are fated to be misleading and misconceived.

We first need to clarify the implications of a focus on globalization and fragmentation for the foregoing discussion of the periodization of the twentieth century. While no claim can be made that these themes are in any way confined to the twentieth century, three arguments can none the less be advanced: that the two forces have intensified during this century; that their mutual interaction has become more conspicuous; and that they have become more explicitly associated with the goals of state policy, rather than being an incidental side effect of other developments. In short, both globalization and fragmentation have become more prominent, the one has reacted more powerfully to the other, and both have been directly stimulated by conscious political action. It is for these reasons that it makes sense to use these as keys to unlocking the century's distinctive features, not least because they encapsulate most of the other forces at work as well.

These assertions conform to the broad claims of globalization theorists. For example, while accepting readily that globalization has been occurring for many centuries, Roland Robertson remains happy to identify its rapid development with the present century: 'its main empirical focus is in line with the increasing acceleration in both concrete global interdependence and consciousness of the global whole in the twentieth century' (Robertson 1992: 8). In turn, he distinguishes three phases of globalization during the century—a take-off phase to the mid-1920s, a struggle-for-hegemony phase to the late 1960s, and an uncertainty phase to the early 1990s (1992: 59). Not only is the century overall identified with globalization but the history of its phases can equally be explained using these terms. Even those writers who remain sceptical of many globalization claims, and certainly about any notion of the automaticity of the process, are prepared to concede that, while not unique to recent times, it is during this period that we have witnessed 'the world-wide spread of such interactions and transactions and, in some cases, their intensification' (Barry Jones 1995: 101).

What is even more important is that this interpretation meshes neatly with other important accounts of the key turning points in international relations. These other accounts will be discussed in detail below. For the moment, it is sufficient to endorse the judgement of Geoffrey Barraclough's pioneering account, written at the height of the cold war, as being fully complementary with the argument of these pages. Barraclough distinguished contemporary from modern history and saw the few years at the turn of the century as representing the watershed between the two. The principal factors which he discerned as underlying this new 'contemporary' history were the industrial and social revolutions of the late nineteenth century and the imperialism associated with them. For him, the twentieth century began around 1900 and did so because it was the 'beginning of the post-European age'. For the next half century, in Barraclough's terms, a new world system struggled to be born while the old European-centred system continued to fight for its life (Barraclough 1967: 110–11). It requires no great stretch of the imagination to incorporate this view into a wider account of globalization.

Another way of addressing the same issue is to ask simply what has *changed* in the course of the twentieth century: the differences between beginning and end provide some crude measure of the key transitions that have taken place. When this is done, the answers are striking. Even Hobsbawm, despite his own ideological account, lists three major changes from century's beginning to end: the end of the Eurocentric world; a globe that has become far more of a single operational unit; and the disintegration of the old patterns of human social relationships (Hobsbawm 1994: 14–15). None of these can be adequately explained by the aforementioned themes that Hobsbawm regards as central to the twentieth century. But the first two can be explained in terms of globalization; and the third by the competing pulls of both globalization and fragmentation.

Likewise, and in denial of Hobsbawm's concentration upon the ideological cleavages wrought by the October Revolution, there is much evidence from the international economic relations of the century that does not fit comfortably into his framework and instead supports an analysis organized around globalization and fragmentation. As Maier points out, 'the central conflict defining the international political economy from World War I until about 1950 was not that between American and Soviet alternatives, between capitalism and communism' (Maier 1987: 182–3). America's fight at that point was against the closed economic systems of Britain, Japan, and Germany in order to maintain pluralist, market-economy liberalism. This in itself represented an embryonic choice in favour of globalization, on America's terms, as against the economic fragmentation through its imperial system now favoured by the old hegemon, Britain, and by the new autarchs, Germany and Japan.

It may seem contrary to conventional wisdom to regard the twentieth century as the age of empire, but the story of empire in the twentieth century is itself central to the dynamics of globalization and fragmentation. The great accretions of territory to the European imperium were already complete before the end of the nineteenth century, even if further divisions of the territorial spoils were conducted after the First World War under the fig-leaf of the Mandates system. And yet it was European war in 1914 that did much to make a reality of empire in a way that had not happened in the nineteenth century: empires were integrated in an unprecedented manner. As has been noted 'the mark of empire on the contemporary world was made in the inter-war period, when local populations were mobilized, regional resources exploited and the general environment—both physical and cultural—altered to suit European needs' (Betts 1985: 11). As will be seen later, the World Wars did much to bring colonial peoples into the global play of forces—into the international economy, into other peoples' wars, into the universalist ideological debates which flourished as the century unfolded, and finally into the state system itself. The last was achieved because the discomfort caused by the closer embrace of empire in the inter-war years, the apogee of empire, hastened imperial fragmentation.

There remain two further, and interconnected, debates which can be clarified by use of the lenses of globalization and fragmentation. These are the attempts to present twentieth-century history as divided starkly into two halves—one of crisis and one of stability. The other is about the significance of the cold war and the meaning of its end. The two issues overlap with each other.

The idea that the twentieth century divides neatly into two halves, the first of crisis and war and the second of stability and peace, is a seductive but ultimately misleading one. And yet it has a strong hold on the historical imagination. Maier writes of a pervasive crisis that endured from about 1905 to 1955, 'the longest period of crisis since the seventeenth century' (Maier 1995: 142). The crisis had two dimensions: the first was an internal crisis of representation as systems of government struggled to respond to the new social structure, and especially to a strong working class; the second was the international, and imperial, rivalry (Maier 1987: 10–11). The First World War did not solve any problems. Instead, according to Maier,

it opened a forty-year period of crisis which was settled only when new hegemons—the United States and Soviet Union—finally displaced both the old imperial leader, Great Britain, and the ambitious challengers of the two world wars, Germany and Japan . . . The period from 1947 to 1954/1957 or so closed the long interval of turmoil that had begun before the First World War. (Maier 1995: 141–2)

Martin Shaw sees the twentieth century as dividing along similar lines when he repeats the verdict that the period from 1890 to the 1950s can be characterized as one of 'total war' because that was its dominant reality. He then asks the question of the latter part of the century, 'whether and in what senses we have superseded, or can supersede, the period of total war' (Shaw 1994*a*: 32). Such a posing of the issue reinforces the impression of a century moving from crisis to stability. The image of a century in two halves once again stands out starkly. Hobsbawm's attempt to depart from such a basic dichotomy is welcome in principle as it provides a more variegated history. However, his tripartite division into an Age of Catastrophe 1914–45, a Golden Age from 1945 to the early 1970s, and an era of Decomposition thereafter (Hobsbawm 1994: 6), creates its own set of problems, not least with the notion that the cold-war period can be regarded as a Golden Age.

This book takes the position that the first half of the century was more diverse than the image of one long, sustained crisis would have us believe. It also takes the view that the second half has been more diverse: it is more than 'the Long Peace'. It therefore dissents from claims that, for example, 'the half century from 1941 to 1991 is best understood as a whole' (Crockatt 1995: 4). On the contrary, that period displays various phases when the precise balance between globalization and fragmentation shifted.

This leads to the second, and related, issue of the cold war and the significance of its end. The artificially strong contrast between an age of total war and an age of tranquil peace encourages the equally stark and false belief that there must either be a reversion to the turmoil of the first half of the century, or that the Long Peace has now become so entrenched that we can assume its indefinite extension. Gaddis (1992*a*: 186) hints at the former possibility: 'What if the long postwar peace should turn out to be just one phase of a long historical cycle, one destined, sooner or later, to bring us back to the circumstances of global depression and war out of which the current international system emerged?' Fukuyama illustrates the second, the secular trend away from nationalistic war. As against the suggestion that post-war integration and stability have been but the side-effects of the cold war, Fukuyama asserts that there has been a more profound transition and, just as religion had earlier been tamed as a source of international conflict, we are now moving into an age when nationalism will cease to cause wars: 'it may turn out that the two world wars played a role similar to the wars of religion in the sixteenth and seventeenth centuries with respect to religion, affecting the consciousness not just of the generation immediately following but of all subsequent generations' (1992: 271). As always, the historical reality is likely to be more mixed and complex than such arguments would suggest: there are intermediate possibilities between a reversion to pre-1939 totalitarian war and the static idyll of the endless democratic peace. It is hoped that this variegation will become more visible when we explore the interplay between globalization and fragmentation throughout the century.

Before the historical analysis can proceed, the first task is to examine more closely the nature of the two processes of globalization and fragmentation, and the debates about the evidence, and reasons, for their occurrence.

1

GLOBALIZATION AND FRAGMENTATION

What is Globalization?

The utility of 'globalization' as a theoretical concept is much disputed. At the same time, there is a surprisingly strong consensus, amongst writers with very different theoretical viewpoints, that globalization and fragmentation are salient themes of the twentieth century. It has, for instance, been asserted that 'globalization may be *the* concept of the 1990s, a key idea by which we understand the transition of human society into the third millennium' (Waters 1995: 1). Indeed, it has been noted that, in the face of the challenges presented by the end of the cold war, globalization 'survived . . . when many of our other ordering and explanatory concepts did not' (Hurrelland Woods 1995: 447). This durability is to be explained, in part, by the great flexibility of the concept and its ability to be accommodated within a broad range of otherwise incompatible theoretical frameworks. Hence, even if each analytical school explains the theme in a different way, and attaches varying significance to it, the assertion of this common analytical motif remains striking: its pervasiveness across intellectual borders suggests that its imagery, for all its imprecision, holds a widespread appeal. The point can be briefly illustrated from such motley writings as those of traditionalist historians, world system theorists, and historical sociologists.[1]

John L. Gaddis has done more than most international historians to give prominence to the themes. He traces a 'fault line' between the 'forces of integration' and the 'forces of fragmentation' back to the eighteenth century. This results from an essential duality in human existence between the integration required 'for the satisfaction of material wants' and the 'particularization . . . that is necessary to satisfy intangible . . . needs' (Gaddis 1992*b*: 32–3). Reformulated, this remains close to the standard dichotomy between the unifying dynamic of the economic universe as against the divisive dynamic of the political realm. Gaddis relates this fault line to the cold war and its aftermath, suggesting that the cold war was a powerful source of integration. But he warns that 'fragmentationist forces have been around much longer than integrationist forces have been, and now that the Cold War is over, they may grow stronger than they have been at any point in

[1] A useful review of the variety of globalization theory can be found in Waters (1995), ch. 3.

the last half-century' (Gaddis 1992*a*: 215). This analysis is important both in that it highlights the centrality of integration to the dynamic of international history and also because it poses the central question about the likely impact of post-cold war developments on future international stability.

Other historians point to a similar duality. Paul Kennedy, in his projections into the next century, stresses how the conjunction of economic activity organized on a global basis with a political structure of fragmenting national units leads to a 'series of jolts and jars and smashes in the social life of humanity' (Kennedy 1993: 329). Pierre Hassner develops the same argument employing the language of 'de-territorialization' and 're-territorialization', and depicts the struggle between these two trends (Hassner 1993: 53). Others again speak of the 'globalization of international economic relations' at the very same time as 'security politics is being fragmented and regionalized' (Dewitt *et al.* 1993: 5). In these various formulations, a recurring antinomy is the favoured analytical device.

This duality is not confined to traditionalist historians: it is equally conspicuous amongst analysts who write from a fundamentally different point of view. For the world system theorists, the dichotomy arises from the central characteristics of the capitalist mode of production and exchange. Such a system, being organized on a global basis, is, by definition, integrated. However, the flotsam and jetsam of states is tossed about on this sea of capitalist exchange relations and the states have ambiguous, but often disintegrative, effects. In the words of its foremost exponent, there is an 'antinomy' between multiple states and the capitalist world-economy (Wallerstein 1991: 39).[2]

Sociologists of international relations have reached similar conclusions, albeit by a different mode of reasoning. They point to the tension between 'the infrastructure of a global social system' and the world of sovereign nation-states (McGrew *et al.* 1992: 2). For many, this tension reveals itself in changing patterns of identity with the state no longer monopolizing human loyalties. In consequence, 'globalization and fragmentation are transforming the nature of political community across the world' (Macmilland and Linklater 1995: 12).

In short, there is pervasive resort to the twin themes of globalization and fragmentation in a wide variety of literature. Does this mean that the terminology is without problem? And does it mean that the significance of these processes for international relations is uncontested?

Unfortunately, discussion of these terms is anything but straightforward. As the following review will reveal, there are several disputed areas: about whether globalization is 'progressive' or not; with regard to its chronology; as to the meaning and central thrust of globalization and fragmentation; as to whether the empirical evidence supports the claims; and, more fundamentally, with respect to any supposed causal relationship between them and international relations.

---

[2] The claim that Wallerstein's theory represents a genuine theory of globalization has been rejected on the grounds that his 'mechanisms of geosystemic integration are exclusively economic' (Waters 1995: 25). Robertson (1992: 15) also argues that 'globalization analysis and world-systems analysis are rival perspectives'.

We need to note the differing contexts in which some of these issues are debated. What, in short, is the significance of the discussion of globalization? To many, it is simply a matter of discerning the main trends in the social, political, and economic organization of the globe. The task is 'objective' and is concerned solely with mapping the relevant 'facts' of the matter. However, as noted above, the analysis of globalization tends often to be cast in a wider normative and ideological context which goes well beyond these parameters: this makes value judgements about economic growth, international stability, the spread of democratic practices, and the possible dangers of regionalism. These debates are not only about whether globalization might be taking place but about what it represents, and whether such a set of developments should be regarded as 'progressive' or not. Thus Hurrell and Woods identify a powerful cluster of liberal assumptions that are attached to the concept of globalization. In their account, the liberal interpretation makes a number of judgements about the beneficial consequences of globalization: it fosters economic efficiency and encourages international institutions and problem-solving. Moreover, for those who see democratic capitalism as the end of history, globalization is to be welcomed for the effect that it has in promoting 'societal convergence built around common recognition of the benefits of markets and liberal democracy' (Hurrell and Woods 1995: 449). In this sense, globalization is not only irresistible, but to be welcomed. Gill, writing from a critical perspective, parodies this ideological subtext when he sets out the view of those supporters of globalization who see in it the 'unfolding of a business Hegelian myth of the capitalist market . . . as the Absolute Idea' (Gill 1995: 406). Thus regarded, much of the literature on globalization has resonances of earlier generations of functionalist writing which argued that technical cooperation in the management of specific material problems would eventually yield a superstructure of political behaviour in which the sovereignty of the nation-state would be steadily eroded and circumvented. It also echoes some of the 1970s literature on the ameliorative impact of interdependence (Barry Jones 1995: 3). The liberal proponents of globalization similarly believe in its progressive impact on economic, political, and social behaviour. It is this set of beneficent assumptions that Hurrell and Woods have sought to question by emphasizing the association between globalization and the perpetuation of inequalities.

In any case, facile value-judgements between globalization and fragmentation should be avoided. They do not represent a contest between good and evil and neither monopolizes moral and political wisdom. To be sure, certain forms of fragmentation, such as the unilateralism of the 1930s, can have highly destructive effects upon human values. However, we should not make blithe assumptions about globalization's progressive role in general: it is itself a politicized process, based in specific conditions, that creates winners as well as losers. Moreover, globalization may itself induce fragmentationist reactions and should not be regarded as a straightforwardly stabilizing force in international relations.

As to chronology, most commentators are content to present globalization as a long-term historical process, however much it may have intensified in the last few decades. Typically, it is asserted that the 'linear extension of globalization that we are currently experiencing began in the fifteenth and sixteenth centuries' (Waters 1995: 4). There are, however, some interpretations that sit uneasily with the perspective set out in this volume. This is the case with those who restrict globalization to the very recent historical period and specifically to the second half of the twentieth century. This can be found in three versions.

Bretherton insists that, to be useful, globalization as a concept must be seen to refer to 'a new, distinct phase in world politics', and hence 'globalization is particularly associated with technological and political developments since the Second World War' (Bretherton and Ponton 1996: 3, 12). On this premise, it becomes impossible, definitionally, to interpret all twentieth-century international history in terms of globalization. Rather than see it as a discontinuous trend which has become more powerful in the second half of the century, this view suggests instead that globalization is a new departure: there may have been integration and extension of international relationships before, but globalization is qualitatively distinct from them. The trouble with such a perspective is that it reinforces the rigidity of the 'century in two halves' image and, if anything, impedes understanding of the post-cold war era. Accordingly, this book takes the wider perspective of globalization as a continuing, if periodically accelerating, aspect of the twentieth century as a whole.

Secondly, there is the distinctively economic conception that globalization denotes a qualitative change from an economy which is simply international. An internationalized economy is one in which, although there is widespread activity among states, the separate national economies continue to predominate, whereas in a globalized economy 'distinct national economies are subsumed and re-articulated into the system by international processes and transactions' (Hirst 1995: 3). Thus Dicken sees globalization as a more advanced form of internationalization, and a more recent form of economic activity, implying 'a degree of functional integration between internationally dispersed economic activities' (Dicken 1992: 1).[3] This integration was both a response to, and a further catalyst for, market convergence and what some economists had discerned to be the emergence of global markets for standardized products.[4] Commentators are mostly agreed that the highest levels of globalization are currently occurring in the world of finance where, coupled with instant world communications, vast dealings can be executed around the clock. For some, this is a cause of concern as they complain about a transnational economy that is 'literally out of control' (Hoffmann 1995: 175).

Thirdly, the notion of a distinctive global economy that has been formed only from the 1970s has been reached by an alternative route. When the liberal international economy of the nineteenth century gave way to a world of rival imperialisms, the system of production became geared to an increasingly internationalized, but still nationally based, world economy. The economic crisis of

---

[3] For a similar argument that 'the term globalisation suggests a quantum leap beyond previous internationalisation stages', see Ruigrok and van Tulder (1995: 119).

[4] See the discussion of the early elaboration of this idea by Theodore Levitt in Ruigrok and van Tulder (1995: 131–2).

1973–4 saw this economic structure increasingly supplanted by one which is typified by 'linking groups of producers and plants in different territorial jurisdictions in order to supply markets in many countries'. This is the 'production mode congruent with interdependence within a global economy' (Cox 1993: 142–3), and this materialized in the 1970s. The disadvantage of this argument is again that, definitionally, it locks us into a concept of globalization that became operative only from the early 1970s, since it was only then that the basis of a truly global economy was achieved. For this reason, the shift from an internationalized to a global economy will be viewed in this book as a gradual change in degree, rather than an abrupt one of kind.

What is globalization and what is its central dynamic? Despite one bold claim that the history of the last two hundred years is one of 'broadening, deepening and accelerating globalization' (Scholte 1993: 8), there is fundamental disagreement about what it is and, indeed, about whether it is actually taking place at all. At the very least, there is recognition that part of the problem in any systematic treatment of globalization is the fact that it is inescapably a multi-faceted process. This in itself fosters a looseness in definition and raises important difficulties in determining whether there is any causal hierarchy among the range of factors involved. Symptomatically, Bretherton herself sees globalization as being a composite of four elements: technological change, the creation of a global economy, political globalization, and a globalization of ideas (Bretherton and Ponton 1996: 3). Such a scheme is helpful but, historically, itself calls into question the notion that 1945 represented some kind of absolute and simultaneous watershed in *all* of these areas. The multi-dimensionality of globalization is also testified to in other accounts which likewise offer a four-part scheme, but with minor variations upon that already described:

First, we are witnessing a dramatic increase in the 'density' and 'depth' of economic interdependence. Second, information technology and the information revolution are playing an especially critical role in diffusing knowledge, technology and ideas. Third, these developments create the material infrastructure for the strengthening of societal interdependence ... Fourth, this is leading to an unprecedented and growing consciousness of 'global problems' . . . and of belonging to a single 'human community'. (Hurrell 1995*a*: 345)[5]

The role of technology is generally regarded as being facilitative, as 'primarily an enabling rather than a determining factor' (Bretherton and Ponton 1996: 3). In this sense, technology is necessary but not sufficient for globalization to take place. This seems a sensible way of conceiving of the issue, leaving open the precise catalytic role of other political and economic factors. Again, however, while in no way disputing the unprecedented development of information and communication technology since 1945, and especially in the last two decades, it is questionable whether it is helpful to divorce this from the more gradual, but still influential, improvements which were set in place from the latter part of the nineteenth century onwards. In any case, as Bretherton concedes, there is a sense in

---

[5] Another variation on this quadripartite scheme is 'polity, economy, communications and world order' (Spybey 1996: 2–3).

which the role of technology is neutral (Bretherton and Ponton 1996: 5), in that it can be both beneficial and hostile to globalization. To the extent that technology is an important source of governmental control over its own citizenry, it can be used to enhance the autarchic isolation of people from wider international currents. In this way, technology made its own sinister contribution to the totalitarian fragmentation of the inter-war period.

The vast majority of globalization theorists present it as a characteristic of economic activity. It is taken to refer to 'the integration and merging of national economies as a result of the transnational activities of firms' (Arzeni 1994: 175).[6] So central are the integrating economic forces described above deemed to be that, in the eyes of some analysts, they are both irresistible and bound to overcome the sources of fragmentation. This can be exemplified in the case of nationalism. If this is understood not as some primordial, and permanent, feature of social existence, then it can be seen as itself an artifact created by the needs of a particular nineteenth-century economic system. At that stage, capitalism required the skills and infrastructure that a national system of organization was best equipped to deliver. Historically, and by extension, it is not unreasonable to suggest that such a remorseless progress of economic activity might in turn destroy its own offspring—the nationally organized economy—by shaping a rudimentary globalized polity to service the needs of a globalized economy. It is some such notion that Francis Fukuyama seems to have in mind. He suggests that nationalism once fulfilled an integrative role that met the needs of early capitalism, but that 'those same economic forces are now encouraging the breakdown of national barriers through the creation of a single, integrated world market' (1992: 275). Globalization, on this account, is manifestly an economic process which contours the political landscape as it surges through it.

What kind of evidence is there to sustain such arguments, and how convincing is it? These issues will be explored further throughout the book. However, by way of introductory summary, the economic arguments concentrate upon the system of manufacture and production (and the extent to which it remains territorially based), on levels of international trade (and how these compare to levels of production), on the extent of international capital flows (and their geographical spread), and on the role of multinational companies. Each issue area is contested. Hirst demonstrates that many of the indices of globalization, such as trade and investment patterns, reveal a stark concentration within the OECD states, and concludes that it 'is the advanced industrial economies that constitute the membership of the "global" economy' (Hirst 1995: 7). This is a much more modest conception of globalization than the rhetoric of its proponents would have us believe. Dicken, while himself accepting the main elements of the globalization thesis, readily concedes that the statistics reveal an overwhelming concentration within the advanced industrial states as the source and destination of foreign direct investment; indeed, some three-quarters of the total (Dicken 1992: 54). On this basis, we should speak of 'Triadization' rather than globalization (Ruigrok

---

[6] See Barry Jones (1995) for detailed discussion of the varieties of economic globalization.

and van Tulder 1995: 151; Spybey 1996: 5). There is also disagreement about the significance of the multinationals. Whilst most economists recognize the scale of their activities (see e.g. Dicken 1992: 47–8; Dunning 1994: 364), they dispute the extent to which they remain nationally identified or genuinely transnational, and also their economic power relative to the states which often set the legal ground-rules for their activities. As against the notion of the transnational corporations (TNCs) as the symbols of globalization, some have concluded that none of these corporations can be regarded as 'global', 'footloose', or 'borderless' (Ruigrok and van Tulder 1995: 168; see also Hirst and Thompson 1996).

Whatever the merits of these specific claims and counter-claims, it is unhelpful to analyse the economic aspects of globalization in isolation. Happily, not all versions of globalization concentrate exclusively on developments in the international economy. Some theorists emphasize evidence from political change and from the development of a global society. This offers a wider understanding of globalization, not confined to economic activity, but affecting the nature of human understanding, types of identity, and the development of the social system as a whole. According to Bretherton, political globalization

refers to a growing tendency for issues to be perceived as global in scope, and hence requiring global solutions, and to the development of international organizations and global institutions which attempt to address such issues. More tentatively, the concept also suggests the development of a global civil society, in which local groups and grassroots organizations from all parts of the world interact. (Bretherton and Ponton 1996: 8)

This tends to separate out a 'political' realm from wider social and cultural change whereas other accounts of globalization see it as 'a social process' (Waters 1995: 3) and thus emphasize the all-encompassing forms of such change. To some, this social change is driven above all by the geographical extension of the impact of industrialization.[7] Such a conception, relating globalization to the broad effects of industrialization, has the virtue of moving us away from the restrictive viewpoint of it as a narrowly post-1945 development. One prominent social theorist, Michael Mann, expresses the point in these terms:

In the twentieth century all of these transformations spread over the globe. Today, we live in a global society. It is not a unitary society, nor is it an ideological community or a state, but it is a single power network. (Mann 1993: 11)

Others agree. Martin Shaw echoes Mann:

We have not just some global connections—these have been developing for centuries—but the clear outlines of a global society. We have a global economic system, with production and markets coordinated on a world scale; elements of a global culture of worldwide networks of communication; globally vibrant political ideas and the possibility of coordinated political action. (Shaw 1994*a*: 3)

Central to many of the sociological interpretations of globalization is the notion of culture, and indeed much of the original theorizing about globalization

---

[7] To this extent, 'modernization' and 'convergence' theory are related to, and in part precursors of, globalization theory. See Waters (1995: ch. 2).

developed in this quarter. Roland Robertson asserts that globalization involves 'the development of something like a global culture' (Robertson 1992: 135). His perspective emphasizes a new-found global 'consciousness', as well as physical compression of the world (1992: 8). This does not necessarily mean a uniform and homogenous culture world-wide, as any such claim would be impossible to sustain. What it implies, in a more modest version, is that cultures become 'relativized' to each other but are not 'unified or centralized' (Waters 1995: 125–6). Culture, in this widest sense, then becomes a potent political force as it may grow to threaten the basis of the current fragmented state system and its panoplies of supporting nationalisms. It potentially challenges statism because 'culture avoids being located and tied down to any definable physical space' (Saurin 1995: 256). At the same time, and paradoxically, nationalism 'is one of the components of culture that has been transmitted around the globe', both 'a globalized and a globalizing phenomenon' (Waters 1995: 136). Such notions are problematic. Many would doubt the viability of the notion of culture without an indentifiable community. This issue will be returned to below when the role of nationalism is discussed in the context of processes of fragmentation.

It thus becomes apparent that, while globalization features prominently as a concept in many disciplines, its manifestations are described in strikingly different terms, as are the bodies of empirical evidence adduced in support. The same diversity can be found in the treatment of its sources.

The Sources of Globalization

What causes globalization? To some historians, this global social integration is no more than the fruits of pervasive Westernization under the impact of the latter's historical dominance. In this account, 'the world revolution of Westernization brought together, in inescapably intimate and virtually instant interaction, all the peoples of the world' (Von Laue 1987: 3).[8] For others, it is simply the spread of the characteristic features of modernity. Giddens identifies these as: the nation-state system; the world capitalist economy; the world military order; and the international division of labour. Thus conceived, modernity comes as a package and it makes little sense to ask which particular element within it enjoys, as it were, causal primacy. One commentator notes that, for Giddens, globalization then becomes '*an enlargement* of modernity, from society to the world. It is modernity on a global scale' (Robertson 1992: 141–2).

As already indicated in the introduction, the main disagreement of concern to this study is whether globalization is an exogenous process with 'its own inexorable logic'[9] (driven by technology, economic organization, and related social

---

[8] Spybey (1996: 34) makes the similar claim that 'Western civilization *is* the world's first truly global culture'.

[9] This is Waters's (1995: 46) description of Robertson's position.

and cultural change)—and to this extent independent of international relations—or whether it is itself a creation of international relations and the behaviour of states. Liberal versions of globalization adhere to the former point of view
in so far as 'states and governments are bystanders to globalisation: the real driving forces are markets' (Hurrell and Woods 1995: 448). If viewed as the latter, it
may well be a discontinuous and reversible process, and it is the argument of this
book that the historical evidence leans towards that point of view.

How then might globalization be shaped by international political forces?
While many writers are sympathetic to such a general perspective, they often
retain substantial disagreements about the precise nature of this relationship. To
illustrate this diversity, we may differentiate among five interpretations of the primarily international political determination of globalization. All will inform the
subsequent historical analysis.

According to the first school, globalization has been shaped by the major international trend of the past several centuries, namely Westernization. It was the
economic and military incorporation of the world by Europe that created the precondition of an integrated global system. As Bull and Watson saw it, 'it was the
expansion of Europe that first brought about the economic and technological
unification of the globe', and they add to this that 'it was the European-dominated
international society of the nineteenth and early twentieth centuries that first
expressed its political unification' (1984: 2).[10] In terms of this perspective, globalization could only develop once the territorial integration of the world had been
wrought by European power and once that world had been subjected to Western
technology and rationality.

A second approach also emphasizes the global balance of power but does so in
a more general sense: globalization was not triggered by a one-off historical
process (Westernization), but is rather fostered and hindered by general fluctuations in the distribution of international power. This is a clear assertion of the
essentially dependent, rather than autonomous, role of globalization:

> The lifetime of a prevailing system of international economic relations in this century has
> been no more than 30–40 years. Such systems have been transformed by major changes in
> the politico-economic balance of power and the conjunctures that have effected these
> shifts have been large scale conflicts between the major powers. In that sense, the world-
> wide international economy has been determined in its structure and the distribution of
> power within it by the major nation states. (Hirst 1995: 2–3)

On this reasoning, it is fallacious to assume a unidirectionality towards increasing globalization: it will wax and wane in accordance with the play of international relations.

A third approach is to emphasize not the balance of power in general, but a specific hegemonic balance in particular. Dominant states, if their interests are
served by 'open' international orders, create by their own national power the
essential precondition and support for the activities that we recognize as consti-

---

[10] Likewise, Waters (1995: 3–4) argues that '[g]lobalization is the direct consequence of the
expansion of European culture across the planet via settlement, colonization and cultural mimesis'.

tuting globalization. Barry Jones gives a detailed account of the necessity of prior political determination before interdependence and globalization can occur. He gives pride of place to 'the central role of political purposes and processes in the generation of contemporary international interdependence and globalisation' (1995: 15). In discussing the historical hegemonies of Britain and the United States, he notes that frequently a sympathetic political environment is created by 'a dominant political and economic actor' (1995: 171–2).

A fourth version of the relationship is less concerned with distributions of power internationally than with the residual, and powerful, resources of states in general. Dicken, himself an exponent of the globalization thesis, none the less remains convinced that states, while constrained by globalized economic activities, are far from powerless in confronting them. On the contrary, globalization is itself directed by 'the varying fortunes of national economies—and the state policies which underpin them' (Dicken 1992: 149). Such a general perspective is given specific illustration by Milward's account of integration in post-war Europe. Rather than seeing a zero-sum relationship between state power and integration, Milward is firmly of the view that the latter is a product of the former and that the two are mutually reinforcing processes: 'Integration was not the supersession of the nation-state by another form of governance as the nation-state became incapable, but was the creation by the European nation-states themselves for their own purposes, an act of national will' (1992: 18). Integration, on this view, reflects state choices and not simply a particular international configuration of power, nor yet an autonomous process over which the states have no control. The same can be said of globalization.

Finally, there are writers whose account of globalization seems initially to be predicated on the determining influence of a global economic system rather than on interstate relations. On closer examination, however, some autonomy of international politics in shaping globalization is preserved, even if in reduced and modified form. R. W. Cox is the best example of this approach. While devoting most of his argument to the transition in the basis of economic organization, he highlights the contradiction that 'the globalizing interdependence principle is strengthened as the territorial national principle is weakened'. The significance of this is that, according to Cox, '*ultimately the security of globalization depends upon military force with a territorial basis*' (Cox 1993: 149, 150; emphasis added). Even as globalization is fostered through the instrumentality of the economic system, it has to be sustained by powerful states willing to take military action to preserve it.

While sharing a view about the essential primacy of political determination, these interpretations retain important nuances of difference. We need not make absolute choices between them. Once again, it is hoped that a loosely corporatist perspective will provide a point of linkage, especially in its attempted integration of the geopolitical aspects of the balance of power and the changing domestic political economy of the states operating within it.

There is one final issue about globalization that needs to be clarified. Is the process of globalization autonomous? It may appear that this is simply to restate the problem, already considered, about the causes of globalization. However, the issues are discrete. Whatever the original motive force of globalization, it is perfectly conceivable that, once initiated, the process may become independent of these factors and develop its own self-perpetuating dynamic. Even if the process requires initial 'political determination', it may thereafter become autonomous, following its own agenda. There might thus be no necessary contradiction between arguing that globalization is politically determined, but also that it becomes an autonomous process. Elsewhere, there has been much interest in the capacity of 'regimes' to outlive their initial circumstances and, for example, in the survivability of the post-war economic and political orders even after the relative decline of the American hegemon, the putative architect of that order (see e.g. Keohane 1984). The problem with globalization is similar: irrespective of initial causes, does it generate its own momentum? And is that momentum reversible or irreversible? The answers to such questions hold important implications for any assessment of the post-cold war world.

The Nature of Fragmentation

Just how resistible, or irresistible, globalization is depends finally upon our understanding of fragmentation, and it is to the exposition of this force that the argument must now turn. Fragmentation expresses itself in many ways: autarchy, unilateralism, disintegration, heterogeneity, and separation. But is it an independent and recurring force? Is it simply the passive reflection of deeper economic and political influences? Is it directly related to globalization?

The initial problem with any analysis of fragmentation is in finding the appropriate level of analysis because, Janus-like, many developments that might be regarded as integrative *at one level* are, at the same time, *fragmentationist* at another. There is no better illustration of this duality than in the role of the state, and of nationalism. It has already been demonstrated that many theories of globalization postulate the state system, in counterpoint to the economic system, as a source of fragmentation. But equally, states, and the official doctrines of nationalism that have succoured many of them since the late nineteenth century, have served as sources of unity and integration within their boundaries. Whether states are integrative, or disintegrative, depends then upon whether one is to consider their external or their internal roles. As Wallerstein has explained, '[i]n one case, they have used their force to create cultural diversity, and in the other case to create cultural uniformity' (1991: 192–3).

This ambiguity can be taken further: the very spread of the state system, geographically, has itself represented a point of global unity, however paradoxical such a suggestion might appear. This is the thrust of the claim that the universalization of the state has 'standardized the form of political life' (Brown 1995: 56). This reveals how difficult it is to make any judgement about globalizing and fragmentationist tendencies, since many real-life events embody elements of both and much depends upon the perspective from which they are addressed. Indeed, much may depend on differing historical experiences. Accordingly, James Mayall nicely captures the ambivalence of humanity's encounter with nationalism and the mixed verdict which history records:

In the West, nationalism is very often considered to be a curse, whereas in the south it is thought of as a blessing. The explanation of this difference in perception can only be historical: in the one case nationalism is associated with war, destruction and irrational intolerance; in the other with progress, the transcendence of parochial loyalties and development. (Mayall 1990: 111)

The experiment with nationalism has been both disintegrative and integrative, and the historian is helpless to find the supreme vantage point from which to make any more authoritative claim.

For the student of international relations, of course, it is not the mere existence of nationalism that is of interest but whether its fragmentationist effects create the potential for instability and conflict. We should, however, be careful to avoid any automatic correspondence between globalization and stability, on the one hand, and fragmentation and instability, on the other. If intensified nationalism is itself a reaction to globalization, then fragmentation is scarcely the fundamental source of any resulting instability.

Some historians do, however, connect nationalism and instability, since the doctrine has become the basic principle of state legitimacy while, in practice, the identity between state and nation can never be more than approximate. It is for this reason that Kedourie, amongst others, dismisses national self-determination as 'a principle of disorder, not of order' (1984: 348–9). And yet Woodrow Wilson, the principle's champion, fought to enshrine it not only as the basis of democratic government domestically, but even more importantly as an essential element within a legitimate and stable *international* order.

Just as there are debates about the autonomy of globalization, likewise there are debates about the autonomy of fragmentation. Does it represent a primordial and inalienable force? Or is it a product of specific historical conditions and of policy choices?

There are intense disagreements about the historical meaning of nationalism. Writers such as Ernest Gellner have identified nationalism with the demands of industrializing economies and thus with specific historic conditions. To become economically competitive, states in the nineteenth century had to organize themselves for the task and create a 'homogenous society with an educational system for all' (Kellas 1981: 42). Nationalism from this perspective is the handmaiden of effective industrialization. Hobsbawm places the emphasis elsewhere. He contends that nationalism initially, in the first half of the nineteenth century, served a positive democratic task in seeking to define the now-sovereign people, but then degenerated later in the century into a narrow ethnic and linguistic form which he thinks disruptive. In neither version is nationalism autonomous but is subsidiary to wider economic and political developments: nationalism is an epiphenomenon of history, not one of its motors.

One way of intitially framing these issues is to explore a view, common in the literature, that fragmentation is a dialectical response to globalization, as opposed to some atavistic relic: the more globalization intensifies, the fiercer will be the pockets of resistance to its intrusive sway. The issue is clearly framed by Smith:

In the era of globalization and transcendence, we find ourselves caught in a maelstrom of conflicts over political indentities and ethnic fragmentation . . . How can this paradox be explained? Is it an inevitable product of a dialectic of cultural globalization which produces a new kind of identity politics . . ., or just a 'survival' from an earlier age of nationalist hatreds and wars? (Smith 1995: 2–3)

The appeal of such an image is that it provides an interesting hypothesis to account for the ebb and flow of periods of both globalization and fragmentation. As the costs and inconveniences of fragmentation arise, there are evoked numerous measures that foster globalization. In turn, when these threaten to become predominant, fragmentationist tendencies reassert themselves: thus is an uneasy equilibrium preserved and the cycle can once more repeat itself. Such self-correction seems too mechanistic and we need to explain it politically. If there is evidence to support such an equilibrium theory, how might it relate to state policies? The image which it presents is of a recurring dialectic, but how might the policy choices of states relate to it?

There are certainly many arguments that explicitly link fragmentation to globalization: fragmentation is a dialectical response to globalization. Succinctly expressed, 'globalization stimulates forces of opposition which may just as readily lead to an increasingly fragmented world' (McGrew *et al.* 1992: 23). Hassner explains this in terms of some deep-seated social-psychological need to differentiate: in the face of the 'powerful homogenizing influence' of the contemporary world, the need for 'diversity and separation' grows (1993: 55).

Robertson portrays this as a major theme of twentieth-century international history. The prime characteristic of the century has been 'global compression' and, accordingly, he sees a variety of ideologies as being evoked in reaction to this trend: he enumerates German fascism, Japanese neo-fascism, communism, and Wilsonian 'self-determinationism' as particularist ideologies stimulated in response to 'the globalization process which had begun in the late nineteenth century' (1992: 18–19).

But how might such a dialectical relationship be explained? Three variations of the argument can be identified to illustrate the possible connections. In the first, and as previously encountered, globalization is understood as Westernization or as the spread of modernity. Accordingly, fragmentation is driven by resistance to the 'hegemony' of this set of ideas and institutional practices. This is the version presented by Rob Walker: 'Resistance to the all-pervasive forces of modernization along Western lines . . . has become a major characteristic of the twentieth century. Concepts of autonomy, nationalism and pluralism have come to challenge the assumed universality of progress towards the "civilization" of the West' (1984: 183).

Secondly, the dialectic is occasionally presented as a necessity of the world capitalist system. It is capitalism itself which generates an ambivalent role for states and the state system, and hence 'both nationalism and internationalism represent politico-ideological responses to the structural conditions implicit in the capital accumulation process' (Wallerstein 1991: 154). Although operating within such a broadly materialist framework, Cox allows that resistance to globalization may possibly emerge from a more 'voluntaristic' form of political action. Dealing with a speculative future, he projects the formation of alliances which might impede the progress of globalization. Envisioning coalitions of the deprived with support from segments of the dominant groups, Cox thinks it possible that there will be secessionist territorial movements away from globalization: 'This reaffirmation of the territorial principle of economic and social organization will be perceived as challenging the structures of global economy' (Cox 1993: 143–4). The opposition to globalization will thus come from the disadvantaged, 'who will affirm the right of social forces to make economy and polity serve their own self-determined goals' (1992: 145).

Thirdly, there is the argument that, rather than in dialectical opposition, the two forces are complementary: indeed, in some cases, they are integral parts of each other. Thus in a reformulation of his own position, Robertson no longer posits fragmentation as a reaction to globalization. Instead, he sees it as 'an aspect—or, indeed, as a creation—of globalization' inasmuch as 'identity declaration is built into the general process of globalization' (1992: 174–5).

Not all, however, subscribe to the view that fragmentation is linked to globalization, regardless of the precise mechanism of which the link is a part. Anthony D. Smith is the most vocal champion of the thesis that nationalism—a potent source of fragmentation—has its own autonomous history and is not a creation of the capitalist system, nor of the course of international relations, and certainly not of globalization itself. Dismissing the wider reverberations of modernity and globalization, he adheres to the view that the key to understanding nationalism 'lies more with the persisting frameworks and legacies of historical cultures and ethnic ties than with the consequences of global interdependence' (Smith 1995: vii–viii): nationalist fragmentation, if thus regarded, is a story apart.

Equally, Smith's is the strongest voice against the view that emerging global cultures may come to replace those currently in existence. Central to his concept of culture is that of collective memory, and since there can be no such 'global memory', it follows that putative images of a globalizing culture must be mere fabrications: 'a timeless global culture answers to no living needs and conjures no memories. If memory is central to identity, we can discern no global identity in-the-making' (Smith 1995: 24).

This returns the argument to the issue of political determination. In Smith's analysis, the elements of global culture owe 'their origins and much of their appeal to the power and prestige of one or other of the great metropolitan power centres' (1995: 18–19): any globalization of culture, induced by international politics, is skin deep and destined to pass away with the next shift in international power. It does not have the resilience of 'true' cultures, based on memory and history. What passes for global culture is no more than the contingent outcome of a moment in international politics: it simply captures the residue of power politics.

Such an analysis seems to follow that earlier, and authoritatively, provided by Bozeman. The argument here is that there is no globally shared system of meaning: each is culture specific. There was, indeed, the semblance of unity from the late nineteenth century until 1945, induced by Westernization, but this has proved illusory. The vestiges of global culture are now being stripped away by the currents of international politics such that, Bozeman warns, 'the de-westernization and de-establishment of the norms and institutions that together had sustained the short-lived global international order constitutes a major challenge for European and American diplomacy' (1984: 404–5). The diagnosis is that an overlay of cultural homogeneity had been forged by international relations but is likewise being removed by it.

Finally, it is perhaps a dangerous assumption that technological developments necessarily favour globalization. Thus Smith challenges yet another of the central premises of globalization theory. The technical accoutrements of communication—the very nervous system of all accounts of globalization—may in fact be more even-handed in their impact on the two processes. There is a tendency to assume—and not to argue—that these communications help break down existing communities in favour of the 'global village'. Smith's contention, however, is that these very instruments also sustain existing social networks; indeed, they may strengthen them. If this be the case, fragmentation is as likely as is globalization to thrive in the communications revolution of the late twentieth century.

While much of the discussion of fragmentation necessarily concentrates upon varieties of nationalism, attention also needs to be drawn briefly to the ambivalent role of regionalism. It is difficult to locate regionalism on a spectrum between fragmentation and globalization. As against nationalist fragmentation, regionalism represents a degree of multilateralism and integration: as against globalization, regionalism may have the appearance of being an oppositional tendency, leading to regional blocs, and countering the formation of globalist institutions or agendas. One analyst suggests that regionalism marks a 'shifting away from "multilateralism" . . . towards a system based upon competing regional blocs', whereas globalization implies that there is 'a general shift underway which has favoured markets and firms rather than states' (Wyatt-Walter 1995: 74–5). This ambivalence is recognized and commentators have suggested that regionalism both fosters, and hinders, wider globalist tendencies.[11] This is a complex relationship and certainly not one in which regionalism can be viewed as the simple anithesis of globalization. One set of studies concludes that contemporary regionalism should be regarded as 'a step towards globalism rather than as an alternative to it' (Gamble and Payne 1996: 251).

What emerges from this review is that the nature and sources of fragmentation are as contested as those of globalization. Fragmentation also takes many diverse forms and is expressed in aspects of political, social, economic, and cultural life. There are deep divisions about whether fragmentation is a kind of 'original sin', or something which is thrown up by more basic political and economic change.

[11]   Hurrell (1995*a*: 345–6). Wyatt-Walter (1995: 77), regards the relationship between regionalization and globalization as 'more symbiotic than contradictory'.

More particularly, there are disputes about whether the balance between fragmentation and globalization is affected by international relations or not. All these
possibilities will be considered in the historical survey which follows.

The Way Ahead

This introductory survey has raised a number of issues and posed a series of questions. It leaves us with an agenda that can be pursued through the remainder of
this work. In summary, the key points to emerge, and to which we will regularly
return are: what forms did globalization and fragmentation take at various junc-
tures throughout the twentieth century; does the evidence support the view that
these are exogenous processes; if not, are they related to specific structures, such
as the economic system; or are they related, and if so how, to the characteristics of
the international system and the goals of the key states within it; how, in turn,
does state behaviour reflect changing domestic agendas; above all, how do globalization and fragmentation relate to each other; does the one cause the other in
dialectical opposition, or are they inextricable facets of the same single process?
Only when we unravel some of these perplexities will we begin to achieve some
wider perspective on the international history of the twentieth century.

The main points in the approach to be adopted in this book can be summarized at this stage. Its perspective shares the view that globalization and fragmentation are multi-faceted: they have important technological, economic, political,
social, and cultural aspects. It rejects a view of historical discontinuity which
posits globalization as a process which can only be so described after 1945 and
prefers, in contrast, to trace the historical evolution of these trends. Their development has not been unidirectional and the balance between globalization and
fragmentation has shifted across various historical periods within the twentieth
century. On this evidence it would be rash to subscribe to any deterministic view
of the irresistible and autonomous drive towards globalization *per se*, let alone to
teleological notions of the unfolding of a grand globalizing design. None the less,
the terminology of globalization and fragmentation, for all its imprecision and
diversity of reference, offers us a scheme through which a central dynamic of the
twentieth century can be explored and better understood.

In particular, while avoiding any crude political determinism, the emphasis in
this book will be upon the voluntaristic impact of state behaviour as a powerful
source of the tendencies towards both globalization and fragmentation, and of
the relative balance between the two. It will concentrate upon the shifts between
globalization and fragmentation, not as some mechanistic device, but as a reflection of the *transference of political costs* as mediated through states: sometimes
globalization has shifted the burden to domestic sectors; at others, domestic
interests have been given priority and international fragmentation has resulted.
None of this is automatic, nor mechanical, but it is explicable in terms of the
working out of political preferences.

In spirit, this is akin to the approach developed by Hurrell and Woods, even if the scope of the present discussion is both wider and more historical in intent. Hurrell and Woods implicitly attack the notion of processes of globalization having 'a logic and dynamic of their own' and seek to 'replace the liberal Kantian image of *progressive enmeshment* with the more complex idea of *coercive socialisation*' (Hurrell and Woods 1995: 451, 457). Key to an understanding of this 'coercive socialization' is the role played by powerful states for whom globalization is to a degree 'a realm of choice'. These choices were made at two levels, some between states and some within them: only by creating a framework which incorporates both, can we make them intelligible. How these choices came to be formulated, and what conditions led to their exercise, can now be examined in the following survey of the twentieth century.

2

THE PARADOXES OF THE PRE-WAR
WORLD, 1900–1914

Few periods reveal such stark paradoxes between globalizing and fragmentationist tendencies as that of the pre-war generation. Historians share a consensus that
the decades around the opening of the new century experienced significant
expansion in the geographical scope of the international system and also momentous increases in the intensity of interactions, and patterns of integration, within
it. This was particularly so with regard to the global scope of the balance of power
(and the new conceptions of it), as well as in the powerful emergence of heightened levels of economic interdependence. The faltering steps through international arbitration towards the Hague Conferences either side of century's turn, as
well as the growth of intergovernmental and non-governmental organizations,
pointed towards future concepts of international governance of varying degrees
of formality and institutionalization. To this extent, the ushering in of the twentieth century marked the beginning of globalized international relations.

At the same time, the drift to cataclysmic war in 1914, and the competitive
nationalisms and social Darwinism of the age, are collectively regarded as the final
apotheosis of that fragmentationist nationalism released by the French
Revolution: it was an age, more conscious than most, of the competitive nature of
international relations and of the shifting balance of economic power. This more
intensely divided international society was also mirrored in the new divisions
within national societies engendered by the effects of industrialization and rapid
social change. Indeed, national foreign policies revealed precisely the intimate
connection between the seemingly more hostile international environment and
the new social and political demands that pressed governments from within. This
chapter will review the international relations of the pre-1914 period from this
twin perspective and explore the extent to which globalization and fragmentation
were dialectically interrelated, the extent to which globalization was induced by
the remorseless logic of exogenous technological and economic development, or
the extent to which it was related to the specific characteristics of international
relations, and the policies of the individual powers, responding to the cross-
cutting pressures of the period.

In fact, it may be erroneous to suggest that the relationship between globalization and fragmentation is paradoxical during this period. We will consider their interrelationship in general terms, and particularly the view that both tendencies were actually the simultaneous and systematic expression of identical pressures: far from being paradoxical, the two were necessary parts of each other.

Many historians strike the note of paradox—of opposed and inconsistent tendencies of development within the pre-war international system. Above all, they tend to emphasize trends towards interdependence and integration, on the one hand, and the contrary development of a self-centred and autonomous pursuit of national economic and security interests, on the other. Michael Howard notes the duality of an emerging transnational order, including peace movements and proletarian labour organizations, as well as the more obvious developments in transport, communications, and banking. He describes the two Hague Conferences as 'the first emergence . . . of a truly transnational search for international security'. As against this, he is also struck by the increasing popularity of 'unilateral solutions' and finds evidence of the retreat from interdependence in the loss of faith in free trade and the new-found vision of autarchic empires (Ahmann *et al.* 1993: 8–9).

There are various ways in which this seemingly contradictory duality might be explained. For some, it is simply the reflection of the interaction of two inconsistent logics—the logic of capitalism versus the logic of a state-centred political system. As the state was rapidly consolidating its sovereign authority, as well as its mechanisms of real social control, it was discovering that it could not monopolize all activities within its confines, and, as Rosenberg remarks, was learning the lesson that 'the economy is not . . . entirely a nationally constituted instrument ready at the disposal of the state' (Rosenberg 1994: 14). But such a crass opposition seems scarcely to go far enough in explaining similarly dualistic tendencies within the economic realm itself. Thus for one economic historian, the striking characteristic of the period was precisely the quest for 'unilateral solutions' in international economic life—the formation of cartels and monopolies, the resort to tariffs to buffer domestic producers, and the organization of the working class (Maier 1985: 107). The contradiction was not then simply one between the economic and political spheres, but pervaded both domains separately.

For others, then, the contradiction needs to be explained by shifts in domestic political balances of power. In one case, it is presented as a kind of dialectical struggle between a seemingly enlightened middle class trying to hold out against the coruscating displays of mass politics:

Everywhere national exclusiveness grew with greater political participation by the bulk of the population, whose ignorance undermined the faint but widespread cosmopolitanism of liberal middle class culture. At a time when worldwide interdependence deepened by leaps and bounds, nation-centred public opinion narrowed the possibilities for peaceful international adjustment. (Von Laue 1987: 47)

On this account, the middle classes served as a point of unity whereas the emerging mass politics thrown up by industrialism was divisive and centrifugal. To be sure, there had been a liberal commercial cosmopolitanism in mid-century but had it survived the depression from the late 1870s onwards? And is it fair to so readily dismiss the cosmopolitan tendencies of the international socialist movement, however ineffective against the nationalist temper it was to prove in 1914? An analysis of the period framed around a stark opposition between the internationalism of the middle classes as against the nationalism of the working classes seems scarcely adequate, but at least begins to draw our attention towards the domestic social tensions which were becoming such an important element of international behaviour.

If one way of conceiving of globalization and fragmentation is as contradictory and oppositional forces, caused by some other factor or factors, then another is to regard them as interacting causes and effects. Two illustrations might be offered to establish such connections. At the most general level, some theorists advance the notion that it was precisely the globalizing tendencies of the period that evoked a defensive fragmentationist consolidation: the state became more generally established, and more effective in its domestic organization, for no other reason than the systemic pressures emanating from the globalization that was taking place. This, at any rate, appears to be the thrust of the claim that 'modern national society was in significant part *produced by* the contingencies of the compression of the world, on the one hand, and the nearly global diffusion of ideas concerning the form that the national society should take, on the other' (Robertson 1992: 142–3).

Elsewhere, the contradiction is equally explained in the specific context of imperialism by positing a direct relationship between the globalizing effects of imperialism and the fragmentationist aspirations which it created. In Barraclough's view, the turn of the century was the great imperial watershed, marking the high-water point of Europe's mastery of the world but also inaugurating a new period that would lead to its inevitable destruction. This was no mere coincidence, nor do we need to appeal to further, and extraneous, factors to account for the change. Rather, the one development necessitated the other. As Barraclough argued, 'it was a paradox of the new imperialism that it released pressures which made its own tenets unworkable. By stirring the outer world into activity it loosened the ties of empire' (Barraclough 1967: 74–5).

Whether they suggest that globalization and fragmentation are merely driven by exogenous forces, or interrelated as cause and effect, the common element to all such accounts is that the two processes are treated as separate tendencies: it follows that the task of the historian is to account for, or explain away, the resultant paradoxes and contradictions entailed by their simultaneous assertion within the same historical period. But there remains one final school of thought which would attack the very notion of paradox and contradiction itself, and this is the view that they are both expressions of a single and consistent logic. Indeed, in these terms, it is questionable whether globalization and fragmentation can be regarded as a duality at all: it is better that they be regarded as one encompassing historical trend. What this suggests is that globalization, whatever else it may have wrought, has been the principal instrument for the spread of a particularist, and ultimately fragmentationist, ideal—the nation-state. Whatever other values might have been spread by globalization, it remains the case that its most impressive lagacy has been the spread of national jurisdictions. What we take to be the special paradox of the pre-war period is then no more than the first appearance of a trend which has characterized the remainder of the century: that globalization has functioned to spread fragmentation. It was during this period that the issue became prominent, but there is nothing *sui generis*, in this regard, about the pre-war period in itself.

This seems to be the argument that is hinted at in the writings of some historical sociologists. It is to be found, if not fully developed, in two key passages in the work of Anthony Giddens. Addressing the development of international organizations in the twentieth century, he offers the following analysis:

It might be thought that what we see emerging here is an increasing movement towards 'one world', in which the nation-state form is likely to become less and less significant in the face of global patterns of organization . . . The sovereignty of the nation-state, I have suggested, does not precede the development of the European state system, or the transferral of the nation-state system to a global plane. State authorities did not hold large areas of sovereign power destined to become increasingly confined by the growing network of international connections and modes of interdependence. On the contrary . . . [t]he period of the burgeoning of international organizations . . . is not one of the growing transcendence of the nation-state. It is one in which the universal scope of the nation-state was established.

Elsewhere, he returns to the same central point and concludes that the coming of the nation-state as the universal political form 'is something inherently connected with, and in substantial degree an outcome of, those very transnational connections that have seemed to many to signal its imminent demise' (Giddens 1985: 263, 291). There is no contradiction, no dialectic, between globalization and fragmentation: they are simply two facets of the same process. And yet, however compelling such an argument might be with respect to the spread of national or state ideologies across the globe, it does not itself explain the fluctuations between periods of pronounced globalization and those of resistant fragmentation: if parts of the same process, how do we account for their relative degrees of prominence?

In order to assess these issues of interpretation, we will finally come back to developments in the role of the state itself during this period. Initially, however, we need to consider the general characteristics of the international relations of the pre-war period and the bodies of evidence that point to the dimensions of globalization and fragmentation respectively.

Globalization in Pre-war International Relations

The first and most obvious manifestation of globalization at the time might be the very culmination of expansionist imperialism. More than any other single development, it was this which brought geographically remote parts of the world into military, political, economic, and cultural contact with each other. And yet it is just as obvious that we cannot fully identify the particularities of late nineteenth-century globalization with the more general process of European expansionism, nor with imperialism old or new, for the very reason that the latter was a long historical process stretching back at least to the sixteenth century.

None the less this expansionism, and the dramatic spurt in territorial partition which occurred in the last quarter of the nineteenth century, provides the essential texture of the period. For purposes of understanding the century, its opening year might be thought a defining moment precisely in terms of the extent of European expansionism. As Hedley Bull has asserted, 'European or Western dominance of the universal international society may be said to have reached its apogee about the year 1900' (Bull and Watson 1984: 219), and this is a sufficiently apocalyptic note on which to open our historical survey.

Some measure of the changing texture of international relations is provided by the growth in numbers of states participating in international meetings but, more especially, in the dilution of their purely European character. At the Congress of Vienna, in 1815, the attendance was exclusively European; at the Congress of Paris, in 1856, the European powers were joined by the Ottoman Empire by courtesy of extending the operations of the European concert to this area. In contrast, the first Hague Conference held in 1899 included also as participants the USA, Mexico, China, Japan, Persia, and Siam, and the second such meeting in 1907 was further joined by sixteen Latin American republics (Bull and Watson 1984: 123). However, this in itself is not a measure of the effects of imperialism alone on the international system as the extra-European powers participating in these meetings were precisely those which had, at least to some degree, either avoided or already escaped the imperial system: the widening membership of international society reflected changes beyond the imperial encounter.

Sadly, the historical analysis of this expansionism, and especially of the new imperialism towards century's end, has been obsessively concerned with its causes at the expense of a wider understanding of its impact on the nature of international relations. Historians have variously championed the views that it was sparked by the domestic condition of the European states themselves, by the pressures of the European balance of power (to which expansion acted as a 'safety valve'), and by developments within the periphery itself which demanded a more assertive imperial presence and which consequently portray European imperial policy as no more than a 'fit of absence of mind'. Most vitriolically, the debate since Hobson and Lenin, and countered by writers such as David Fieldhouse, has been about the importance of economic factors, especially movements of capital and the quest for trade.[1]

Each of these interpretations has strengths and weaknesses. It may well be that interests in France sought colonies as a sop for damaged pride after the humiliating defeat of 1871 at Prussian hands, and interests within Germany as a means of reconciling agrarian, industrialist, and working-class tensions. This can hardly be

---

[1] Much of this is succinctly summarized in Lowe (1994).

a sufficient account on its own without the opportunities presented on the periphery and the permissive circumstances within Europe as a whole. Thus, as against the safety-valve notion, Bartlett is correct to emphasize that it was perhaps less the dangers within Europe that contributed to overseas expansion and more the reassurance offered 'by the relative calm in Europe so that they felt free to pursue their ambitions in the wider world' (Bartlett 1994: 15). For Germany, whatever the press of domestic politics, it was also the tangible feeling of continental encirclement by the Franco-Russian entente which rendered credible the programme for a break-out into colonies and spheres of economic interest, especially in the Near East (Lowe 1994: 14). It may also be significant that the pursuit of these imperial interests seldom brought the powers to the brink of crisis: Bartlett regards the Central Asian Penjdeh crisis of 1885 and the North African Fashoda crisis in 1898 as the only noteworthy exceptions (Bartlett 1994: 24).

The detail of the disputes about the economic sources of imperialism need not detain us. What is more important for our purpose than an analysis of the causes of late nineteenth-century imperialism is an assessment of its effects. For the moment two may be noted. The first draws our attention to a seemingly paradoxical interplay between globalization and fragmentation. To the extent that economic factors were important in the new imperialism, it has been argued that they reflected the newly competitive mood of the Great Depression of the late 1870s and 1880s. This bore particularly on a British economy already losing its edge: of major concern was the flight from free trade, leaving Britain as the last redoubt of this cause and exposing it to the chill winds of protectionism elsewhere (Lowe 1994: 77). Paradoxically, to the extent that this impinged upon British imperial expansion, it also served to develop the notion of Empire as a single living organism: fragmentation in the international economy, as well perhaps as in international security, thus helped foster an integrated concept of Empire as an economic and strategic entity, ideas which took increasing hold in the early years of the new century. As Paul Kennedy remarks:

Just as Britain could send aid to its overseas possessions, so they . . . could assist the imperial power with troops, ships, raw materials, and money—and this was an age when politicians in Whitehall were carefully cultivating their kinsmen overseas in the cause of a more organized 'imperial defense'. (Kennedy 1988: 230–1)

Secondly, the *indirect* effect of the imperial temper of the period was the embroilment of the powers in a number of significant encounters in East Asia. It was here that the emerging changes in the structure of international power were to make themselves felt. Politically and diplomatically, the distinctive form which globalization took at the turn of the century was not the accretion of territory, gradual or dramatic, which had been a feature of Europe's encounter with the rest of the world for centuries but, more particularly, an integrated and reciprocal interaction between the traditional European balance of power and events in East Asia and, thereby, an extension in the scope of the balance of power itself. It is to this process that one writer draws attention in his observation that the seriousness of the clashes in East Asia testified to 'the global nature of the imperial rivalries in this period' (Lowe 1994: 109), but this would not be sufficient to explain the events if the international field of forces had remained constant. In fact, it extended, even if only temporarily. It is to the significance of this expansion of the balance of power that we must turn.

Globalization of the Balance of Power

Many historians have pointed to the years 1895–1905 as an important transitional phase towards the final realization of a globalized international system. Looking back from the vantage point of the high cold war, Barraclough felt able to describe the transition as one in which 'the system of balance of power, European in origin and dependent for its continuance upon the pre-eminence of Europe, gave way to the system of world polarity', and from that distinctive perspective it was a change which would culminate in the 'establishment of great self-contained, continent-wide power blocks, from which iron curtains excluded all extraneous powers' (Barraclough 1967: 108). While, with our hindsight, this was manifestly not the end of history, Barraclough's central contention has much force and others make essentially the same point. Bartlett contents himself by saying that all the great powers 'were profoundly influenced' by the events in East Asia (1994: 25). This claims too little. Langhorne more accurately depicts the structural transformation that was underway when he notes of the international developments in East Asia that they 'were independently acquiring their own momentum, beyond the ability of the great powers to control'. Moreover, he sees this contact between the European concert and an East Asian 'international system in embryo' as fatally damaging to the former precisely because of its inability to control the new forces in this region (Langhorne 1981: 8, 21–2).

The same process can be traced in the intellectual or cultural history of the evolving international system. Thus far, the international system had been basically divided between the European and non-European worlds, with the latter an appendage of the former. By the end of the century, the test for admission into the international society was the 'standard of civilization'. Its historian makes the following suggestive observations:

Dramatic evidence that control of the balance of power no longer resided solely in Europe came with the rise of two non-European great powers, the United States and Japan. The entry of these two Pacific powers onto the international scene during 1895–1905 constituted a major element of change for the international system. It hastened the process by which the the standard of 'civilization' emerged. That the United States and Japan joined the international society during the same years as the standard of 'civilization' emerged as an explicit legal concept was more than a symbolic coincidence. (Gong 1984: 41)

The events themselves can be summarized as follows. Their central dynamic was created by the steady disintegration of political control in Imperial China which, in turn, drew the attention of near neighbours, Russia and Japan, but also that of the emerging Pacific power, the United States, as well as the custodians of the *status quo*, the European great powers. Japan's military defeat of China in 1895 encouraged the Triple Intervention by Russia, France, and Germany to compel Japan to disgorge some of its territorial spoils, in particular the Liaotung peninsula. During 1897–8, China came under renewed pressure as first Germany, followed by Russia, Britain, and France, secured their own particular concessions. The episode evoked the famous Hay Notes by the US Secretary of State in which American commitment to the Open Door in China was reasserted but it was scarcely this which saved China from the fate of Africa. By 1902, the entanglement of East Asia in an increasingly globally conceived balance of power was further demonstrated by the alliance struck between Britain and Japan, confirmation indeed that the latter had now arrived and been accepted into society, a point dramatically underscored by its defeat of Russia in 1905.

It is relatively straightforward in seeking to understand these events to draw the links between Pacific and European developments, as if thereby to imply that Europe still pulled the strings. Certainly, Europe's Triple Intervention against Japan seems to fit with such a view. Again, the fact that Germany participated in this, as also Germany's initiation of the 1897 scramble by its seizure of Kiao Chow, can both be explained by Germany's wish to distract Russia into Far Eastern ventures and thus relieve the European constraints of the Franco-Russian entente. Germany did, in fact, gain from this distraction by feeling safe enough from the Russian army in Europe to transfer funding away from its own army and in favour of its naval build-up (Bartlett 1994: 59). The Anglo-Japanese alliance, in turn, had either a central or a passing impact upon Anglo-French relations, to ensure that they would not be drawn into conflict with each other on the coat-tails of their eastern partners. Finally, Russia's defeat at the hands of Japan incapacitated a key player in the European system with incalculable consequences for the chain of European diplomacy over the subsequent decade (Bridge and Bullen 1980: 156).

The momentous development, of course, was in how these events were perceived at the time. For Britain, the problems which it faced, even if these should not be overstated, were increasingly regarded as part of a single, coherent whole: there were no longer discrete regional balances of military power but a unified world-wide imperial predicament. Britain's commercial dominance in China was threatened by the new territorial acquisitiveness; it continued to face colonial rivalries with its traditional protagonists Russia and France; if Germany was a potential threat to the European balance, the USA was already a real threat to British commercial and financial leadership of the world. In straitened circumstances, Britain had to engage in creative burden-sharing for imperial defence, either by recruiting new allies, as with Japan, or by defusing the points of tension, as with both France and Russia.

Britain's global strategy was as real as that of Imperial Russia, which also had no choice but to play both the parts of European and East Asian proactivist. Surprisingly, it is Germany's global policy that has grabbed the historical headlines: and yet it gained its substance only as a symptom of the globalization of the balance of power that had already taken place but to which it was not itself a contributary factor. For all the diversity of historical accounts of German *Weltpolitik*, their point of unity is the perception that the game had already moved on from the struggle for mastery in Europe and had become a global struggle between the world empires, including the USA, Russia, and Britain. Barraclough insists that it was this perception which gave the urgency to German policy in the first half of the twentieth century, based on a realization that Germany had limited time in which to secure its right to participate in this game ('win our freedom to participate in world politics'), let alone to win it (1967: 115). If this is accepted, Germany must be viewed as reacting to a new condition of the balance of power which had already emerged, rather than as initiating it.

There is ample support for such a view in the literature. Kennedy summarizes Germany's unique predicament as that of being a 'new comer' Great Power and, moreover, one which, if it expanded, could 'only do so at the expense of powerful neighbours' (1988: 214–15). Others have made the same point in noting that 'while Britain came to preside over half the globe, and both Russia and the United States relentlessly filled out their continental hinterlands, Germany was expected to remain locked within the tight frame of Europe's traditional balance of power' (Calleo 1978: 5). This was unacceptable to Germany and the frustration which it created contributed to the reckless quality of German policy. But what this emphasizes is that *Weltpolitik*, however imperfectly thought out and inconsistently pursued, was itself a reflection of the globalization of the balance of power and not a cause of it. Indeed, it was to be the obsession with German power in the first half of the twentieth century that was responsible for the illusion that such a shift in world power had *not* occurred, and that the game of international politics in the 1920s and 1930s could be played in self-contained European fashion according to the old rule book.

The singular development of the period, even if its full effects were to be obscured for some time, was the emergence of the United States as a great power: this, more than any other, symbolized the globalization of the balance of power. Industrial trends, as Kennedy demonstrates (1988: 244), were already destined to make America the leading economic power by the 1920s even before that process was hastened by the effects of the First World War. At the turn of the century, its growth was impressive but had certainly not been translated into effective military power. The vehicle for this transition was to be naval power which absorbed some 6.9 per cent of government spending in 1890 but had swelled to 19 per cent by 1914. Ultimately by the Second World War, this presence was to be decisive; for the time being, it remained potential at best. As noted, the preservation of the Open Door in China cannot be accounted for alone by the vigour of American diplomacy on its behalf. What ensured the notional territorial integrity of China was the much more complex balance of power operating in East Asia at century's end and of which the United States was only one element.

The Alliance Systems and Integration

Although the core of the alliance systems, and especially the Dual Alliance of Germany and Austro-Hungary, was located in Europe, it also responded to wider global developments. As suggested above, Britain's alliance with Japan, and its ententes with France and Russia, are not explicable in exclusively European terms. However, the issue that needs to be addressed is the general impact of the alliances on the international relations of the period, particularly their integrative effects, and their ability to channel tensions from one part of the international system to the remainder.

Ever since President Woodrow Wilson singled out the alliances as the characteristic vice of the old diplomacy, they have been assigned a special responsibility for the outbreak of the war. Most recently, Henry Kissinger has subscribed to the same view in presenting the image of the alliances as the key element of a political Doomsday Machine that rendered war almost inevitable. His main argument, and unlike that of Wilson, is not that the alliances operated as part of a highly unstable balance of power but rather that they introduced a degree of rigidity which *prevented* the balance of power from operating as it should. It is thus the lack of flexibility which he sees as the prime cause of the breakdown, and all attempts (particularly by Germany) to undermine the alliances served only to reinforce them. He thus argues that whereas '[h]istorically, alliances had been formed to augment a nation's strength in case of war; as World War I approached, the primary motive for war was to strengthen the alliances' (Kissinger 1995: 200).

None the less, it remains misleading to view the alliances as the key determinant of war, even if they had a powerful effect upon the nature of the war that eventually resulted. As important as the specific commitments entailed by the various alliances was the degree of open-ended support which the parties chose to lend to their various clients, largely for other reasons. Thus it was not simply a matter of Germany's commitments to Austria, which had existed since 1879 and had effectively restrained Austrian policy in the past, but the fact that Germany's sense of isolation (itself the creation of Germany's own reckless policy) made Germany ever more dependent on retaining Austria's goodwill. Similarly, France could not abandon its ally Russia even though the latter was now pursuing a more dangerous game of courting pan-Slav sentiment in the Balkans as an alternative to the expansion of its sphere of influence in East Asia, which had been prematurely interrupted by its defeat at the hands of Japan. Thus it was the changed context in which the alliances operated that was to be so decisive, and destructive, in the summer of 1914.

That said, it certainly remains the case that the alliances were to have a profound impact on the nature of the war which then started. This was so in at least two respects. First, the operation of the alliance commitments, and in particular the military strategies devised to cope with these, ensured that the war could not be localized. Any war which broke out in 1914 was inevitably to be a general war and this in itself says something of importance about the integrative effects of the alliances. Secondly, because this in turn ensured a clash of two substantial coalitions, in which ultimately the overall resources available would be crucial, it was never likely that the war could be quickly won by either side:

Thus, the alliance system itself virtually guaranteed that the war would *not* be swiftly decided, and meant in turn that victory in this lengthy duel would go . . . to the side whose combination of both military/naval *and* financial/industrial/technological resources was the greatest. (Kennedy 1988: 256)

A Globalized System?

If the evidence for a globalized international system is not to be found exclusively in the imperial expansion of the late nineteenth century, its most likely source is in the economic developments of the period.

To many economic historians, it was the nineteenth century that realized the achievement of an integrated global economy. For Ashworth, the 'outstanding characteristic of the late nineteenth century' was dramatic productive and commercial expansion which led to 'the binding of the whole world into something very close to an economic unit' (1975: 219). This is believed to be so for a number of reasons, foremost amongst which are the rapid expansion of foreign trade, the export of capital, and the creation of international financial institutions and means of international settlement.

The century as a whole witnessed dramatic surges in the volume and value of foreign trade. Much of the increase, especially in the middle decades of the century, can be accounted for by reductions in both tariffs and transport costs. This volume of trading activity necessitated more sophisticated financial institutions. During the century, a complex clearing system developed, based on bills drawn on the London market. The foreign exchange system was also increasingly formalized after the 1870s with widespread adoption of the gold standard. As one economist has noted, '[t]he thirty years before the First World War saw the establishment and working of an international fixed exchange regime, unprecedented in history' (Foreman-Peck 1983: 182). Additionally, the turn of the century represented a high point in the mobility of capital. What collectively is the significance of these trends for our understanding of the globalizing forces at work during this period?

Barraclough felt confident enough to make the categorical assertion that by the end of the nineteenth century 'more of the world was more closely interlocked, economically and financially, than at any time before', and he regarded this as the product of the second (scientific) industrial revolution that left its imprint on the final decades (1967: 55). The most frequently cited evidence for this interlocking was the increased salience of international trade within the world economy.

The standard interpretation of the period presents a very straightforward, and positive, picture in this respect. Not only is the growth in foreign trade seen to be increasing at a rate higher than that of production, but the system achieved a degree of 'openness' comparable with that attained in the dramatic post-1945 period. For instance, we have the following summary judgement:

the European and the world economies were quite open to the movement of goods and people by 1910. Low rail and steam-ship transport costs, and economic policies that, in historical perspective, were still liberal, underlay these highly internationalised economic relations . . . [B]y 1913 Europe's trade/gross national product ratio, at a peak not achieved again until the 1960s and 1970s, indicated that the late nineteenth century nationalist/ liberal international order supported markets at least as free as those created by the post-1945 institutions of GATT and the IMF. (Foreman-Peck 1995: 116)

To this general picture is added the specific statistic that of the sixteen leading economies of the period, growth in output increased by 1.5 per cent per annum from 1870 to 1913, whereas growth in world trade averaged 3.3 per cent across the same period, a performance judged by the analyst as 'remarkable' (Foreman-Peck 1995: 91). This is presented as telling evidence of the increasingly integrated nature of the world trading system.

In one sense, this overall achievement is surprising because, for one of the fastest growing economies, namely the United States, the salience of foreign trade was less dramatic, given the importance of its own domestic market. Thus, inclusion of the United States pulls down the average overall. Kennedy, for example, notes that in 1913, foreign trade accounted for a mere 8 per cent of America's GNP compared with a figure of 26 per cent for Britain at the same time (1988: 244). Indeed, it was protection of the home market which allowed the growth in US exports to spur ahead of growth in imports during this period (Kennedy 1988: 245). None the less, this very imbalance in US trade may itself be thought to have contributed to the world-wide integration of the trading system in that it was to play an important structural role in the system as a whole. In Kennedy's view, Europe's deficit with the United States was met by capital flows to the United States which, in turn, was running a deficit with raw-material supplying countries, and thus served as a financial link in the global pattern (1988: 145).

There has been at least one dissenting voice which challenges the uniformity of this overall account. In his own review of the pertinent statistics, Panic reaches a more nuanced and differentiated interpretation. He contends that the liberal trading order of the period 1860–80 was succeeded by one less so, from the 1880s, with the return of protective tariffs. This was particularly the case with respect to industrial manufacture and trade. Accordingly, he asserts that 'the pace of international integration slackened sharply during the thirty years just before the First World War', on the grounds that rates of manufacturing production increased faster than growth in manufacturing trade. He concedes, however, that the reverse was true in primary commodities, and hence any assessment of the 'openness' and integration of the trading system has to be a variegated one (Panic 1988: 163–4).

There is greater consensus on the integration of world capital markets. On the figures provided by Panic, long-term capital exports as a percentage of GNP remained at unprecedentedly high levels throughout the pre-war generation. He cites a figure of 3.8 per cent in 1870 and 4.9 per cent in 1913 (contrasted with figures of 1.0 per cent or less ever since) (1988: 172). Obviously such statistics must be approached with caution as, in absolute terms, figures in the 1950s and 1960s are high, but simply dwarfed by the explosion in GNP itself. None the less, they provide a telling measure of a major development. Kennedy demonstrates how such capital flows became an important element in the geopolitical fabric. In the case of France, its loans not only gave practical demonstration to its strategic alliance with Russia but were used to unsettle the Italian commitment to the Dual Alliance and to compete with Germany for influence in Turkey and the Balkans (Kennedy 1988: 221). In that sense, the globalization of capital was certainly not a tale that can be divorced from the everyday international politics of the period. The combined effect, however, was to yield a situation in which 'a world capital market integrated a large number of national markets by the last quarter of the nineteenth century' (Foreman-Peck 1995: 120).

What was true for the movement of capital was equally true for the movement of populations. Again, there is broad agreement about the unusually favourable circumstances which facilitated migration, namely improvements in, and reduced costs of, transport coupled with relatively liberal immigration policies. This issued in 'the greatest migration of people . . . the world had ever experienced' (Foreman-Peck 1995: 152). Panic agrees and calculates that the period 1880 to 1913 saw immigration running at an average of 11.3 per cent of increase in world population, compared with 5.3 per cent in 1860–80, 6.2 per cent 1911–30, and a mere 0.9 per cent in 1931–40 (1988: 172).

The final piece of evidence pertaining to a more integrated and 'formally structured' international economic system was its means for managing stable exchange rates, and here there is substantial agreement about the effectiveness of the arrangements in the latter part of the nineteenth century. Indeed, one historian sees this as the foundation stone of the increasing interdependence in such other areas as trade and capital flows, and describes the exchange rate system as 'remarkably stable' (Milward 1992: 9). The key to this was the gold standard system which, by encouraging stability, also reduced the risks of trade and investment and thereby served to stimulate them (Foreman-Peck 1995: 154). Panic, however, notes that the gold standard system was itself under stress by 1914 and could probably not have survived, even if the First World War had not intervened and brought it to an end (1988: 181–2). Its collapse in 1914 was the result of a long-developing crisis within the system, and when the tree finally fell, it was already 'rotten' (Cecco 1974: ix, 128).

It is possible to regard much of the internationalization of economic activities in the late nineteenth century as simply the spin-off of technological developments, particularly in transport and communications. Moreover, some of these developments were themselves to shape the conduct of international relations. For instance, one need only mention the impact of railroad development on military strategy and upon geopolitical calculations, and the reduced autonomy of far-flung ambassadors in conducting their personalized diplomacy wrought by the inception of the telegraph. None the less, the idea that technological development by itself determines the internationalization or globalization of economic activities must surely be erroneous as this cannot account for the subsequent periods of relative closure in the international economy during which these self-same technological influences remained equally active. In short, the technological infrastructure is a necessary but not sufficient condition of globalization. It did, for all that, serve as a major predispositional factor to openness during the pre-war generation.

For Barraclough, it was the decisive breakthrough in world communications of this period which was radically to transform international politics and initiate the age of the global system. At first, the Europeans saw this as bringing the world closer to them, and thereby increasing their ability to shape it as they wished, while in the longer term the actual effect was 'to bring them face to face with powers of continental stature, which overshadowed them' (Barraclough 1967: 103–4). In part, this was the case because of the heightened speed with which technological developments could now be transferred from one national economy to another: competitive emulation itself guaranteed diffusion of such skills and, by the last quarter of the century, this process was becoming an intercontinental one (Kennedy 1988: 198).

In turn, the revolution in transport and communication was to have a pronounced impact upon industrial organization. Craig Murphy argues that, in the American context, breakthroughs in both areas provided the infrastructure for the second industrial revolution by creating a continent-wide market and professional, bureaucratic business management. Perhaps even more importantly, in the European context, they stimulated rationalization as 'international agreements had been needed before continental rail and telegraph systems could operate' (Murphy 1994: 120–1). As regards agriculture, reduced freight rates, and refrigeration techniques, gave the period what has been called a 'historically unique character' because vast areas of temperate land could now bring food to a world market (Foreman-Peck 1995: 97–8).

The diffusion taking place during these years went well beyond that of technology and industrial practices. It must also be considered how far a process of cutural globalization was advanced by the combined impact of imperialism, a global field of power politics, an internationalized market for goods, capital, and people, as well as by the infrastructural changes in transport and communication. More importantly, should any such tendencies be described as globalization or as enforced Westernization? Hobsbawm makes the connection in his suggestion that there was really no choice: for most of the twentieth century, the West has offered the only model to be imitated elsewhere. If there was to be globalization, then it necessarily would take the form of Westernization (Hobsbawm 1994: 200). In this process, which certainly was a long one extending back well before the period under review, it none the less is the case that the turn of the century represented a particularly formative epoch. Roland Robertson, following Gong, maintains that it was early in the twentieth century that the idea of civilization 'became central to international relations' and also became 'for a critical historical moment a, perhaps the, central ingredient in the globalization process' (Robertson 1992: 121,

115). The standard of civilization became the test for admission to international society: this was itself a form of European coercion but some states, and Robertson cites the obvious example of Japan, voluntarily sought to conform to it. Above all, what was coming to be globalized by this process was the culture of the modern bureaucratic and technocratic state which, by force of example, was demonstrating that herein lay the key to national economic success and to national power. Gong himself had subscribed to a two-stage version of the argument. For him, the various instrumentalities of European imperialism in the nineteenth century, such as unequal treaties and protectorates, had already drawn the regions of the Levant, Asia, and Africa 'into the framework of what became the first global international system in history' (Gong 1984: 4). Subsequently, however, the standard of civilization rationalized, and legitimized, that *de facto* incorporation. In doing so, he suggests, the standard solved the philosophical problem 'of determining which countries deserved legal recognition and legal personality in international law' (Gong 1984: 24). To the extent that it did so, this must surely represent the development of a more sophisticated, and legally based, notion of a global international system than that which had already been put in place: but it remained a clear instance of 'coercive socialization' despite that legal veneer.

Renewed Fragmentation

In stark contrast to the various evidences of globalization considered above, we have the revealing judgement of the period offered by Kennedy:

there existed in governing élites, military circles, and imperialist organizations a prevailing view of the world order which stressed struggle, change, competition, the use of force, and the organization of national resources to enhance state power. (Kennedy 1988: 196)

The comment suggests that whatever the development of globalization, there was another reality to the international relations of the time: a climate of fragmentation. Of this, the assertion of a more intensive mood of nationalism, or at any rate a mutation in the nature of nationalism itself, was without doubt the most potent, even if, at the individual state level, that very nationalism served an integrative role.

Historians have been at pains to document the transformations in nationalism at the end of the nineteenth century, depicting them as a move away from the liberal nationalisms of the century's earlier decades. At its turn, Hobsbawm argues, nationalism had taken on a number of new characteristics: it became an ideal adopted by the political right; it called for self-determination regardless of political and economic viability; it asserted full national independence as the only acceptable form of that self-determination; and it was coming for the first time to be defined in terms of ethnicity and language (Hobsbawm 1987: 144). Such developments impacted upon the nature of states. However, it was also the changing nature of states that created a new social role for these very doctrines of nationalism.

Many associate this with the effects of industrialization. States became more powerful, both as a result of the new resources which industrialization gave them, but also because industrialization compelled them to act more intrusively in the social sphere if the state was to be successful in international competition. 'Because almost all valued the increasing collective powers of an industrial society,' Michael Mann has argued, 'they urged the state on toward greater social coordination. In turn, state infrastructures enhanced the density of social interaction, but bounded by the state's territorial reach' (1993: 730). Social coordination, domestically, translated into social disintegration internationally. In the oft-repeated, if trite, observation, 1914 witnessed the victory of nationalism over proletarian internationalism, confirming fragmentation's tangible constraint on the process of globalization.

Such trends were evidenced in two developments of the period. The first was the more obtrusive militarization of the national societies, at least in so far as it is measured by the statistics on sizes of armed forces and on national expenditures on defence. Bartlett notes that growth in these areas in the last quarter of the nineteenth century was 'disturbing', Germany's establishment having almost trebled to 3.4 million, France's doubled to 3.5 million, and those of Austria-Hungary and Russia by a similar measure to 2.6 million and 4 million respectively. Over the same period, expenditure on armed forces rose by some 80 per cent in the cases of Germany and Russia and by about 45 per cent in the cases of Britain and France (Bartlett 1994: 7).

If this militarization epitomized the competitive social Darwinism of the age, the other area to reveal a similar trend was that of national economic policies. Notwithstanding the integrative tendencies discussed above, it is also the case that the closer identification between national power and national economic success, combined with a neo-mercantilist doctrine of the survival of the economically fittest, exacerbated international tensions. As against the mid-nineteenth century Cobdenite vision of international economic activity spilling over into more harmonious international relations, the state's clearer perception of the basis of its own national power generated 'a competitive kind of official nationalism' in the economic sphere (Murphy 1994: 137), even if we must be careful not to imagine a post-Second World War governmental management of the economy at this stage (Hobsbawm 1987: 54–5). The partial flight from free trade was but one manifestation of this tendency. The 're-invention' of nationalism in the late nineteenth century is thus to be explained by the social dynamics which underlay it— the threat to traditional sectors and non-traditional urban classes alike from the onset of the new industrialism, and also as a response to the large-scale migrations of populations which the period had encouraged (Hobsbawm 1990: 109). To this extent, it is evident that the new fragmentation was itself in some measure a conscious reaction to the globalizing pressures of the industrial economy and of the rapid movements of population in response to its new demands and opportunities. We thus have the paradox of a world both integrating and disintegrating at the same time.

States, International Relations, and the Globalization/Fragmentation Paradox

One historian has offered a neat resolution of the paradox. He suggests that as states took on new *domestic* responsibilities, they were led into policies of internationalization and of international cooperation. But, according to Richard Langhorne, we should not be misled by the significance of this evidence, which he sees as 'making states less and not more willing to take combined action in the political sphere: the very closeness of the relationship between states in some matters only served to increase their self-consciousness over the vital issues' (1981: 64). If this is accepted, then the paradox dissolves in that the evidence of globalization in some spheres is perfectly compatible with a fragmentation of state interests on the core matters of national power. To investigate this hypothesis, we need to move beyond international relations, to the changing nature of states and their domestic circumstances.

The most obvious application of such a shift, as regards the pre-war period, is in the attempt to offer a domestically grounded theory of German foreign policy. The controversial position of Fritz Fischer, and the consequent debates about the *Primat der Innenpolitik*, focus our attention in this direction. The state of this debate is conveniently summarized by Lowe. He sets out the standard argument about a link between Wilhelm II's *Weltpolitik* and the domestic situation inasmuch as social tensions required the Kaiser to find new popularity by a foreign policy that would appeal across the social divides (Lowe 1994: 14). This was all the more necessary because of Germany's fundamental problem that its political system had not kept pace with its very rapid industrial development, and equally rapid social change. In short, the compressed nature of the experience had been such that it 'permitted the survival of influential pre-industrial élites and an authoritarian power structure' (Lowe 1994: 144)—although Lowe himself dissents from specific aspects of the argument, such as the claimed attempt to use naval policy and tariffs as the basis for creating a coalition between the two powerful interests of the new industrialists and the old agrarians (1994: 145–6).

However, if Langhorne's more general thesis is to be sustained, it must rest not upon a view of the German problem as *sui generis* but rather on developments in the state practices of the key powers collectively. Why should key élites in control of them have felt the need to intensify their hold over national power? It has been boldly asserted that 'in this period, states became large, socially relevant, and distinctively "modern"' (Mann 1993: 727). This presumably refers to the new salience of the state's managerial and bureaucratic structures, its greater social impact, and, above all, the problems faced by the state in coping with the new social interests, and consequent social conflicts, engendered by industrialization. It is part of Langhorne's thesis that emerging social, economic, and technological agendas were leading states to cooperate internationally in their management. But these self-same issues represented a threat to state power domestically and hence they responded by shoring up their powers in other aspects of their international relations.

Many analysts identify the effects of industrialization at the turn of the century as the key element in the 'modernity' of state development. In this sense, the great transition to be wrought was the transfer of power away from the traditional landed and aristocratic élites and the collapse of the old social order associated with them. Historians continue to argue about this large issue and about whether the old order died in 1914 or fought a major comeback in the inter-war period. None the less, the important issue for our purposes is the extent to which the political power of these traditional élites was threatened by the new industrialization and whether foreign policies were then pursued as a means of addressing this domestic social and political issue. Robert W. Cox sets out this theme with reference to Germany, but sees it as being broadly applicable elsewhere:

Bismarck was among the first national leaders to understand that the new industrial working class had to be incorporated within the nation in order to enhance state power. He made overtures to the nascent German socialist movement, introduced a whole series of social insurance measures, and formulated a concept of corporatism, linking workers and employers with the state, as a basis for his drive for German unification and primacy in Europe. The same broad tendency, through national corporatism or tripartism, culminated in the welfare states of the post-World War II period. (Cox 1993: 145)

In other instances, the social tensions thrown up by industrialization were regional rather than class based, as in the case of Italy (Kennedy 1988: 205).

The thrust of the argument is that social tensions spilled over into more assertive foreign policies as a means of stabilizing the domestic situation. Unfortunately, in some cases, the strain to compete on the international stage had the opposite effect of exacerbating domestic tensions. Thus, in the example of Russia, the state-induced industrialization of the period under finance minister, Count Witte, was designed to enhance Russia's external power and especially its military programme (Kennedy 1988: 235). Unfortunately, it required ever-increasing levels of domestic extraction to fund the borrowed capital which, in turn, raised levels of rural discontent (Lowe 1994: 9). Russia then faced its twin nemeses in war and revolution in 1905, instead of preparations for the former serving as antidote to the latter.

Nor was the strategy any more successful across Europe as a whole (see Murphy 1994: 46). The strengthening of states neither saved the old order, nor could it prevent the fragmentation of the international system. Indeed, as Langhorne suggests, the remnants of liberal internationalism simply placed greater stress on the areas of acute competition.

The paradoxes of the age are thus to be accounted for by the complex interplay of the two dialectical processes—between an open and closed international system, on the one hand, and between the old and the new social orders, on the other. It was the attempt to solve the problems of the latter by the enhancement of state power, and through the modality of the new nationalism, that tipped the scales of the former away from open internationalism and towards destructive fragmentation. The very globalization that had hitherto represented an extension of state power had come to be regarded as a threat to its bases of domestic control. It was thus through the medium of changing state practice that the new mood of international relations was to find its expression: the need for domestic accommodations reduced the scope for international concessions on the key issues affecting the external standing of these states.

3

THE IMPACT OF WAR, 1914–1919

The Ambivalence of War

The ambivalent trends towards globalization and fragmentation of the pre-war era were simply reformulated, if reinvigorated, by the experience of war itself. Otherwise expressed, the analytical problem for the historian to disentangle is the extent to which the war was an independent cause of new directions in global interactions, or whether the outbreak of war was itself the symptom of deep-seated, and longer-term, forces *already* at work.

The argument can be introduced with reference to the British economist and official John Maynard Keynes's pessimistic diagnosis made after Versailles:

The Treaty includes no provisions for the economic rehabilitation of Europe—nothing to make the defeated Central Empires into good neighbours, nothing to stabilise the new States of Europe, nothing to reclaim Russia; nor does it promote in any way a compact of economic solidarity amongst the Allies themselves; no arrangement was reached at Paris for restoring the disordered finances of France and Italy, or to adjust the systems of the Old World and the New. (Keynes 1919: 211)

The question is whether, to the extent that Keynes's gloomy assessment of international political and economic fragmentation was justified, this was a consequence of the war or of ongoing changes that would have surfaced in any event.

According to the former interpretation, the war should be regarded as a 'voluntarist' political intrusion into the spheres of economic interdependence and interaction: it then becomes necessary to identify precisely how the dynamics of war intensified either the forces of globalization or of fragmentation, and on the Kenynesian estimation the fragmentationist impact would predominate. According to the latter interpretation, the fragmentationist tendencies within the international economy should rather be regarded as being caused by forces already immanent within the pre-war international system, and of which the outbreak of war was itself a clear indication: these tendencies did not originate in the war. Ashworth hints at such an account of the international economy when he notes 'the deeper economic changes that were beginning to appear before 1914 and became gradually more pervasive' (1975: 227). This latter view, in turn, is compatible with those historical accounts which tend to be dismissive of the fundamental changes wrought by war: the less instrumental the war, the more obviously do post-war developments link back to pre-war tensions. Maier, for instance, argues for the relative superficiality of the social and political consequences of the war (1989: 131–2).

Whatever the causal view, there can be little disagreement with the claim that ambivalent trends persisted through, or were further fostered by, the experiences of war. Many commentators draw attention to this ambiguity in the war's effects, whether in terms of the actual economic and strategic policies pursued by states, or in terms of the new-found rhetoric in which the political issues of the day were to be debated. Thus one historian of Woodrow Wilson's diplomacy places it in the context of the duality of war-time experience characterized by both 'centralization and diversity', and which 'witnessed the simultaneous flourishing of internationalism and nationalism' (Ambrosius 1987: ix). Writing from a quite different sociological perspective, Giddens none the less fastens upon the very same duality:

Wilsonian doctrines, with their emphasis upon national sovereignty within a global community of states, were in some substantial part a reaction against the enormous devastation of the War. But they also expressed an acknowledgement of a heightened level of interdependency in the world system, which the activities of the participant states had stimulated away from the war zones themselves. (Giddens 1985: 238)

Others again point to the same essential ambivalence with regard to the articulation, at war's end, of a universalist aspiration to self-determination, which has been neatly captured—revealing the intimate connection between globalization and fragmentation—as a 'universalistic entitlement to particularism' (Robertson 1992: 19).

This ambiguity becomes especially germane for understanding the interplay between globalization and state policies within the context of various areas of recent historical research. It will be suggested later that globalization was given a pronounced stimulus after 1945 by the policy adopted by the leading power at the time, namely the United States. It is, of course, the conventional wisdom that the policy of the United States after the First World War was sharply at odds with that after the Second World War (indeed, lessons were learned from the former to apply to the latter), and this represented a diplomatic revolution on the part of the United States. Such a view is epitomized by the general perception of American 'retreat into isolationism' during the inter-war period.

Such a view is now increasingly questioned by historians who have been more inclined to emphasize the elements of continuity in American policy between both periods and to move away from the thesis of radical discontinuity in American foreign affairs. But it is not only in the context of American policy that such revisionism has surfaced: it is to be found also in the study of French policy, in the background of European integration and, more pervasively, within the study of changes in the political fabric of the state itself. These areas of historical revisionism, briefly sketched at this point, are central to any analysis of the causes of globalization because they provide an insight into the multi-layered interconnections between wartime experience, political change within states, the orientation of foreign and economic policies, and the dynamics of globalization and fragmentation. Put bluntly, the historical puzzle is how to explain the differing outcomes of the two post-war periods if it is now accepted that there was substantial continuity between them; and in particular how to account for the dominance of fragmentation in the inter-war period, as against the dominance of globalization after 1945. The new historical research poses the issue starkly but, in turn, offers the possibility of a deeper understanding of the interplay between exogenous pressures and international political voluntarism.

Three areas in which such revisionism has taken place are: American foreign policy and European reconstruction; French reparations policy and the quest for integrated international economic policies; and the development of the corporatist state as a forerunner of post-1945 welfarism. Although, taken separately, these might seem to be narrow and specialized historical issues, placed together they are highly revealing of wider concerns about the relationship between national policies and the creation of distinctive international political and economic orders. They thus become central to any explanation of the setbacks to globalization during the inter-war period.

We will return to detailed analyses of American post-war economic policy, and the role of dollar diplomacy in the 1920s, in the next chapter. For the moment it is enough to say that historians now recognize the early beginnings of the full-blown post-Second World War reconstructionist policies of the United States, and in particular of the Marshall Plan, in US activities in 1918–19, and again in the latter half of the 1920s (see esp. Hogan 1987). The argument is to be found in specific, and more general, versions. Some have seen the food aid and relief programme run by Herbert Hoover in the immediate aftermath of war as an early harbinger of subsequent US policies:

In the last analysis, this Hoover-directed program of anti-Bolshevik food relief, with its emphasis on the breaking down of nationalistic barriers to trade and economic recovery, was a classic expression of the more general proto-Marshall Plan tendency of Wilson and his advisers to use America's expansionist economic power in the postwar period to establish international liberal-capitalist stability. (Levin 1968: 191)

Others have explained the same Hoover programme in a less grandiose and altruistic way as short-term self-interest grounded in the 'need to sell American farm surpluses' (Offer 1989: 6).

The wider argument, of which the Hoover relief is but a small part, is about the recognition within the United States of the the need for it to play a role in European stabilization and reconstruction, and to generate a zone 'free from the extremes of both xenophobic nationalism and Bolshevism' (Stevenson 1988: 247). The significance of this interpretation is that it displaces the view of 1945 as the turning-point in American foreign policy and, in its stead, accepts 1917 as the watershed year: 'Wilsonianism laid the foundation of a modern American foreign policy whose main thrust, from 1917 on, may be characterized as an effort to construct a stable world order of liberal-capitalist internationalism . . . safe from both the threat of imperialism on the Right and the danger of revolution on the Left' (Levin 1968: 1).

The second area in which some continuity has been identified is that of French policy about the terms of the peace. Historians have now softened the formerly dominant view of the purely punitive attitude of France towards Germany, at least as the initial policy, in its demand for the highest possible level of reparations. In its place, they have suggested that France sought a complex series of international economic cooperative arrangements which would serve as a geopolitical constraint on Germany while also nurturing French interests within a grouping of Allied powers. The embryonic logic of this is so close to that developed from 1950 onwards that historians speak of the 'early traces of the more imaginative responses to the "German problem" that emerged in the post-1945 period' (Sharp 1991: 99–100).

Marc Trachtenberg is the principal revisionist in this area. His argument is that France did not look first to reparations for its salvation, but did so only as a fall-back position when the alternative failed. The preferred solution lay not in Germany but with France's allies (Trachtenberg 1980: 1). He demonstrates that France did not initially press for reparations:

Allied 'cooperation' would see France through the period of reconstruction, but it was a permanent economic bloc and not just a temporary continuation of the wartime regime that was needed. The aim was not to crush Germany, but rather to provide a framework for the ultimate reintegration of Germany into the international economic system: the system itself would restrain German ambitions. (Trachtenberg 1980: 15–16)

It might again appear that this is a narrow historical disagreement about the basis of French reparations policy and indeed Trachtenberg's thesis has been criticized on the obvious grounds that he relies overly much on the position of Clémentel, and the Ministry of Finance, as the exponents of this policy—which was not necessarily shared in other sectors of French government. However, the wider issue at stake is the French quest for a kind of Allied integrated economic system—at the time resisted by Washington—but which in the longer term was to become the nucleus of the post-1945 Western economic order and which itself did so much to foster the globalization of economic activity. Hence, the reasons for the failure to create such a post-1919 economic system in themselves provide a large part of the explanation for the shift to fragmentation in the inter-war years.

The final area of continuity is in the domestic politics of the belligerent states themselves. Although historians are generally interested in analysing the social and political impact of the war on the states which participated in it, there is one particular strand of the argument which touches directly on the present issue. The thesis which Charles S. Maier has made his own is that the economic policies pursued in the aftermath of the First World War were devised with one eye to their effects on the domestic situation and particularly to the balance of domestic social forces. There is thus an intimate connection between foreign and economic policy, on the one hand, and the social basis of the state, on the other. Allowing this connection, transnational processes of globalization can be understood fully only within the context of the specific state policies which encourage them and, in turn, these policies are a reflection of transformation in the structural basis of the state itself. This transformation has been summed up by some as the development of corporatism, which, while already underway, was further stimulated by the wartime 'integration of labor into a bargaining system supervised by the state' and by the 'erosion of the distinction between private and public sectors' (Maier 1989: 137–8).[1] When finally the United States was led to encourage post-Second World War financial policies for European reconstruction, it did so in part by attempting to initiate structural change within the European states themselves. There was a complex interaction which strengthened the view that 'some restoration of pre-war trade and capital flows was needed', but this was in order 'to rebuild not merely currency balances but the old equilibrium of social classes' (Maier 1989: 147–8). The development of an open international economic order thus had complex origins, partly in the social structures of states, and indeed it was this fact that was to contribute to the dislocations of the inter-war period.

Before any attempt is made to distinguish the specific impact of war on processes of globalization, we must begin with a more general review of the major effects of war on the international system as a whole.

It has been suggested that one of the ironies of the war was that the very intensification of forces that might have been expected to work against its outbreak simply increased the scale of its horrors once underway. Thus Stevenson identifies economic interdependence, democratization, the military revolution, and the global extension of the balance of power as forces that should have helped deter war. Instead, once war had been initiated, these selfsame forces gave it its deadly dynamic and 'magnified the scale of the disaster' (Stevenson 1988: 10). However, the mechanism by which the war was concluded ensured that, while German power was contained, it had not been destroyed: many of the disequilibria which had contributed to war in 1914 thereby persisted. Fundamental to these was the central role of Germany within the balance of power, as the history of the inter-war period was to reveal. German power remained pivotal. While it was checked, other sources of challenge could also be contained. It was German revival that allowed Mussolini to engage in active revisionism, just as it was German power which presented Japan with its opportunity in the Pacific (Stevenson 1988: 311–12).

If, in retrospect, it is thought that the armistice was premature and that German power should have been more directly assaulted in 1918, then this ignores the political and social context in which war came to an end. Its final stages were conducted with the very real risk of social revolution: to extend the war to extirpate German power might have been to unleash domestic revolutions in central Europe (Bell 1992: 144). There was also a second reason for seeking a speedy termination of war in that, the longer it continued, the more influential the Americans became. This was no particular cause for comfort for the other Allies, wary of Wilsonian rhetoric and its implication for wartime secret deals, as well as for the future of empires, including the division of Germany's.

---

[1] On corporatism generally, see also Hogan (1991); Leffler (1979).

Britain especially harboured ambivalent feelings about the American role. No country more bitterly resented the respective economic outcomes of war upon itself and the United States. Britain expended much of its national wealth in the war effort while the American economy prospered and became the source of loans to the other impoverished Allies. Thus Britain remained wary of any extension of American influence which a continuation of the war would have encouraged (Bartlett 1994: 102). As against this, however, Britain also needed to exploit American power to maintain a European and global balance of power in the straitened circumstances in which it now found itself. Accordingly, it has been noted that an 'absorption of American power into the maintenance of a moderately punitive European settlement had been a dominant goal of British policy at Paris', and this contributed to the mixed outcome of Versailles and the League, part 'idealist' and part 'realist', as leaders sought both to transform and transcend traditional power politics, while remaining rooted in the necessities of their dictates (Levin 1968: 124–5). They discovered ultimately that, to their cost, they had neither enforced the peace nor found an alternative that would avoid the necessity of doing so. The problem, as French leaders realized, remained that of German power and not that of bringing about a transformation in international relations (Holsti 1991: 189).

But if German power was one dimension of the post-war balance, the other was conspicuously that of the United States. Only the latter had the potential to transform the international system into an open liberal order in which globalization could spread. We can, therefore, agree with Immanuel Wallerstein, albeit for different reasons, about the significance of 1917 as a watershed year. That year was important, Wallerstein contends, less because of the Bolshevik revolution than because of America's entry into the war. He then grandly interprets the war, at this stage, as one 'between the US and Germany to control the world-system in the next era' (Wallerstein 1991: 4). This may be too formulaic an analysis. However, in one specific sense Wallerstein is correct: that war was to resume in 1941, and whether or not it was about 'control of the world-system', the clash between a policy for an internationalized world economy and a policy for autarchy and closure was one that was to shape the balance between globalization and fragmentation for the remainder of the century.

Amongst the salient effects of war were the collapse of several empires and the emergence of a new territorial settlement. These impinged on international relations in sundry ways. In the case of Russia, its collapse reduced its geopolitical presence in eastern Europe by the recreation of Poland, diminished its strategic involvement in the international system, and thereby intensified France's security problem in the face of German revisionism. In the case of the Habsburg empire, its collapse and dismemberment served the wider cause of sanctifying the national state, while simultaneously compounding the economic dislocation for central Europe that war had brought in its wake. The demise of the Ottoman empire gave rise to mutually exclusive nationalisms in the Middle East, while in practice extending the imperial sways of both Britain and France. If the main territorial changes took place within Europe, none the less the impact of war was experienced much more extensively, so much so that one historian sees the First World War as initiating a new phase in the 'world revolution of Westernization' in that the 'ambitions of global power became yet more universal and ruthless' and the 'impact on unprepared peripheral societies more intense' (Von Laue 1987: 51).

The economic ramifications of war were manifold and will be addressed at length below. In general outline, the war disrupted traditional patterns of trade and commerce and interrupted the established flows of capital and people. The consequence of naval blockade and of attacks on shipping was to dislocate the normal commerce in goods (Foreman-Peck 1995: 177). Most important of all, however, were the effects on international investment and lending, as Europe moved from being supplier to consumer of spare capital. Simultaneously, the United States became the principal creditor, the value of its foreign assets doubling from $3.5 billion to $7.0 billion between 1914 and 1919 (Hardach 1977: 290). Wartime borrowing by governments, coupled with the collapse of the gold standard, destroyed confidence in international exchanges on which trade was dependent:

As a result of the First World War, there was not only a global depreciation in the value of currencies, which had repercussions in terms of currency instability in the inter-war years, but also a decentralization of the international economy. Europe's share of world production and trade fell through the stimulus afforded non-European competitors. (Beckett 1989: 34)

But if the war had its impact on the economy, just as important was the impact that the economy had on war. If it is true that 'the ability of modern economies to sustain long wars came as a surprise' (Bartlett 1994: 88), it none the less revealed the intimate connection between the organization of the economy and the capacity to make war. Modern states could mobilize vast economic resources but the effort to do so had to be organized bureaucratically and that in itself impinged on the powers of the state. One little statistic provides a powerful insight into the modern state at war: the British army went to war with 100 lorries but ended it with 60,000 (Bond 1984: 102). Resources had not simply to be commanded; they had to be deployed to the field of battle. In every sense it was a 'war of resources' (Bell 1992: 135).

The very outcome of the war was to be determined critically by this resource war. Some historians now see the Allied victory as being inevitable because of this factor, and especially after the entry of the United States. In one bold account, it was the access of the Allies to the resources of the transoceanic societies (United States, Canada, and Australia) that gave them the edge over the Central Powers (Offer 1989: 1). By contrast, the landlocked Central Powers 'were handicapped by their comparatively small area of supply and lack of access to overseas raw materials' (Bond 1984: 116). But even more important than just the Allies' access to raw materials was the specific manner of international integration by means of which the Allied success was to be achieved. This served as a powerful model for future international economic organization. Its basic elements were French reliance on imports of materials and machinery from Britain and the United States, and British and French reliance upon loans from the United States (Bell 1992: 135–6). Here, in embryo, was a closely integrated and orchestrated international economy, that greatly benefited the United States but was sufficiently attractive to France for it to wish to preserve it into the post-war period as a means of controlling Germany. If access to the resources of an expansive global economy was the secret which won the war, there should be no surprise that such a project retained a powerful hold over the imagination of some who thought about survival in the post-war peace.

There is one final association between economy and victory which has been drawn by historians and, once again, this was important for the kind of social compact noted by theorists of corporatism. Social historians have recently emphasized the management of health and welfare, and consequent demographic trends, during the First World War, and have regarded this as one important aspect of the total war effort. According to Jay Winter, it was 'precisely on the level of defending civilian living standards that Britain and France succeeded whereas Germany and her allies failed' (1988: 11). National leaders could have transferred a greater share of the burdens of warfare to the population at large but chose not to in order to defend welfare and living standards. This too was to be an important indicator for the future, even if the attempted maintenance of such a social contract was not to survive the dislocations of the post-war international economy.

Thus far, it has been suggested that the war had an ambivalent impact on post-war international relations. Before proceeding to examine these effects in detail, some attempt will be made to explain this ambivalence. In brief, three interpretations can be considered. The first focuses upon the United States's policy and suggests that this policy itself was a volatile compound of nationalist and internationalist elements; the second focuses upon the domestic social orders of the post-war states and emphasizes their precarious balance between national cohesion and social divisiveness; the third dwells on the changing structure of the international order itself and suggests that the ambivalence of the wartime experience was a function of its location in the transitional phase between two hegemonic patterns, the declining one related to Britain and the emerging one of the United States.

According to the first account, a study of the United States—especially as the key player that could shape the wider international configuration—serves as a microcosm for the study of the international system itself. Thus conceived, the impact of war was genuinely contradictory, simultaneously reinforcing tendencies towards narrow national exclusiveness but also towards wider frameworks of international order in which such goals might best be fostered. It is thus misleading to regard the latter as mere ideological window-dressing to conceal the true motives of the former: the essence of the argument is that both were equally genuine aspects of American policy. The ambivalence is neatly captured in the following interpretation:

Global interdependence and pluralism combined to create a fundamental dilemma for the United States in the twentieth century. This nation could no longer maintain its traditional isolation from the Old World, yet neither could it expect universal acceptance of its own ideals and practices by other nations. Wilson attempted to resolve this dilemma with the League. It promised a global environment in which the United States could protect its vital interests. It would, in his view, permit American control over foreign affairs. (Ambrosius 1987: ix–x)

More pointedly, the League would permit 'universal and unilateral tendencies to coexist harmoniously' in American foreign policy (Ambrosius 1987: 290). Levin had earlier pointed to the interplay between the same two 'inclusive' and 'exclusive' tendencies (Levin 1968: 147).

That there was an inclusive and universalist dimension to American policy is not in doubt. Moreover, historians of American foreign policy are agreed that the themes articulated by Wilson in 1919 were to become recurrent *motifs* in the decades to come. To that extent, they reflected an emerging tradition. Two key aspects are prominent in Wilson's articulation of the new League-based world order. The first was concerned with the purely interstate basis of order and sought to replace the haphazard balance of power by 'an inclusive concert of liberal powers into which a reformed Germany could eventually be reintegrated' (Levin 1968: 177). Latent in this idea is the notion that international order can be constructed, not on the basis of negative opposition of interest to interest, but only on a positively managed network of mutually reinforcing economic and political goals. The second aspect, although here historians are less agreed, concerns the domestic social basis of order and Wilson's presentation of his new diplomacy as an explicit counter to Bolshevism. In this context 'Wilson's efforts to transform the Entente's struggle against the Central Powers into a crusade for international-liberalism was in direct opposition to Lenin's desire to transform the war into a world revolution' (Levin 1968: 6).

If this internationalism was genuine enough, so was the national and exclusive interest on which it was based. The United States profited enormously from the war but faced the real prospect of major recession when the post-war dampening of international markets asserted itself. There was also a good prospect of profitable investment in European reconstruction, but only if the European economies could service their loans and only if political stability was not threatened by revolutionary social unrest. Cain and Hopkins note that, during the war, the US share of world exports increased from 13.5 per cent in 1913 to over 25 per cent by 1920, and they conclude from this that it 'may not be too cynical to suggest that the motive for American intervention on the Allied side was to safeguard her loans and her burgeoning export markets' (Cain and Hopkins 1993: 59–60). Whether Wilson himself was a party to this reasoning or, as has been suggested, delegated such business at Versailles because 'economic questions interested him little', there is at least agreement that the effect was the same, namely, to give a free hand to his experts 'to pursue a course of American economic nationalism that harmed his broader goals' (Stevenson 1988: 245).

The second interpretation of the ambivalent impact of war relates to its domestic social and political effects. The experience of war, at least in its early years, contributed significantly to social cohesion. In the words of Cox, it 'mobilized all social forces behind the nation-state, and in so doing reaffirmed . . . the supremacy of the Bismarckian union of nationalism and welfare over class conflict' (1987: 158). In order to achieve this balance, the state acquired new competencies in the direction of the national economy. The problem was that this transformation in state functions left it terribly exposed as the broker between demands for national welfarism and the pressures of adjustment to the international economy. These dual pressures aggravated the ambivalence of state policies, pushing them in both internationalist and unilateralist directions. If welfarism after 1945 was to be an important ingredient of social stability which helped to nurture the international economy and thus to sustain these domestic bargains, in 1919 it stood as a less harmonious element within post-war reconstruction.

Finally, there is the argument that the post-war international economy found itself suspended uneasily between antagonistic poles of integration and disintegration for the very reason that there was an interregnum between the passing of British economic hegemony and the establishment of the American alternative. Such a view, in turn, is based on the wider conception that it is the task of the hegemon to establish the basis of of an open and internationalized economy whereas, in the absence of such leadership, it will revert to its natural state of closure and disintegration. Although inter-war fragmentation is implicit in most versions of hegemonic stability theory, its specific application to the end of the First World War has been made in the following account which sets out a generalized theory of globalization and of fragmentation. In hegemonic orders

production in particular countries becomes connected through the mechanisms of a world economy and linked into world systems of production . . . An incipient world society grows up around the interstate system, and states themselves become internationalized . . . In nonhegemonic phases of world order these tendencies are reversed. Social classes and the organization of production revolve more exclusively around the state. States advance and protect the interests of particular national social classes and production organizations, using all the political, economic, and military means at their disposal as necessary. (Cox 1987: 7–8)

The three interpretations mentioned need not be viewed as mutually exclusive: indeed, in important respects they are interconnected. Collectively, they suggest that tendencies towards globalization and fragmentation (or, in this case, an uneasy coexistence between both) will tend to be fostered by the combined effects of their domestic social circumstances, their consequent policies internationally, and the wider setting of international relations within which the degree of hegemony will be an important element. With these as the background schemes of analysis, we can now proceed to an assessment of the impacts of war on globalization and its alternative.

The First World War and Globalization

The globalizing impact of war can be considered in two broad categories, one ideological and the other material. Within the first, we need to consider the universalizing and integrative effects of the ideas unleashed as part of the total war
effort. Within the second, account has to be taken of the integration achieved by
the strategic and economic effects of war.

The first outcome of war is perhaps the most paradoxical in effect—
Robertson's 'universalistic entitlement to particularism'. There can be no doubt
that Wilson's rhetorical promulgation of national self-determination had a profound impact on the subsequent international system. At one level, it might be
thought that this was simply to enshrine and legitimize fragmentation on a
nation-state basis. But while this is indeed a part of the complex reality, its less visible aspect was that such a principle was being *universalized*. In other words, a
common political form, long accepted *de facto*, was now to be encouraged *de jure*
in all parts of the world. The League, as an institution of sovereign states, became
the international pressure group which would proselytize towards this goal. Thus
Giddens insists that the profound and longer-term effect of the League was not to
diminish the role of the separate state but, on the contrary, lay in 'consolidating
conceptions of national sovereignty as the "natural" political condition of
humankind, via a particular interpretation of the sovereignty–citizenship–
nationalism relation'. In short, it stimulated 'the primacy of the nation-state as the
universal political form of the current era' (Giddens 1985: 259, 258).

Wilsonian self-determination came as part of a package of universalist ideas,
many of which were pitched at an international audience, at least in part as a
counter to the similar appeal of Bolshevism. Their contribution to globalization
lies precisely in their attempt to articulate the prerequisites of a world order in
which all peoples would have an entitled place and a role to play. Given that its
overarching philosophy, once suitable democratic forms had been adopted, was
inclusivist (and only within such a setting did collective security make any kind
of theoretical sense), it must be said that Wilsonianism held an ideological commitment to globalization. In no other way can his appeals to a world community
of peoples be understood. Moreover, his doctrine of collective security, in so far
as it required acceptance of the notion that the fate of any one state was the fate
of all—and hence its attempt to instil an ethic of universal responsibility—was
likewise globalist in inspiration.

Part of the American rhetoric was related to the domestic imperatives of finding a way to bring a reluctant country into the war. It was certainly true, if by no
means absolutely the case, that the war had had an undertone of liberalism versus autocracy throughout (Stevenson 1988: 137–8), although this was easier to
sustain after the fall of the Tsar. However, for the United States, such an image
became an essential part of the politics of becoming a belligerent. That is not to
say that it was the compelling motive. It is surely correct that the decisive consideration for Wilson was to have a commanding influence over the peace settlement

and, for this to be done, belligerency was the *sine qua non*. Concerns about the peace, as Stevenson claims, were more important for US entry than any 'solidarity with the Western Europeans' (1988: 79–80).

However, after the US entry there can be no doubt that this ideological aspect of the conflict—and its associated universalist underpinnings—was given much greater prominence (Levin 1968: 55–6). As has been noted,

The entry of the United States thus helped to ensure that the war was continued. It also brought another change in its character, emphasizing still further the 'moral' or abstract element in Allied war aims . . . Once again the stakes were raised, and the Central Powers were given a further incentive to try once more for victory. (Bell 1992: 143)

Whatever the motives underlying Wilson's pronouncements, they were certainly universal in their potential appeal. Thus it has been said of Wilson's programme, as of Lenin's, that it was not 'European-centred but world-embracing' (Barraclough 1967: 121), testifying to the globalist notions with which it was associated. Indeed, it was world embracing not only in appeal but in its instrumentality, in that world public opinion was believed to be an important means by which peace would be preserved. '[S]anctions for correct behaviour,' Holsti observes, 'would derive from morality and world public opinion' (1991: 182–3). The idea of such a monolithic world opinion, sharing similar values and making similar judgements about what constitutes aggression, itself rests upon a globalized conception of world affairs. Moreover, to be effective, it hinges upon the spread of a uniform democratic political practice: the democratization of the globe is thus the implicit programme for peace as, without it, 'global underlying harmony cannot find expression if the constituent units of the international system are represented by autocratic and militarist governments' (Holsti 1991: 182–3).

This is not to suggest the absence of self-interested considerations underlying such universalist aspirations. Without doubt, the need to present an ideological counter to Leninism was omnipresent, if by no means the sole or decisive concern (cf. Mayer 1959, 1968). Similarly, American anxieties extended not only to the new ideological competition from Bolshevism but to the more traditional economic and imperial competition from Britain. It is reported that Colonel House, Wilson's close adviser, and not himself unsympathetic to Britain, warned of the dangers of a decisive war leaving Britain in too dominant a position: the wartime expansion of the American fleet was an insurance policy against any eventuality (Bartlett 1994: 95). But even at the level of self-interest, the judgement about American policy needs to be qualified. John L. Gaddis claims that Wilsonian policy was too ideological for its own good and in its rejection of Bolshevism neglected its own power-political interests (shared with the Soviet Union) in restraining Germany (1992*a*: 12).

There is one final ideological issue in which the matter of universalism arises, and this was the attempt, sponsored largely by Japan, to secure recognition of a principle of equal racial treatment. An unfettered universalism, and a full acceptance of such equality, would have had no difficulty in acceding to such a demand, but in this respect, as in others, Wilson was no free agent. He resisted the Japanese request for fear of the domestic backlash which any dilution of America's restrictive immigration policy would provoke, especially in California (Walworth 1986: 38). Wilson knew how to be a 'particularist' when he had to be.

That said, Levin is undoubtedly correct in his overall assessment of the Wilsonian legacy to American foreign policy in the twentieth century: 'Wilson established the main drift toward an American liberal globalism,' he avers, 'hostile both to traditional imperialism and to revolutionary socialism' (1968: 260). Since the former had been, and the latter was to become, a bastion of global fragmentation, Wilsonian universalism must be adjudged a bulwark of incipient globalization, even if the implementation of such a programme was not to be immediate.

If Wilsonianism was one universalist legacy of the war, Leninism was its counterpart and rival. No less than Wilson's was Lenin's a blueprint for a new world order and was thus inherently globalist in inspiration and intent. Indeed, there was substantial overlap between the two programmes: both were avowedly anti-imperialist; both sought peace; both favoured national self-determination; and both sought to promote a universal model of political development based on indigenous experience. They were projected as rival and competing political programmes precisely because they had so much in common, each seeking if by different means to create a 'classless society in a warless world' (Mayer 1959: 393).

The Leninist claim to universalism is readily established. It derives, of course, in however adapted a form, from a Marxist paternity which emphasized the universal form of history, with its schematic sequence of class stages, and its ultimate teleology. Like Wilson's Fourteen Points, Lenin advanced the appeal of a non-annexationist peace. More generally, peace would be established by the overthrow of the class-based state policies which created war and, as in the liberal tradition, would follow naturally from the introduction of genuinely popular foreign policies. His views on the need to destroy the bourgeois state and replace it by the dictatorship of the proletariat were meaningless if not considered as a revolutionary appeal to be replicated elsewhere, and were thus, and seen to be, a siren-call for world revolution—the view expressed in the 'Riga Axioms' that took hold in Western policy circles at the time (Yergin 1980: ch. 1). Lenin, of course, is most closely associated with his theory of imperialism as a necessary stage of a collapsing capitalism: world revolution would thereby not simply overthrow the capitalist system but the entire imperial edifice which it had created. It was hardly surprising that such doctrines encouraged a whole generation of colonial nationalists and revolutionaries. And finally, the Leninist programme was to be advanced around the world through its own institutionalized mechanism, the Comintern.

These parallels are striking enough. Additionally, however, Leninism, like Wilsonianism, heartily embraced a universalism combined with a deep-seated defence of particularism: both presented ideological frameworks, of general applicability, but in which nationalism itself could be nurtured (Iriye 1985: 37). In large measure, Lenin's espousal of nationalism was tactical, but no less successful for that: it allowed communism 'to pose as the friend of oppressed nationalism everywhere' (Ulam 1968: 18). In this form also was a future source of fragmentation carried forward at the very heart of proposals for revolutionary internationalism.

If this is the case with the idological impact of war, did its material impact point also in a globalist direction? There is one very obvious sense in which such an image is presented. Isn't the very nomenclature of a *World* War suggestive of an integrative effect? How accurate then, as opposed to hyperbolic, is the description of the war as the first to involve the world?

Historians return a mixed verdict, ranging from yes to no, with a compromise position—of a local war at the outset becoming a global war by its end—somewhere in the middle of the spectrum. Brian Bond seems inclined to accept the validity of the description as the statistics he offers point in that direction. He notes that eventually twenty-eight states were involved as belligerents and repeats the claim that of a world population of 1.6 billion, 1.4 billion were formally at war: on this accounting, any description of the war as less than world-wide in scope would be an understatement (Bond 1984: 133). Others disagree. Despite his listing of the campaigns on the western and eastern fronts, in Italy, Turkey, the Caucasus, Palestine and Mesopotamia, Africa, China, New Guinea, and the Pacific, one historian none the less concludes that 'it must be doubted whether these campaigns outside Europe really merit the designation of the conflict as a "world war"—Europe was always the true centre' (Bell 1992: 132–3). Bartlett occupies the middle ground in claiming that the 'global dimension' had not been present at the outset, certainly not in German minds, but that eventually a war 'sparked off by primarily European causes' was to be largely won 'by a non-European power' (1994: 89, 94). Beckett also portrays it as having been 'global in scope' even if having begun as a European conflict (1989: 31).

But much of this is to miss the essential point. To the extent that the war became progressively global in scope (even if the premature retiral of Russia might be thought to have narrowed it), this was not an accidental by-product but intrinsic to the changes in the balance of power that had already preceded its outbreak and which had contributed to the dislocated context in which the events leading to war had taken place. Stevenson speculates that the geographical extension of the war might be regarded as the consequence of recurrent attempts to overcome the stalemate on the western front by an indirect strategy of encirclement. But he is right to dismiss this thesis. In its stead, he points out that the new entrants into the war became involved for their own independent reasons, and not as the mere shadow play of the existing contestants. Thus he compellingly explains the expansion of war as a reflection of the 'decentralization of the balance of power': 'That the war had become global,' he concludes, 'testified to the existence of a global balance of power' (Stevenson 1988: 42, 86). In this respect then the war did not create a globalized international system but took the course that it did because the system, as argued above, had already become globalized: the war was a symptom, not a cause, of this change.

But in other respects, there can be little doubt that the war had its own independent causal effects. The most visible of these, with reference to the globalizing tendencies they induced, were upon the economics and strategy of empire, as well as upon the global spread of the experience of combat. This last, while it may be viewed as a shared and totalizing experience, was, of course, to lead ultimately to fragmentationist conclusions.

As in other areas of international exchange, as will be noted below, the impact of war was to be disruptive. However, in the short term, the war can also be said to have had an integrative effect upon the European empires, in some cases giving rise for the first time to cohesive imperial strategies. It was the war, and the need to mobilize the resources and populations of empire for war, that gave rise to these schemes:

The extraordinary mobilization and the productivity that the war generated demonstrated . . . the ability of the local economies to serve European needs. As the imperialist state intruded more boldly into colonial affairs, the first suggestions for economic planning were adumbrated. It has been suggested that the genesis of the Sarraut plan for economic development . . . occurred during the war. (Betts 1985: 45)

Of the various forms of mobilization, the recruitment of soldiers to fight in the war was perhaps the one with the largest impact. France was the most assiduous in this endeavour in its drafting of an African force, but by no means stood alone. Britain, of course, could draw on the white dominions, as well as upon the vast manpower reserves of India. Rough estimates suggest over 800,000 drawn from Canada, over 400,000 from Australia, almost 1.5 million from India, some 170,000 from Algeria, and 160,000 from French West Africa (Betts 1985: 14).

Participation in war was a uniquely globalizing experience, especially for those drawn from societies which seemed many times removed from the causes of conflict. But few were to remain untouched by the experience. It has been estimated that roughly 2 million Africans saw service in the war and some 200,000 to 250,000 of these lost their lives. The author notes that for a continent on the scale of Africa, the figure 'seems low', but he adds pertinently that 'the impact on a whole variety of peoples who were only marginally involved in the politics of the conflict was great' (Page 1987: 14). He elaborates:

For these African combatants, and for the frontiers and villages they left behind, the Great War was not merely a European civil conflict. It was instead a maelstrom of gigantic proportions, one which pulled them—many for the first time—into a world of diverse races and experiences, wreaking havoc with the societies of their ancestors in which they felt at home. (Page 1987: 1–2)

It is hard to imagine a more tangible expression of globalization on the lives of ordinary people: if globalization means the compression of all life, and the creation of networks to transfer impacts from one part of the system to another, then the First World War certainly attained this condition, over a greater geographical span, than had any similar military encounter over the centuries.

The First World War and Fragmentation

Whatever the globalizing effect wrought by the war, it is unquestionably the case that its disintegrative and fragmentationist impact was the greater. These themes can be illustrated by the experience of post-war Europe and by the impact on far-flung empires.

The collapse of empires within Europe was sanctioned on the principle of nationality which now reached its symbolic apogee. Curiously, a world which had seen the fires of war stoked by nationalist passion now sought redemption in the tighter embrace of that very sentiment. Hobsbawm sees this twist in fortunes as being largely fortuitous:

If there was a moment when the nineteenth-century 'principle of nationality' triumphed it was at the end of World War I, even though this was neither predictable, nor the intention of the future victors. In fact, it was the result of two unintended developments: the collapse of the great multinational empires of central and eastern Europe and the Russian Revolution which made it desirable for the Allies to play the Wilsonian card against the Bolshevik card. (Hobsbawm 1990: 131)

Thus did globalist universalism conspire to engender localist particularism.

This fragmentation was carved most deeply in central Europe out of the Habsburg empire. A series of successor states—Hungary, Czechoslovakia, Yugoslavia—joined others, such as Poland, in the interstices of receding German and Russian power. However, even Wilson recognized that the principle of self-determination could be applied half-heartedly at best. It had to be joined also by balance-of-power considerations which mandated tolerably strong states to check Bolshevism and to offer France the option of a residual 'eastern' alliance. And so the new nations were, by default, themselves amalgamations of ethnic groups. Some who had enjoyed a faltering protection within the grander imperial whole now found themselves more acutely exposed to the rule of others. 'The Versailles Treaty,' it has been said, 'in seeking to embody the principle of self-determination, actually created more, not fewer, minorities, and much angrier ones', and this for the reason that the new nationalist regimes 'could afford to be far less tolerant than the old empires' (Johnson 1991: 38). Indeed, Hobsbawm reasonably speculates that the Russian empire also would have succumbed to fragmentationist nationalism, as it was to do after 1989, had not the Bolshevik revolution supervened (1994: 372–3).

The fruits of the new self-determination were, therefore, mixed and, in some cases, short-lived—even if the effects of this essay in liberal nationalism were to endure and re-emerge in sinister form at the century's end. But apart from the issue of protecting minority ethnic rights in the successor states, the region suffered a second form of fragmentation in its loss of economic cohesion. In thrall to the idea of nationalism, the peace-makers committed the sin in central Europe of neglecting 'the economic unity of European regions, which they disrupted by creating new states, hedged with barriers to trade and investment' (Foreman-Peck

1995: 178; see also Ashworth 1975: 230). States which struggled to find political-civil legitimacy in the eyes of all their citizens had to carry the additional burden of coping with a dislocated economic infrastructure as well.

As to the empires outside Europe, the new diplomacy made token recognition of the changed atmosphere in instituting its system of mandates for their governance: accountability was asserting its right to sit beside imperial fiat. Even this symbolic change, however, given its limited practical effects, could do little to disguise the reality that the major empires of Britain and France emerged from war with the imperium expanded, and the will to empire largely intact where it had not been actually intensified. For this reason, Mayall is correct to point to the stark inconsistency between the treatment of empire within Europe and of that without. 'It is a major paradox in the history of national self-determination,' he writes, 'that the struggle for political liberty in Europe coincided with the expansion of European power to every corner of the globe' (Mayall 1990: 45). If this refers generally to the nineteenth century, its sentiment remains apposite to the disposition of empire in 1919. However, that there was little slackening in the reins of empire in the metropolitan centres does not imply that the war was without impact on the colonial periphery.

Universalist ideals were to be turned to fragmentationist purposes. There is perhaps too strong a tendency to portray the impact on empire in ideological terms. One account, for instance, explains the seed of imperial disintegration in such terms: 'everywhere non-Westerners appalled by the slaughter had lost faith in the moral superiority of Europe. They became more self-assertive, more than ever guided by the Western ideals of self-determination and national power' (Von Laue 1987: 57).

In reality, developments on the ground were driven as much by pragmatism and opportunism. It was perhaps less the loss of European moral authority in the abstract, and more the local opportunities to substitute for withdrawn colonial personnel, as well as to exploit the economic void, that enhanced self-assertiveness. Even more important still in encouraging a new consciousness was the disturbance of traditional imperial management, and in particular of the political powers of local élites, by the heavier intrusion of the imperial presence into the colonies, either to protect them physically, or to mobilize their resources for the war. It was these élites, from Egypt to India, which saw their position threatened on two fronts—by the imperial masters and by popular nationalist agitation engendered by the hardship of wartime economic conditions. The analysis of post-war Egypt's reaction to its protectorate status is symptomatic:

The traditional leaderships within indigenous society therefore felt that they were being hemmed in by British supervision . . . and they sought to stem these encroachments on their privileges by manipulating popular disturbances. (Holland 1985: 17)

The pattern was repeated in India, where 'it had been the pressures of war imperialism—with its conscriptions, taxes, and other regimentation—which had upset the old compromises between British rulers and established interests' (Holland 1985: 18). However, even if this disabuses us of any notion of the war creating a cohesive outpouring of nationalist fervour in the colonies, the disaffection of the local élites was itself more damaging for the longer-term survival of empires: based in self-interest, rather than on Western liberal ideals, their disenchantment with empire was all the more potent.

Reactions to the war occasionally took the form of popular demonstration, often about the drafting of recruits to fight in it. In some cases, there can be no doubt that this constitutes a formative 'nationalist' experience. Despite the large numbers of Australians who fought in the war, and had their baptism by fire at Gallipoli, the introduction of conscription was sternly resisted and defeated, an action which in imperial terms was 'an expression of Australia's growing national awareness' (Betts 1985: 39). In Africa there was some armed resistance to recruitment, with rebellions, for instance, in Mozambique and Nyasaland. Although these reflected wider discontent with colonial rule, their historian comments that 'it was the Great War, and particularly wartime conscription, which focused such grievances so clearly as to demand action' (Page 1987: 7).

If the war created fissures in empire (even if they were not to become open cracks for another three decades or more), it had its most profound fragmentationist impact on the international economy as a whole. It contributed to the 'disintegration' of the liberal-capitalist world economy 'due not so much to the working of economic laws as to political action' (Hardach 1977: 226). This can be illustrated in the areas of foreign trade, investment, credit, foreign exchange, and disputes among the Allies about the bases of post-war economic policy. However, Maynard Keynes should perhaps be allowed the first word because he gets to the heart of the problem when he describes the war's destruction of the delicate, but complex, organizational infrastructure on which the continent of Europe depended for its survival:

Europe consists of the densest aggregation of population in the history of the world . . . In relation to other continents Europe is not self-sufficient; in particular it cannot feed itself. Internally the population is not evenly distributed, but much of it is crowded into a relatively small number of dense industrial centres. This population secured for itself a livelihood before the War, without much margin of surplus, by means of a delicate and immensely complicated organisation, of which the foundations were supported by coal, iron, transport, and an unbroken supply of imported food and raw materials from other continents. By the destruction of this organisation . . . a part of this population is deprived of its means of livelihood. (Keynes 1919: 212–13)

In these understated terms, Keynes draws attention to the potential horror of the dislocation brought by war. If nobody had anticipated the duration of the war, neither had anyone foreseen the profundity of its economic impact. At first, the effects had seemed minor and likely to be temporary. It was only, as Ashworth notes, as the scope of the war increased that its imprint deepened. At first it disrupted trade and investment and the gold standard was abandoned. This led to a search for new markets until it became clear that the demands of war left decreasingly little surplus to export. In the case of Britain, the proportion of its manufacturing production for export had fallen by a half between 1913 and 1918 (Ashworth 1975: 228–9). Capital outflows from Europe halted before being reversed. By the end of the war, all the economies suffered from acute inflation as the costs of war had been met by borrowing rather than by taxation. New producers grasped the markets vacated by their former suppliers, with Japan asserting itself in China, India, and Russia (Bell 1992: 145). Fledgeling industries established during the war now demanded tariff protection at war's end to secure their survival (Marwick 1991: 26–7).

Dislocation of traditional patterns of economic activity does not, of course, by itself amount to fragmentation. What was so striking were the attitudes stimulated by war and which survived its end. It is thus possible to detect the changing winds of economic policy in wartime planning and discussions. The stress throughout, at least on the European side, was on the quest for self-sufficiency, protection, and where necessity demanded international activity, its organization on a government-imposed and institutionalized form, rather than a return to reliance upon the market itself. Thus it has been observed that 'during most of the War, the British Government concentrated on making postwar British trade secure and on planning for national self-sufficiency . . . after the war' (Bunselmeyer 1975: 14). There were many suggestions that this might be done within an imperial framework. None the less, Leo Amery was not alone in arguing that 'the great lesson brought home by the war to every combatant and neutral is the necessity of being self-contained' (as quoted in Bunselmeyer 1975: 23). Such autarchic conceptions were scarcely compatible with the restoration of an open, free-trading international economy, even if the direst versions of such schemes fell away as the war came to an end.

Faced with inflation and massive borrowing at home, trade deficits with suppliers such as the United States, and external indebtedness to the United States, the Allies had two choices for economic salvation in 1919. They must hope for economic largess from the United States; or they must exact tribute from Germany. The future of the international order hung in the balance as the peacemakers confronted the complex, and interwoven, issues of credit, loans, foreign exchange, and reparations in order to rehabilitate the world's economic system.

The root problems for a restoration of international trade were the inability of most of the Europeans to pay for their imports, as well as the difficulty of making foreign payments without the stability of the gold standard mechanism, and especially in a period of high inflation. Much of this, in turn, was associated with the 'financial chaos' brought about by 'huge budget deficits' from the war (Ashworth 1975: 229). Without a restoration of stability to the financial system, it was difficult to see how international trade could recover; but likewise, for many of the European belligerents who had lost large proportions of their overseas capital stock, it was hard to see how their finances could be stabilized without export earnings: the vicious circle was complete. Already Congress had authorized war loans amounting to some US$10 billion, most of which had been allocated by the end of the war but some of which might be needed to meet import bills for essential supplies in the months thereafter (Walworth 1986: 164).

As noted above, the two possible solutions lay in indemnity from Germany or in some kind of economic assistance from the United States. The evidence of fundamental dislocation in the international economy can thus be reviewed by examining the Allied deliberations about reparations and war debts, on the one hand, and about the wider structure of post-war economic policy, and the role of the United States, on the other.

Total Allied war debts amounted to some US$26.5 billion, the majority owed to the United States; although Britain, while owing the USA some US$4.7 billion remained a net creditor overall (Pollard 1993: 164). Most of the Europeans argued that, if the debts were to be repaid, there would need to be reparations exacted from Germany at high levels, but that in justice they need not be paid at all as the Allies had already paid the costs of war in kind. Only the United States could have relieved this log jam by rescinding all debts, as Keynes strenuously urged (1919: 262–3), but this it steadfastly refused to do. Thus the USA too was committed to reparations, not because it sought payments for itself but because, indirectly, it required a German economy healthy enough to make payments to the other Allies in order that they might pay off their war loans (Walworth 1986: 169–70). What this entailed was an American policy of seeking a limit on German reparations that approximated what its economy could reasonably afford to pay (Sharp 1991: 99). Britain's Prime Minister Lloyd George, in the meantime, was increasingly pressurized to increase his demands, both for domestic political reasons, and to take account of demands from parts of the empire which feared that they would receive no compensation whatsoever. According to Marc Trachtenberg, it was therefore largely as a result of British intransigence that no agreement could be reached on a reparations figure and no fixed amount was included in the Versailles Treaty. He points out that this was deeply damaging to Germany, and hence to the rest of the international economy, because 'no one would lend Germany anything . . . if the amount due for reparation were not limited' (Trachtenberg 1980: 63). The French, on the other hand, and as argued above, were forced into a position of raising their own demands but as a fall-back position and, tactically, 'as a lever more against the Americans than the Germans' (Sharp 1991: 83). It was from the Americans, and the wider post-war economic framework, that ultimate salvation was sought.

British officials had, during the war, laid the groundwork for a post-war economic system which would continue a kind of economic war against Germany into the peace: only thus was it believed that British economic security might be preserved. Some of these intentions were agreed with the French in the Paris Economic Resolutions of 1916. However, by the end of the war the British government had come round to support of reparations as a substitute for such measures, not least because it doubted the willingness of the United States to go along with them. The historian of this British planning therefore concludes that 'trade war was thereby renounced in favor of direct compensation from Germany' (Bunselmeyer 1975: 46). In short, British policy moved from a conception of close Allied economic cooperation, designed to constrain Germany, towards the alternative of reparations. British feelings were heavily coloured by suspicions, and resentment, of the new American economic influence.

For France, however, and according to Trachtenberg's thesis, the espousal of reparations was largely a recognition of its failure to secure agreement for its project of continued inter-Allied economic cooperation: tactically, it was used to persuade the Americans to think again (1980: viii). What French finance minister Clémentel wanted to construct was a *dirigiste* Allied economic system that would secure French needs but also create the basis for an orderly expansion of trade (Trachtenberg 1980: 3–4). The Americans refused to participate in such a scheme and immediately after the war dismantled the Allied control agencies that had operated in wartime. Wilson's concern was for a 'return to the prewar structure of free markets and commercial equality' (Trachtenberg 1980: 22).

What does all this tell us about the fragmentationist impact of the Great War? The United States walked a thin line between two forms of economic closure, one that would exclude Germany from international economic participation through severity of reparations, and one that would construct a kind of 'economic entente' for the post-war period. The keys for the preservation of an open, inclusive, and expansionary economic system lay in American hands. That this did not eventuate can in part be attributed to the narrow economic nationalism that was prevalent in Washington and New York. More fundamentally, however, and unlike the period after 1945, there was no basis on which a 'transatlantic bargain' could be struck: the failure of the Allies to agree on a post-war economic system revealed the limited possibilities for accommodation of their disparate interests. Without this, the international order suffered not only from a hegemonic interregnum but from a lack of international leadership of any kind.

States of War and States at Peace

If this establishes the international configuration which was to hold globalization in check for most of the next generation, it none the less does not go quite far enough in accounting for these state preferences. To accomplish this, and to unravel finally the ambivalent outcomes of war, we need to turn to the domestic aspect. Here, as much as in the international sphere, there was to be much dislocation, innovation, and compromise. Allied governments failed to agree on a new international economic order because they were caught between what their domestic constituencies demanded and what the international system would allow.

In much of the literature, the domestic impact of the war has tended to be assessed in two areas—the extent of government intervention in the economy and its wider social consequences. It was perhaps the first that caught the earliest attention. Noting both the eventual Keynesian management of the economy, and the wider social responsibility of government associated with welfarism from the 1940s, historians have tended to trace the development of these managerial and welfare functions from the experience of the two World Wars. It was widely assumed that the war had at least hastened, even if it had not entirely caused, this trend. Thus, as Robert W. Cox suggests, based on their experiences of coordinating industrial production during the war, there emerged thereafter 'national economic planning, or state capitalism' (1987: 161). For instance, in the British case, allocation of resources and price-fixing began with munitions and was extended to other areas, so much so that by war's end 'two-thirds of the economy and nine-tenths of imports were subject to direction by bodies authorised by government' (Cain and Hopkins 1993: 49). However, more recent research has tended to question the permanency of such changes and it is recognized that much contemporary opinion, whatever its mood during the war, had by its end envisaged a return to normalcy and thus 'viewed the state's intrusion into economic life in wartime as being temporary and accidental' (Wall and Winter 1988: 4).

The historiography of war and social change in the twentieth century has moved in similar directions. As against those who pointed to the radically transformative impact of war—on class divisions, gender roles, political participation, welfare—there has developed a more sceptical approach, regarding the effects of war as being far from durable or unidirectional: some have indeed argued that the war's impact was socially regressive. Typically, a specialist survey of war and the family suggests that it had a temporary dislocative effect but that 'in terms of the social history of the European family, the First World War was more a conservative than a revolutionary force' (Wall and Winter 1988: 4).

However, by far the most interesting area of recent historical research has been that which brings changes in the role of the state, and in its social basis, into clear relationship with the international situation. As noted above, this has been done under the concept of corporatism. This is the analytical point at which international politics, state policies, and domestic social forces come together in such a way that the full dynamic of the setback to post-First World War globalization can best be understood.

The most powerful expression of the corporatist thesis is that offered by Charles S. Maier. Its central propositions are as follows. Such had been the internal political strains generated by the long period of warfare, so necessary had a state managerial style become to the war effort, and so relatively important had become the maintenance of class cohesion that a form of political economy based on 'new interest-group compromises' was developed (Maier 1989: 132). This corporatist approach to some extent bypassed elected representatives and officials and fostered direct bargaining between state, employers, and workers. Another writer attributes the adoption of this model to the 'increase in working-class strength brought about through the war', and even suggests that corporatism found institutional embodiment in the post-war *international* system in the shape of the International Labour Organization (Cox 1987: 180, 182–3).

For the present purpose, corporatism, whatever its limits, is a revealing concept for understanding the tensions between globalization and fragmentation that became apparent in the aftermath of war, and the reasons why the inter-war period gradually saw the scales tipped in favour of fragmentation. The essential idea behind corporatism is that it was a political strategy for generating domestic stability by co-opting potentially dissident classes to the national cause, especially at a time when revolutionary disenchantment was a very real prospect. In order to achieve this stability, domestic economic concessions had to be made. In particular, wartime governments found it politically attractive to run with inflationary borrowing, rather than attempt to impose the real costs of war on their populations. The problem with such domestic accommodations was that they were finally constrained by international pressures. As Maier suggested, '[e]quilibrium remained hostage to the discrepancy between the demands of the international economy and the pressures for compromise between groups at home' (1989: 147). Inflation and deficits might be attractive domestically but they flew in the face of the restoration of a viable system of international trade and finance, without which real economic recovery was not possible.

Even more pointedly, it was not just that European corporatist strategies came into conflict with the demands of an international economy in the abstract, they came into conflict with the particular expression of these demands emanating from Washington: corporatism could not be reconciled with America's prerequisites for reviving the international economy. All the tensions and ambivalence of the war experience are encapsulated in this central contradiction:

The overriding thrust toward monetary stabilization came in part from across the Atlantic. The economic trends of the second half of the 1920s reflected American conditions for alleviating the balance-of-payments difficulties that impeded capitalist stability. Since Woodrow Wilson's intervention in 1917, the United States had sought to secure a liberal democratic and capitalist comity of nations . . . It was apparent that the United States had become the guarantor of such a political economy. (Maier 1989: 147)

But the guarantee was conditional and thus the potential of a liberal capitalist comity of nations was not immediately to be realized. What it fell foul of was the real world of international politics inhabited by the Europeans (fears of Germany, Bolshevism, unconsummated desires for security, psychological needs for self-sufficiency, imperial distractions, jealousies of American economic success, and the rest) as well as of their domestic political and economic imperatives. There was not yet either a sufficient comity of international interests, or a United States with enough power and conviction of its own to impose one. In the absence of these conditions, further globalization had to await the ultimate working out of the logic of fragmentation: only then would such comity be assured.

4

THE FRAGMENTATION OF
THE INTER-WAR ERA, 1919–1939

There is a suggestion that the forces of globalization and fragmentation are engaged in a perpetual and dynamic self-correcting relationship: once a certain point is reached the balance moves back in the opposite direction. Some such notion was hinted at by the Cambridge historian, E. H. Carr, in his account of the inter-war crisis. He noted the longer-term tendency towards 'integration and the formation of ever larger political units' which set in during the later nineteenth century, and was associated with developments in capitalism, industrialism, and the technology of communication. As against this, he also recognized the persistence of 'disintegrating forces'. These, he speculated, might be governed by some law of size and become virulent when certain orders of magnitude were exceeded. When this happened, they would provoke 'a recrudescence of disintegrating tendencies' (Carr 1940: 293–5).

The inter-war period certainly witnessed the reassertion of such disintegrative trends. As such, the period offers a fascinating interpretive challenge, and has been the subject of considerable revision in recent decades: out of this emerges the view of the 1920s as the critical stepping stone between pre-1914 concepts of international stability and their final redefinition after 1945 (Jacobson 1983: 623). These wider debates about the period can be applied to the discussion of the causes of fragmentation. Did fragmentation prevail because the economic and technical sources of globalization faltered? Did fragmentation revive, as Carr hints, because of some dynamic law which ensures that a dominant trend is periodically corrected? To what extent were the forces of globalization thrown off course by the exogenous shock of the events of the First World War? Can it be argued that during this phase, certain social and political forces were unleashed which, once established as state policies, demonstrated that political voluntarism is always capable of overturning what might appear to be secular and predetermined technological and economic trends?

The inter-war era, or at least the 1920s, represented a more complex interplay between globalization and fragmentation than these remarks might imply. There was certainly no instant nor uniform return to disintegration. As already discussed above, the First World War gave rise to a rhetorical and ideological presentation of international affairs that pointedly emphasized the universal and notions of an integrated and cohesive world order: the emphasis on collective international responses was itself intended to reflect an integrated concept of community which was dependent upon a single security structure. To be sure, much of the rhetoric was self-interested, and only selectively accepted and applied, but this should not detract from the symbolic importance of this ideological strategy: such notions could have had no potential appeal had there not been thought to be an emerging constituency persuaded of a changing international reality.

The paradox of the age was that this emphasis on internationalism and universalism had to coexist with a sharpened sense of nationalism and particularism. The League of Nations was created not simply to avert future wars but out of recognition that the international system was now a much more complex web of interactions, requiring more conscious management than had been practised in the nineteenth century. As Zara Steiner argues, the proliferation of specialized agencies in the 1920s 'corresponded to the increasing interdependence of the states' (1993: 69). At the same time, the League followed Wilson's Fourteen Points in sanctifying the principle of national self-determination, thus pushing into uncomfortable juxtaposition the twin ideals of supranationalism and nationalism. Wallerstein regards this as the characteristic tension of the period:

Overall then, the thrust of the historical developments of the period was a contradictory one. It involved on the one hand the attempt at the elaboration of a supranational political apparatus implying a limitation on state authorities, and on the other the extension of nationalist demands and of the principle of national self-determination. (Wallerstein 1991: 151)

Revealingly, as will be discussed below, this tension was to be displayed in both spheres of international economy and international security.

In one specific respect, the inter-war period appeared to signify an important measure of de-globalization. It was suggested above that, at the turn of the century, there was an extension of the European balance of power to incorporate other extra-European powers and that this had led to a more complex configuration than had prevailed for most of the preceding century. Superficially, at least, the inter-war period seemed to betoken a reversal of this trend and a reassertion of European primacy and insularity. Thus one writer claims of the period that it suspended what had been believed to be some inexorable nineteenth century trends, foremost amongst which was the evolution from a European to 'a global balance of power' (Stevenson 1988: 321).

Such a suspension was more apparent than real. By most objective measures, the world was a less Eurocentric place in 1919 than it had been before the war. Economic historians consistently point to Europe's loss of primacy during this period as measured by trade and production statistics. Relatively, Europe's performance declined, especially compared with that of the United States and Japan (Aldcroft 1977: 33–4). Europe's share of world trade fell: the US share was 32.1 per cent in 1920 as against 22.4 per cent in 1913, and Europe's declined from 58.4

per cent to 49.2 per cent (Aldcroft 1993: 13–14). Of great importance for what was to follow, this dropping off was especially marked in terms of Europe's share of the US market where the share in the 1920s fell to some 30 per cent compared to over 50 per cent before the war (Keylor 1984: 99). As regards manufacturing production, a similar story unfolds. In the period 1913 to 1925, European manufacturing output grew by 22 per cent. Aldcroft notes, however, that the 'contrast between Europe and the rest of the world is striking'. Over the same period, the following gains were recorded: USA (48 per cent); Japan (122 per cent); Australia (41 per cent); India (32 per cent); New Zealand (36 per cent); and South Africa (304 per cent) (Aldcroft 1977: 98–9).

Certainly this picture of general European decline has been challenged by some recent historical writing. In the case of Britain, it is suggested, rumours of the country's terminal weakness have been much exaggerated. Cain and Hopkins vigorously argue for a Britain still pre-eminent in 1914, straitened but still relatively strong in the 1920s, and fit enough to come through the slump and challenge some American positions in the 1930s (1993: 3–6). But, even conceding this qualification, the general picture of Europe's relative economic decline, not to mention its loss of moral authority, broadly stands.

And yet the perception, if not the reality, was of an inter-war international system dominated by Europe and European concerns. Marks comments of the peace settlement in 1919 that 'although it dealt with the entire globe' it 'was a peculiarly European peace, written largely by the European victors to their own benefit'. Elsewhere, she notes of the League that it was a 'European club, dominated by European statesmen, European assumptions, and European issues most of the time' (Marks 1976: 26, 29). How are we to explain this perception and the seeming suspension of the trend towards a global system? The answer is straightforward enough and lies in the coincidental distractions and preoccupations of the other potential great powers. Russia and China were beset by civil war and the United States pursued an arm's length policy which concealed its emerging status. In short, there is an impressive historical consensus that the shift to globalism was not so much halted or suspended but merely *disguised* during the inter-war period. Richard Overy notes the incipient problems for Britain and France in defending global empires and records that only the defeat of the Central Powers and Russia's temporary eclipse 'disguised the fact' (1987: 7). Kennedy similarly notes of the period that 'in a curious . . . and artificial way . . . it still seemed a Eurocentric world' (1988: 277). To this extent, the Eurocentricity of the age was the negative by-product of what the other world powers could not, or would not, do. The illusion was compounded also by artifice. Sally Marks makes the telling suggestion that the European great powers (namely Britain and France), which were less than enamoured of the security responsibilities which the League structure bestowed upon them, were none the less assuaged by the status which the League also conferred. To this extent, the League itself concealed the realities of the age in that it 'disguised the transfers of power taking place in the world and reinforced Europe's view of its role' (Marks 1976: 30).

However, the drift towards fragmentation in the inter-war period amounted to more than the disguising of the ongoing process of global dissemination of power: the age also witnessed fundamental shocks to the processes of international integration, cultural unity, and the multilateralization of economic and security management. How are we to account for such massive dislocations? The analysis of the setbacks to globalization overlaps with other central questions about the period. For instance, was the depression and its ensuing deep-seated economic fragmentation the result simply of cyclical economic conditions and structural problems, or was it the consequence of external shocks, such as those represented by the war and by fundamentalist nationalist political doctrines? Alternatively conceived, was the breakdown of the international political and economic order in the 1930s the consequence of fortuitous circumstance or was it the inevitable result of the failure to deal, in 1919, with profound systemic imbalances of both an economic and military nature? Such debates are familiar in the literature but it will be the function of this chapter to reappraise them for the light that they shed on the less familiar issue of the causes of fragmentation.

The first debate is more narrowly economic and is largely concerned with the causes of the economic slump and depression. Structurally, the arguments are similar to those which revolve around the issue of the collapse of the political and security order. Aldcroft clearly articulates the stark choices. According to the first view,

we are justified in treating the war as a large exogenous shock which so upset the pattern of development and its underlying equilibrium that it eventually resulted in the breakdown of the type of integrated international framework which characterized the nineteenth century.

According to the second,

the war may be seen as an initial shock which for a time disturbed both cyclical and secular processes of economic development, but . . . after a short adjustment stage economies reverted to their previous trends . . . In this case the impact of the war had little bearing on the 1929 downturn in economic activity and the subsequent disintegration of the international economy. (Aldcroft 1977: 1)

In outline, the respective positions are that the war introduced fundamental disequilibria into the system, partially concealed in the 1920s, but which eventually emerged in the stark collapse of the international economic order by 1930. As with the political domain, the history of the inter-war period is one of the stripping away of the 'illusions' of the post-war decade (the view most clearly expressed in Marks 1976). The seeming return to prosperity in the late 1920s simply disguised the fact that 'the structural supports were too weak', as the 1929 collapse revealed (Aldcroft 1993: 1). Accordingly, the disaster of 1929 was endemic in the conditions generated in 1919. In contrast, the second view holds that there was material change and progress in the 1920s and that therefore the final collapse has to be explained either by the onset of *new* conditions (not directly related to the war) or at least by the failure of the government strategies designed to cope with these conditions. Monetarist accounts of the depression would obviously fall into this second category (see Kindleberger 1987: 3). Likewise, those accounts which emphasize the natural rhythm of the business cycle (that one was due by the end of the decade in any event) thereby distance themselves from the exogenous impact of the war's disruptive effects (Aldcroft 1993: 65–6).

Very similar positions are held with regard to the disintegration of the security order. Bell thus identifies a Thirty Year War perspective:

a school of thought has developed which regards the Second World War as the culmination of a disintegration of the European order, begun in the First World War and continued by the abortive peace, which left the Continent in a state of chronic instability. (1986: 14)

Given that conflict was endemic in this system, the 1920s presented only the illusion of peace. What was wrong in 1919 was the failure to tackle the fundamental disequilibrium represented by Germany's disproportionate power. This view has received trenchant recent support in a formidable account of the Second World War. There was in 1919 no thought of the radical breakup of the German state and yet, geopolitically, German power was strengthened, not weakened, by the Versailles settlement. While the revival of Poland shielded Germany from Russia, the emergence of the successor states in central and Eastern Europe removed any potential restraint on Germany and, in effect, set in place an embryonic German sphere of influence not far removed from the *Mitteleuropa* ambitions propagated under the Kaiser (Weinberg 1994: 15).

As against this notion that the Second World War was caused by the first, there is an alternative point of view:

Instead of the continuation of the First World War, arising almost inevitably out of the effects of that war and the instability of the peace settlement, there appears the outline of a successful European recovery, cut off in its prime by the great depression and its dreadful consequence, the advent of Hitler. (Bell 1986: 38)

This is the view that, but for the depression, 'there would certainly have been no Hitler' and, more generally, that 'the Great Slump destroyed economic liberalism for half a century' (Hobsbawm 1994: 86, 94–5). The depression takes on the status of an independent causal factor—rather than being viewed as an integral part of the settlement of 1919—itself tearing down the security order, but as a consequence of shorter-term economic conditions and not as part of an overall crisis of the inter-war period. The debates about the origins of the Second World War thus replicate the format of the debates about the causes of the depression.

Striking as these interpretive parallels may be, they would be little more than matters of intellectual curiosity did they not serve to crystallize the central issues for an understanding of the inter-war period. In accordance with the principal argument of this book, it can now be suggested that this period provides graphic illustration of the role of politics and of political voluntarism in disrupting what might be thought to be deterministic trends. Likewise, the powerful political forces unleashed after 1919 were themselves a mixture of international and domestic concerns, and indeed of the interplay between them. Once again, the fate of globalization and fragmentation was to be shaped by the manner in which state élites sought to manoeuvre, squeezed as they were between international pressures and irresistible domestic priorities: the history of fragmentation at this point becomes the history of state structures adrift in a hostile international environment. There was to be a dynamic interplay between the ways in which that environment uniformly encouraged *étatisme*, at its best, and totalitarian extremism, at its worst, and the ways in which these developments at the state level reinforced the severity of the international conditions. That political voluntarism then confounded the processes of globalization is hardly in dispute. As Milward contends, '[i]nterdependence can be rejected by an act of national political will . . . The case of Germany under the national-socialist regime would seem an irrefutable proof of this, that of Russia in 1917 another' (1992: 8). What is at issue, and what needs to be understood, is why during the inter-war period national political will sought salvation in policies of fragmentation rather than in any possible alternative.

The Period in Overview

Versailles bestowed an inauspicious beginning on the period in that it failed to construct what, in Henry Kissinger's words, might be called a legitimate international order. This was so in the sense that its terms reflected the interests of a small number of victor and *status quo* powers but left outwith the settlement the interests of several other great powers. It is for this reason that it has been said of the inter-war system that 'there never existed any firm foundation for permanent peace since three of the four strongest continental powers were intensely dissatisfied with the *status quo*' (Marks 1976: 143). To Italy, Germany, and Russia in a European perspective must be added also Japan in a wider global context.

It was perhaps out of some such subconscious realization that the early years of the period were given over to attempts to enforce the settlement, not least because the period 1919–22 saw a spate of wars and border disputes as various disaffected parties sought to exploit the vacuum on the ground left by the aftermath of war. 'By that time the world had learned,' Marks wryly comments, 'that peace treaties are easier to write than to implement' (1976: 32).

In any event, and as often remarked, there was much in the settlement and in the design of the League that was backward looking: the League was intended to prevent the outbreak of the First World War and the settlement was designed to perpetuate the specific *status quo* which had emerged at the war's end. Neither of such preoccupations, however understandable in the context of the time, served well to establish the institutions that would be required to allow for adaptation, or to prevent wars that might result from other than accident or secret diplomacy, or be prosecuted in the teeth of world opinion. Indeed, the most potent legacy of war, and the very underpinning of its new security concept, was the need to avoid the recurrence of war. This imperative explains most of what needs to be known about the tragedy of the 1930s but the reluctance to contemplate war was itself a severe limitation upon the efficacy of the new collective security. Many League supporters 'so hated war that they never wanted to fight another, not even a League war' (Northedge 1986: 2), thus fostering the illusion that what was unthinkable had thereby been eliminated.

Sadly, security became collective only in the sense that it became the responsibility of nobody in particular. Britain had perhaps aquiesced without enthusiasm in some of Wilson's more extravagant proposals if for no other reason than the expectation that the USA might thereby be recruited to British ends (Bartlett 1994: 114), not least in sharing the burdens of psychological reassurance to the French. Without US membership of the League, and with the consequent lapsing of American guarantees to France, Britain was driven to trim its commitments and responsibilities to the new realities. In any case, and presumably for historical reasons, Britain regarded France as the now-dominant continental power, more than able to look after its own interests. In this way, there opened the perceptual gap that was to divide the Western powers and to destroy any possibility of their joint action to maintain the balance of power. Symptomatically, the French took unilateral enforcement action in the Ruhr in 1923 while Britain ducked from the commitments that might have been entailed by the Draft Treaty of Mutual Assistance and the Geneva Protocol of 1924 (Kissinger 1995: 254). 'As the peace settlement crumbled,' Marks observes, 'the fear-driven French became sticklers for at least a modicum of enforcement, while the British, who were having second thoughts about many aspects of the settlement, encouraged the crumbling process' (Marks 1976: 34).

Such stabilization as was achieved by the mid-1920s was based on the Anglo-American preference for revision rather than on the French preference for enforcement. The twin monuments of the period—the Dawes Plan of 1924 and the Locarno Treaty of 1925—both symbolized acceptance of the process of revisionism in the reparations and territorial spheres. None the less, they gave precious hope to a generation who saw in them German acceptance of a final settlement, such as had not been forthcoming in 1919. The restructuring of German reparations proposed by the committee working under the US banker, Charles Dawes, was the basis on which currency stabilization in Central Europe was to be achieved and was accompanied by the beginning of the return to gold. Above all, only with this solution could private investors be tempted to transfer funds to Germany on the scale required for recovery and reconstruction. Locarno was its political counterpart, signalling political rehabilitation in Germany's acceptance of its western border, guaranteed by Britain and Italy, early removal of occupation forces from the Rhineland, and German admission to the League as a permanent Council member.

It is on the interpretation of these events that many of the above debates hinge. On the economic front, they are regarded by some as the final failure to confront the radically altered circumstances wrought by war. Hence, Dawes and the return to gold created the 'initial conditions from which the world depression of 1929 emerged' (Kindleberger 1987: 14–15). Others see these as the basis of a new stability and prosperity, however fragile, which unhappily was to be overturned at decade's end, but for different and unforeseeable reasons. The judgements of

Locarno are similarly divided. It is either seen as confirmation of the myopia of 1919 and hence as an essential instrument in transmitting the dislocations of 1919 into the 1930s or, alternatively, as a real chance for peace subsequently lost through economic and social collapse.

Locarno demonstrated that coercion of Germany would now be abandoned in favour of cooperative 'fulfilment' (Ross 1983: 10). But it was at best a lopsided agreement. In a sense, as Kissinger pointedly remarks, it simply confirmed the result of the last war in that 'Germany had been defeated in the West but had over-come Russia in the East'. By ignoring the sanctity of Germany's eastern borders, Locarno thereby 'laid the basis for Germany's ultimate assault on the Eastern set-tlement' (Kissinger 1995: 275). For all that, the agreement received the benign blessing of the United States for which it represented the final consummation of post-war policy:

the Americans welcomed the Locarno agreements because they seemed to constitute a framework for a new era of stability in Europe, an era based on orderly change and the imperatives of modern capitalist economies. In the view of American policymakers, Locarno accomplished the elusive task of enhancing French security without emasculat-ing Germany's economic potential or compromising America's independence of action. (Leffler 1979: 119)

To most historians, Locarno was more of a mixed blessing than this would sug-gest. Locarno's contribution lay mainly in what it did to stimulate hopes for the future and, in this, certainly encouraged a semblance of peace. Even here, how-ever, it must be conceded that its contribution was made at the expense of the League: the agreement was a traditionalist arrangement that should have been unnecessary if there was credence in the Covenant, and its regionalism detracted from the universalism of the general guarantees of the League (Steiner 1993: 48). Others, while admitting its improvement of atmospherics, assess its contribution above all to have been in furthering the illusions of the period (Marks 1976: 74).

These illusions were stripped away in the 1930s. Symptomatically, the League's disarmament endeavours finally faltered early in the decade. The consensual revi-sionism of the second half of the 1920s, associated with German chancellor Gustav Stresemann, gave way in style, if not much in substance, to the unilateral revisionism of the 1930s. Revision of the 1919 settlements was as major a feature of the Pacific theatre as of the European at this time. Whilst Japan had operated within the constraints of the Washington system since 1922, the new decade opened with the overt challenge to it in the occupation of Manchuria. There was little pretence that the League could take any real action over this matter and the overlay of collective security, that had coexisted in the 1920s with more tradi-tionalist alliances, was progressively stripped away to reveal the salience under-neath of that erstwhile dominant form of security. France added Russia to its existing, and questionable, treaty arrangements with Poland and the Little Entente in the East. The problem for Britain was not so much the abandonment of the League but the simple shortage of prospective partners with whom a viable coalition might be forged—Japan, Italy, the Soviet Union, and the United States all either defected or stood aside (Kennedy 1988: 317–18). With the last of these, Britain enjoyed a relationship of 'mutual suspicion', especially about the potential economic costs of salvation by Washington, and this persuaded Chamberlain that appeasement of Germany was the lesser of the two evils (Cain and Hopkins 1993: 102).

But is the story of the inter-war period one in which internationalism was espoused in the 1920s, only to be rejected by the crises of the 1930s? Or was the situation more nuanced than such an account would suggest? Was multilateralism essayed and abandoned, or did it fail because its implementation had been little more than fainthearted in the first place? These questions can best be addressed by exploring the balance beteen globalization and fragmentation in the economic and security policies of the powers in the 1920s.

The Return to Internationalism?

There is a tendency to present a stark contrast between the resumed hopes of the 1920s and the disillusionment of the 1930s. While accurate in essence, such a depiction misses some important features of the 1920s and runs the risk of leading to misunderstandings of the inter-war period as a whole. While there can be little dissenting from the picture of fragmentation, closure, and unilateralism which was to characterize the 1930s, the 1920s were less wholeheartedly the sponsor of globalization, openness, and multilateralism than any such contrast would imply. Its record was more variegated and while there was unquestionably some enfeebled endeavour to return to the internationalism of the pre-war system, any full accounting of the period must note also the constraints on such a return that existed from the outset. In short, autarchy did not replace multilateralism at the turn of the decade but, instead, was a latent feature of the period from its very beginning. From 1919, nationalism vied robustly with internationalism and, while contained in some respects, was to be a dynamic presence in the inter-war period as a whole.

This argument can be made by exploring both the security and the economic arrangements that were set in place. As noted, there is a striking similarity between the two: in both spheres, there was an aspiration to, and a rhetoric of, internationalism and collectivism while, in practice, nationalist dissension and unilateralism tended to prevail. None the less, the aspiration to internationalism cannot be discounted: it represented a tangible element in the psychological and political make-up of the age and all practitioners had to operate with at least one eye to its requirements. What was different about this internationalism in the two spheres was that, as regards the international economy, the wish was for a return to a system that was believed to have created an earlier golden age whereas, as regards security, the surge of collectivism constituted a vision for the future and a rejection of a past that was deemed to have failed. The contrast is no accident. For American ideologists, amongst others, it was clear that the political domain would avoid the turmoil of war only when it had adopted the sensible rationalism that prevailed in an orderly international economic system. Thus collective security was little more than an extension of the order that had been established in the domestic economy and that had worked so well in the pre-war international economy.

What were the constraints upon genuine internationalism in the new security order? Marks raises the general point succinctly in her lament that 'the theory of collective security assumed an astonishing amount of agreement and altruism among men and nations, an unfailing willingness to sacrifice and die for strangers' (1976: 31). The point is well taken. Indeed, those who have lived through the 1990s can be more readily sympathetic to this reality having themselves witnessed the inevitable scarcity of such willingness to sacrifice. However, this will always be an obstacle to collective security and its generality tells us little about the distinctive temper of the inter-war age. In part, at that time, the unwillingness was itself a manifestation of the memory of the Great War, the shadow of which lay across the entire period. This sentiment intermingled with the artificiality of the power balance—the illusion that the *status quo* powers *could* prevent change—to erode confidence in the provision of security by community means. The result, understandably, was a reversion to the typical security arrangements of the nineteenth century, such as France's 'pactomania', which was itself a 'forlorn effort to conceal power relationships that they realized were unfavourable to them behind a thick foliage of paper guarantees' (DePorte 1979: 28). This was the counterpart to economic nationalism, a rhetorical commitment to internationalism bolstered by healthy doses of self-help and unilateral action.

As with any mixed system, the danger was that it would produce the worst of both worlds, a collectivized security without real substance and an individualized security prosecuted without sufficient conviction because it seemed just a shade less necessary. Kennedy thus concludes that the main effect of the League's existence was to cause 'cabinets and foreign ministers to wobble between the "old" and the "new" diplomacy, usually securing the benefits of neither' (1988: 290). The same wobbling occurred in the disarmament field. There were few more stalwart supporters of generalized disarmament at the end of the war than President Wilson himself: arms races, after all, were a symptom of the diseased European polities as well as an independent cause of war. But even Wilson could not desist from endorsing a new naval contruction bill in 1919 (Iriye 1993: 74).

One of the most popular historical counterfactuals is the suggestion that the return to unilateralism might have been avoided had the United States not defected from the League. Such suggestions seem misplaced. They assume that the fact of League membership in itself would have resulted in a different American calculation of interests and in a different American domestic balance of power. This is surely naïve and Northedge was right to cast cold water upon it (1986: 286). Given the domestic composition of forces, the United States would have acted on the basis of consensual agreement about its interests, not in response to paper commitments. Such American unilateralism could not be overturned simply by League membership. Indeed, some have pointed to the tenacity of the USA in securing its interests, especially in the Pacific. 'The Washington Conference showed how far she was prepared to go,' Ross observed, 'in promoting a major political settlement and a disarmament agreement outside the League' (1983: 113). If there is an argument that American participation in the League might have made inter-war collective security more effective, it must rest less on any likely transformation in American policy and more on the bolstering effect which this might have had on the policy of other states, such as Britain. Like international financial arrangements, collective security is almost wholly a matter of confidence in the system and in the behaviour of others.

It is readily understandable that statesmen were reluctant to entrust national security to a new and untested system. It is perhaps more difficult to comprehend the sluggish reluctance with which the same statesmen took measures to return to what was deemed to be the highly successful multilateralized pre-1914 international economic system. What was it, then, that constrained the return to economic internationalism?

There were specific, and material, economic obstacles to doing so and they will be addressed below. But these constitute only a partial answer to the question. Beyond them, it is necessary to take stock of the new political arrangements, and above all of the pervasive new political attitudes, which gave the 1920s a different appearance from pre-war, however much the rhetorical commitment to a return to normalcy might be expressed. Of these political attitudes, the reassertion of a 'nationalist' perspective seems the most fundamental. One historian bemoans the failure to recognize 'that national economies operated in an interdependent global network' and attributes the failure to the 'spirit of nationalism' fostered by the war (Von Laue 1987: 97). Likewise E. H. Carr suggests that nationalism has variously played an integrative and a disintegrative role, and points to the post-war period as one 'when nationalism momentarily resumed its disintegrating role'. He berates those who lost the peace by continuing 'to pursue a principle of political and economic disintegration in an age which called for larger and larger units' (Carr 1940: 293–4). There seem to be two broad reasons why such economic nationalism asserted itself after 1919, both related to facets of wartime experience. The first was the lesson of self-reliance that the war had reinforced, namely 'the military advantages of economic self-sufficiency and the danger of dependence on foreign markets and sources of supply' (Keylor 1984: 96). If this was a sentiment that was to be found mainly amongst the core of the former belligerents, the other source of economic nationalism was that to be found amongst those who had benefited from Europe's turmoil. New industries had emerged to substitute for those of Europe in countries such as Japan, India, Australia, and Latin America. The threat of post-war revival of Europe's producers ensured a clamour to protect these infant enterprises (Kenwood and Lougheed 1992: 175).

That there were straightforward economic obstacles to a return to openness is not in doubt. Most economic historians point to a combination of four factors: the technical difficulties in restoring the gold standard; the constraints on international trade; problems of primary producers; and the overhang of issues related to reparations and war debts.

There was a talismanic faith in restoration of the pre-war gold standard as the fundamental measure of all economic recovery: once this system had been recreated there would be stability and prosperity. In reality, while the pre-war gold standard certainly contributed to the efficacy of the economic system, it was in turn also dependent upon other beneficent conditions. Thus if the gold standard fostered financial stability, it was also parasitic upon it. Consequently, statesmen found an obstinate reluctance to resurrect the system, and perhaps failed to understand that this was because the supportive conditions of the earlier period no longer existed. Hence it was not the failure to restore an effective gold standard that thwarted economic stability but rather the reverse: 'The inability to restore these ideal conditions in the post-war period,' Aldcroft suggests, 'was one of the main reasons for the failure to recreate a viable gold standard in the 1920s' (1977: 166–7).

None the less, the inability to restore currency and exchange stability unqestionably hampered the revival of international trade which continued to lag behind production. Between 1913 and 1929 world manufacturing production grew by 2.7 per cent annually but trade grew by only 1.6 per cent per annum (Aldcroft 1977: 306). The reasons for this were multiple but the absence of an efficient and reliable system of international settlement was of prime importance. Aldcroft himself attributes the sluggish revival of trade to 'uncertainty engendered by currency instability' (1993: 34). Assuredly, there were other contributory factors: protectionism, if not at the levels to be attained in the 1930s, was still markedly higher than before the war (Kindleberger 1987: 61), both in Europe and elsewhere; and trade with the Soviet Union was lost as long as the Bolsheviks refused to countenance compensation for debt default and nationalization of foreign assets (Arter 1993: 56–7).

Additionally, there were the particular problems experienced during the 1920s by primary producers. Many have held that there was an endemic crisis of overproduction brought about by the wartime expansion of agricultural acreage, technical improvements in farming, and then the recovery of European farm production. Historians speak of 'a huge potential for overproduction' (Pollard 1993: 159), and of a 'tendency for supply to outrun demand' (Kenwood and Lougheed 1992: 164). Aldcroft had earlier questioned whether the fall in commodity prices was attributable to excess production (1977: 231), but has more recently commented that 'the vast expansion of wheat production in North America and Australia and sugar in Cuba would have spelt ruin for high-cost European producers but for tariff protectionism' (1993: 15). At the very least there is agreement that the terms of trade shifted adversely against primary producers and that this played a strategic role in the depression even if, as Kindleberger concludes, 'it is an open question whether an independent depression in agriculture helped to cause the stock market crash' (1987: 70).

Finally, the return to normalcy was inhibited by the very real presence of new international disequilibria in the shape of reparations transfers and war-debt payments. There is no need in these pages to rehearse the many vexed, and vituperative, disputes about these issues. It is sufficient to note that their very existence cast a shadow over other economic problems and themselves encouraged narrow, self-interested, and unilateralist frames of mind. No party was immune to their contagious effects. They thus served to poison the atmosphere and ironically very little was to be paid over in either quarter despite the time and energy devoted to both issues throughout the decade (Aldcroft 1977: 96).

To these 'technical' economic issues (although few of them were other than politically driven) must be added the overtly political sources of dissension which counteracted any speedy return to internationalism. Within Europe, the territorial settlement in the East played its part. Sidney Pollard lambasts the disruptive economic effects of the new territorial boundaries which helped make the new states 'aggressively nationalist, protectionist, and unwilling to contemplate any form of economic interdependence' (1993: 161). To survive at all, the successor states adopted severe tariffs—that of Czechoslovakia in the mid-1920s was set at almost double that of the old Empire (Aldcroft 1993: 36–7).

Nor can it be said that US policy in the early 1920s, whatever its intentions, actually contributed to the revival of multilateralism. The US role as international lender, and the accumulation of war debts in its favour, gave the United States considerable leverage in the immediate post-war years. From the point of view of the US Treasury, this leverage could be used to induce on the part of the Europeans forms of economic and financial behaviour favoured by Washington. Thus the Treasury opposed proposals (such as that of Britain in 1922) for debt cancellation as its officials saw debt repayment as a form of external discipline to persuade the Europeans to balance budgets, cut armaments, and abandon discriminatory commercial practices (Leffler 1979: 23). Whatever the intent, this programme aroused European suspicions of American financial hegemony and, if anything, persuaded them of the virtues of unilateralism.

In any event, American post-war policy itself appeared manifestly to be driven by domestic priorities and it was the practical example, rather than the rhetorical exhortations, which the Europeans were more inclined to follow. The basis of American policy has been definitively set out by Melvyn P. Leffler. There was assuredly no turning of America's back on European reconstruction, but the American role would be confined to the private financial sector and would represent a balance between internationalist needs and domestic priorities. Where politics dictated, as on tariffs, President Warren Harding accepted the high levels on which Congress insisted (Leffler 1979: 53). Where politics demanded, as on immigration, the US administration adopted new restrictive measures. The contours of a policy had emerged in which 'the American contribution to Europe's reconstruction was limited to the financial and economic spheres, circumscribed by domestic considerations, and influenced by the perceived value of European stability to American self-interest' (Leffler 1979: 43). This was not isolationism, but if it was internationalism, it was little more than half-hearted.

Paradise Regained?

And yet the 1920s did witness the restoration of an internationalism of a kind. Akira Iriye writes of the period that, though it 'had not been free from economic nationalism, the basic rules of multilateralism, symbolised by the gold exchange standard, had been accepted by all' (1993: 19). Whatever its limitations, multilateralism had been recreated and the key element of this was the return to gold, albeit it in a much-modified form. The readoption of a gold parity exchange rate, strongly encouraged by the United States, began in the mid-1920s and was substantially in place before the end of the decade. As foreseen, it facilitated the sought-after revival of international trade which increased by some 21 per cent between 1925 and 1929 (Aldcroft 1977: 188). Some have insisted that the 'major beneficiary' of this was the United States because monetary stabilization gave 'American capital and trade the chance to begin an economic invasion of Europe' (Cain and Hopkins 1993: 72). But others gained as well, at least in the short term. The return to prosperity, if illusory, was an image that took hold well beyond the United States.

As all are now agreed, the return to gold was not an unmixed blessing. The favourable conditions of the pre-1914 period had vanished and the standard could not operate as some magical invisible hand to create a stability that was otherwise not there. In any event, there was no full return to gold and banks held a much larger share of foreign exchange as part of their reserves, a fact which itself increased exposure and potential volatility. Moreover, countries rejoined the system at an array of parities, some deemed to be too high and some benefiting from a parity thought to be too low. Aldcroft's summary judgement is largely negative. 'Far from correcting the underlying maladjustments the restored gold standard itself was subject to serious strains from the start, and it disintegrated soon after it had been re-established' (Aldcroft 1993: 53–4). Indeed, while the case for a re-affirmation of economic multilateralism must rest in large measure upon the symbolic place of the gold standard, there is good reason to question just how international and multilateral were the means by which the system was re-established. Paradoxically, when this is examined, one discovers that the gold standard was as much an act of nationalism, as of internationalism, and what was put in place was less a universal system than a series of *ad hoc* and unilateral measures, disguised as a regulatory mechanism. The process was 'piecemeal' and 'uncoordinated', and carried out 'as an act of national sovereignty, with each country acting independently with little regard to the resulting interrelationship of currency values' (Aldcroft 1977: 154).

The last feature of the 1920s to be considered is the most portentous, both in its short-term effects and in its longer-term implications. This is the matter of US capital investment, in Europe and elsewhere, and of its central role in what was to become post-1945 globalization. If American policy represents the key to understanding twentieth-century globalization—in that it powerfully brought together the strategic, political, economic, and cultural aspects—then a study of the 1920s becomes crucial for the historian of that process. From this period we can gain an insight into how one phase of American expansionism resulted in fragmentation whereas a later phase was to provide the springboard to globalization.

The significance of the 1920s is now generally accepted amongst historians but this is a comparatively recent development. Conventional historiography dismissed the 1920s as America's age of isolationism, to which post-war American expansionism or globalism served as a counterpoint. That antithesis is now largely discredited and, as has been well expressed, 'isolationism and expansionism . . . were mutually reinforcing rather than contradictory principles' (Crockatt 1995: 20). The 1920s were, then, neither an age of isolationism nor of the fully developed globalism of the post-1945 variety, but rather an intermediate stage in which the extent of unilateralism almost overshadowed the global dimensions which were developing. The point is well captured by Leffler:

The period 1919 to 1933 remains of great interest to students of American foreign policy because it constituted a transitional phase in the evolution of American diplomacy. During that time policymakers grasped the growing interdependence of the world economy and sought to establish a stable liberal capitalist community in Western Europe. (Leffler 1979: 368)

What remains in dispute was the extent of US economic primacy, and of the opportunity for it to impose its own preferences, in the 1920s. Some regard the claims of incipient US hegemony as overdrawn. Thus Charles Kindleberger dissents from the revisionist accounts of US primacy (1987: 296–7), and others disparage the terminology of a new 'American-shaped world order' (Kenwood and Lougheed 1992, criticizing Costigliola 1984). But the proponents of continuity have had the louder voice, while writing from disparate positions. The British leftist historian, Eric Hobsbawm, is drawn to conclude that 'after the end of the First World War the USA was in many ways as internationally dominant an economy as it once again became after the Second World War' (1994: 97). The American post-revisionist, John L. Gaddis, holds the position that America's role in European rehabilitation after 1919 'now seems comparable in importance to their better-known activities there after 1945' (1992a: 6). Above all, Michael J. Hogan's corporatism compels him to argue for significant continuities between 1919 and 1945 which 'put to rest forever . . . the legend of isolationism' (1991: 211) and through which 'the Marshall Plan can be seen as a logical extension of domestic—and foreign—policy developments going back to the first American effort to reconstruct war-torn Europe' (1987: 18–19).

The Dawes Plan of 1924 was the critical step in allowing for a marked acceleration of American investment, especially to Germany and central Europe. During the decade American long-term investments rose by nearly US$9 billion, much of this in the second half of the 1920s (Aldcroft 1977: 241, 248). It was this American money that was to fund the alleviation of German reparations payments and thus construct the political context in which Franco-German accommodation would be made possible: US dollars would perform the task that US military force would not. Fortunately, Germany's Gustav Stresemann accepted the logic of the US position, as did France's Prime Minister, Aristide Briand, after the Dawes Plan removed France's unilateralist enforcement option recently exercised in the occupation of the Ruhr. Accordingly, all key players were content to sign up to an American-driven financial framework that was the architectural design for the new political arrangements of Europe. Like the Marshall Plan after it, the Dawes Plan, while economic in overt content, was implicitly a much broader political and strategic design as well: it envisaged a recovered Germany in a stabilized western Europe.

Economically, the financial arrangements of the mid-1920s were not sustainable in the longer term, or at least, were acutely vulnerable to external shocks. The circular flow of dollars from American investing houses, to Germany, to the Allies, and then repatriated once again to the United States, provided an effective economic merry-go-round while it lasted. But it could last only as long as the availability of an outflow of surplus US dollars to sustain it. The stock market boom of the late 1920s, and high domestic interest rates, had already jeopardized this flow before the final crash of 1929 brought the whole edifice tumbling down:

the international lending of the 1920s created an illusion of soundness and stability that did not in fact exist. So long as the flow of capital to debtor countries continued the cracks in the international economic structure remained concealed. Yet at the same time the process of lending served to widen the cracks so that once the flow was cut off the superficial stability of the system was undermined completely. (Aldcroft 1993: 61–2)

In another important respect, the implications of which will be addressed below, US lending added to problems because its recipients were not so much primary producers as other industrial competitors (Kenwood and Lougheed 1992: 184). How these were to earn enough dollars to pay back debts given the restricted and highly competitive nature of the US domestic market was a difficulty that could only increase over time.

Apart from the direct export of American goods and capital, there is also an argument that the US at this period contributed to globalization through the export of its ideas and values: these came to be increasingly internationalized and encouraged the development of a common stock of cultural images and beliefs. At one level, these ideas related directly to the ethic of business which America purveyed. Iriye holds that a 'philosophy of business civilization' took hold as an underpinning of government and foreign affairs, and he emphasizes its 'model of rational action' (1993: 96–7). It was an image which certainly had appeal in a war-torn world and, associated as it was with American economic success, it offered a messianic vision of the future. European business leaders drew the comparison between the fragmented, old-fashioned European economy and the integrated and modernized economy of the United States and wished to replicate such a United States of Europe (Arter 1993: 60–1). They had seen the future and it worked.

At a second level, both deeper and more widespread, Iriye also speaks of a process of cultural Americanization. This did not begin after the war but was accelerated by it: 'America, virtually unscathed by war,' he contends, 'was more than ever before the symbol of the new material and popular culture' (Iriye 1993: 113). The instruments of this process were the automobile, the motion picture, and the radio. As a result of their spread during this period, there was 'a cultural Americanization of the world during the 1920s' (1993: 113), the beginnings of a 'global cultural order' (1993: 115). There is a superficial validity to this picture but it is much overdrawn. Whatever impact all this might have had in metropolitan Europe, segments of Latin America and pockets of Asia, it is to be doubted that the vast majority of the world's population was even aware of these new developments, let alone culturally assimilated by them.

In sum, America's policy was only halfheartedly internationalist, constrained by domestic imperatives. Paradoxically, its main venture into globalism, through private investment, fostered a short-term illusion of a return to multilateralism, only for this to give way to an even more virulent form of fragmentation. Iriye asks if US policies in the 1920s promoted 'the further interdependence of the world economy'. His answer, typically, is that the picture was mixed and was so because the policy itself embodied a tension between 'economic internationalism and economic nationalism' (1993: 98–9). To this extent, American policy exactly mirrored conditions in the world outside but could do little to reshape or modify them. And so the quest for a revived multilateralism faltered and was replaced by policies of fragmentation to which all states soon subscribed without inhibition.

A World Fragmented

Before turning to the overwhelming evidence for fragmentation in the 1930s, there is need for brief consideration of the few remaining vestiges of multilateralism, or new forms of global interconnection, which managed to survive in this hostile climate. Even at the height of the disintegration of the depression, it would be inaccurate to imagine that all areas of interdependence and cross-national activity, material and ideological, were closed down. But significant as some of this evidence is, it does little to alter the fundamental reality of widespread fragmentation.

One historian of transnational business activity gives an account of the inter-war period from which the scars of the depression seem to be absent. The inter-war period saw rapid growth in international investment in manufacturing, the United States leading the field by 1939 (Dicken 1992: 13). This may be true in the aggregate but it takes little account of the peaks and troughs in this activity during the 1930s and there is no convincing evidence that international conditions were such as positively to promote TNCs during this period: such growth as there was occurred in spite of, and not because of, the international economic environment.

More convincing is the simple proposition that the nature of the depression was itself powerful evidence of the economic networks and interconnections that continued to characterize the inter-war economy: had it not become so interdependent, the depression's effects would have been more selective and there would have been national insulation against it. As it was, perhaps only the self-contained USSR avoided its dire effects. 'The reason why the depression was so universal and so severe,' Marks reminds us, 'was that, in the twentieth century, the world's financial structure had become entirely interlocking' (1976: 122).

In another respect, it could be held that there was developing a more globalized ideological polarity during the 1930s. To an extent the depression itself fostered this because it lent some credibility to claims for the bright future of the communist system and to claims for the imminent demise of capitalism. But beyond the accuracy of these specific prognoses, there was a sense in which the world's political future was coming to be conceived within the structured parameters of these two alternatives. This was not entirely new but certainly took on a novel prominence during the decade. Hobsbawm presents such a characterization, speaking of an 'international ideological civil war', but which he extends beyond communism and capitalism to encompass the wider clash between 'progress' and 'reaction'. This he sees as more significant than the mere balance of power within the inter-state system (Hobsbawm 1994: 144). Inasmuch as this image draws our attention to the important developments linking domestic to international policies (in both directions), Hobsbawm's argument is appealing. And yet on the specifics, it must surely be recalled that the directions within the 'balance of power', and particularly in Soviet policy itself, were precisely intended to soften and erode such a polarity. It was after all the Soviet Union which, in the mid-1930s, swam against the tide when it 'turned to multilateralism' while all else were heading in the opposite direction (Ahmann *et al.* 1993: 12).

Beyond this again, there is evidence of a renewal of regionalism. Whether such a develoment, or its aspiration, is to be regarded as a source of integration or disintegration is very much a matter of perspective: it might be thought integrative in being an antidote to national autarchy but disintegrative against the alternative of global interdependence. There were certainly attempts, but without much success, to institute such regional groupings during the inter-war period, for instance in the Baltic, the Danube, and the Balkans (Arter 1993: 64). But Carr is largely correct in his assessment that the sentiment behind such ventures was the logic of autarchy rather than the logic of multilateralism. Reviewing the emergence of distinctive economic blocs associated with the United States, Britain, Germany, the USSR, and Japan in the 1930s, he comments that 'the more autarchy is regarded as the goal, the larger the units must become' (Carr 1940: 294). For all their 'internationalization' of economic activity, regional blocs were not exercises in globalization on a small scale, but acts of closure and inwardness. Far from representing exceptional departures from the main tendencies of the 1930s, they turn out to be additional confirmations of them.

What then was the dominant temper of the 1930s? There is little dissent from the image of near-universal fragmentation:

1933 marked the end, for the time being, of a fully organised international economic system . . . International considerations were almost completely subordinated to national financial and recovery policies in this period. (Ashworth 1975: 228)

Kindleberger paints a similarly apocalyptic picture:

the world economy lost its cohesion. The gold bloc sank still further into depression. Germany and Italy of the Axis pursued independent economic paths, cut off from the world economy by a system of controls. On the other side of the world, Japan was recovering on its own with speed and verve. The British Commonwealth, together with a number of other countries linked to sterling, proceeded, turning inward along its own recovery path . . . The world capital market was moribund. (Kindleberger 1987: 230)

In short, any form of international economic activity was a high risk for government because of the domestic impact that it would have. Unwilling to pay such high political costs domestically, governments sought to extricate national economies from the international. Thus was fragmentation sought as a conscious act of national policies.

Three examples illustrate the general trend. First, the states of central and eastern Europe, heavily in debt and struggling to find markets for their primary products, were acutely exposed to the icy winds of depression and the drying up of international capital. This evoked a raft of defensive measures, including tariffs and currency controls. In the absence of effective instruments of international settlement, there was widespread resort to barter as the only viable form of trade.

Secondly, the United States was by no means the first country to adopt a 'domestic first' strategy, but when it did the example was portentous and the effects widespread. Its repatriation of capital had commenced from 1928 but it was in the early 1930s that 'official' policy itself adapted to the changed circumstances. Many historians take what has been presented as President Franklyn Roosevelt's 'wrecking of the World Economic Conference of 1933' as symptomatic of the new mood when he asserted that he 'was going to ensure the restoration of equilibrium in the domestic economy before worrying about the international economy' (Foreman-Peck 1995: 221). An American policy that had thus far, in Leffler's terms, sought to balance domestic needs with European stabilization was highjacked by a policy of New Dealers which 'combined economic isolationism with a crude neo-mercantilism' (Hogan 1987: 16; see also Leffler 1979: 359–60). Roosevelt's inaugural speech at the beginning of 1933 had unveiled the new direction:

Our international relations, though vastly important, are in point of time and necessity secondary to the establishment of a sound national economy. I favor as a practical policy the putting of first things first. (quoted in Kindleberger 1987: 278)

Thirdly, Germany's turn inwards was, of course, much more severe by an order of magnitude: it was also driven by a strategic concept largely absent in the American case. By act of national policy, Nazi Germany progressively detached itself from the wider international economy, developing its own increasingly exclusive economic sphere of influence in central and eastern Europe. This policy of autarchy was formalized, and taken to its extreme conclusions, in the Four-Year Plan adopted in 1936, the thrust of which was to make Germany 'entirely independent of markets and resources outside its political and economic orbit' (Keylor 1984: 142). This programme was driven by shortages emerging in the rapid militarization of the German economy but also recalled the vulnerabilities of the First World War. Then the land-locked German war machine had been exposed to enemy blockade, and Hitler, determined not to repeat the same mistake, sought to protect his sinews of war by a state-initiated programme of self-sufficiency (Keylor 1984: 165).

Cumulatively, these and other national decisions tore the heart out of what remained of internationalism. Most evidently, this can be seen in the fracturing of the international trading and monetary systems: the former shrank and retreated into blocs; the latter collapsed and sought refuge in various currency zones (Panic 1988: 183).

Tariffs and quota restrictions became a feature of the depression years, and were not reduced even in the years of recovery. Other countries set the trend, but America's Smoot-Hawley tariff of 1930 did little to discourage it. By 1935, world trade had fallen to one-third of its 1929 level (Foreman-Peck 1995: 200). Of that trade, much was bilateral rather than multilateral, and where multilateral was largely carried on within blocs (Kindleberger 1987: 278). Trade protection had its counterpart in monetary protection with the abandonment of the gold standard and resort to widespread exchange controls, the objectives of which changed and expanded to include a range of nationalist commercial goals (Kenwood and Lougheed 1992: 198). The effects were contagious. When sterling left gold in 1931 and depreciated, others followed suit for fear of being placed at a trading disadvantage.

The world fragmented into sundry currency zones: the dollar area; sterling; those still on gold, including France; the German-dominated central European bloc; and that of the yen in Pacific Asia. If the economic motor of globalization in the late nineteenth century had been the creation of an integrated, and increasingly widespread, financial system, then the 1930s saw that system pulled asunder. The erstwhile architect of that earlier system now sought a more modest leadership within the sterling area and within the confines of imperial preference. 'If, by 1931, they could no longer manage a world economy,' it has been noted sardonically, 'the British still aspired to run an empire' (Cain and Hopkins 1993: 73). If imperial preference rested upon a trend which had been developing previously, the emergence of a sterling area 'was a spontaneous piece of crisis management' (Cain and Hopkins 1993: 36–8, 93–4).

Each aspect of fragmentation compounded the others. Given the drying up of dollar imports, Europe faced insuperable difficulties in servicing its debts to the United States. Unable to export directly to America, neither could it pay indirectly by exports to other primary producing areas (Kenwood and Lougheed 1992: 192). Default, deflation, and depreciation offered only short-term palliatives and at the cost of yet more international instability. There was no effective international response to the depression. Indeed, it has also been maintained that when slow recovery began, this also owed nothing to international policy (Aldcroft 1993: 78). Why was there no international policy for recovery? It is to these underlying causes that we must turn to comprehend why fragmentation was to run its course, unchecked, throughout the remainder of the decade.

The Sources of Fragmentation

Although the evidence for fragmentation has mainly been presented from the economic realm, the return to unilateralism in security matters was just as apparent. It is then the argument of this chapter that we should not look for narrow economic sources of state behaviour in the inter-war period. Both in the economic and in the security spheres, there were deep-seated forces at work. These forces were part of the very fabric of international relations and, in turn, international relations was a reflection of deep-seated domestic tensions and political problems. We must resist the notion that the inter-war collapse was the result of technical economic problems, just as we must resist the notion that the story of interstate politics can be told in separation from the profound domestic social and political developments of the period. Only a fully integrated historical perspective can account persuasively for the lurch to fragmentation that was so much the salient characteristic of the age.

As always, there are longer-term and shorter-term factors which place this in perspective. To be sure, the First World War left its own distinctive impression on all that was to follow. We have seen that although there was a quantitative resurgence of nationalist policies in the 1930s, these were not wholly the creation of the economic problems of the depression; on the contrary, these forces had been latent throughout the 1920s as well and had already done much to undermine confidence in multilateralist solutions in both the economic and security spheres. To this extent, there is considerable continuity throughout both decades, rather than the stereotypical notion of an 'age of recovery' yielding suddenly to an 'age of collapse'. There was an aggravation and acceleration of these trends in the 1930s, but the rapidity of the flight from internationalism is surely suggestive of the powerful predispositon thereto that was already in being.

Indeed, in some respects, the continuities stretch back further into the late nineteenth and early twentieth centuries. It was earlier noted that while this period experienced considerable globalization, there was a not insignificant counter-current pulling in the opposite direction: competitiveness, nationalism, Darwinianism were not the products of 1914, but in substantial measure the backdrop to those fateful events. And so the search for the inter-war mood links back to the tensions of that earlier age: the increasingly competitive process of industrialization; the feeling of interstate insecurity; anxieties about the transformation of a European-based system into an extended global one and about the nature of the balance of power under these new arrangements; and the domestic social and political cleavages spawned by 'modernity'. None of these issues had been resolved by the war and many had been magnified. To that extent, fragmentation in the inter-war era was the product not of a new agenda, but of a pre-existing one that clamoured for attention and resolution.

As to the short term, these were as much symptom as cause. When the historical explanations for the failures of the 1930s are reviewed, they again display considerable identity in the economic and security spheres. Collective security could not be made to work because the system was flawed from the outset, because of Anglo-French differences, or because of a failure of American leadership. Diagnoses of the economic ills take much the same form: the renewed international economic system was flawed from the outset; Britain and France quarrelled over reparations and gold; and the United States was unable to give leadership. There are elements of truth in all of these but they describe events rather than explain them. In all cases, what was really at stake was the domestic costs of alternative courses of action: the costs of making collective security work or of abandoning appeasement; the costs of staying with gold; and the costs to the United States of playing its hand differently.

Much emphasis is placed on the lack of leadership in the inter-war period. Kindleberger's is the classical economic rendition, although his judgement is equally applicable to the security realm:

It is the theme of this book that part of the reason for the length and most of the explanation for the depth of the world depression was the inability of the British to continue their role of underwriter to the system and the reluctance of the United States to take it on until 1936. (Kindleberger 1987: 229)

In security affairs US reluctance persisted much longer, and many would dissent from the effectiveness of US economic leadership from 1936. Be that as it may, the key causal explanation is to be found in the hegemonic structure of the international system, or more accurately in the absence of one. If the facts of the matter are relatively straightforward in the British case (Reynolds 1991), what more can be said in the American? Why was America reluctant? And what might this tell us more generally about the voluntarist rejection of globalization at this time?

In amplification, Kindleberger tells us only that Roosevelt's administration 'had little interest in or knowledge of the world economy, and it lacked confidence in facing it' (1987: 229). This suggests policy by omission and neglect, rather than by conscious choice between alternatives, and is not supported by other writers. We must turn to Leffler for another version. It was not that international demands went unconsidered, but rather that, in competition with domestic ones, they were found wanting. 'The decision to forgo strategic commitments abroad,' Leffler informs us, 'reveals that American officials did not consider the nation's vital interests, either strategic or economic, to be at stake in Europe' (1979: 362–4). And so the United States had no compelling reason to sit, Canute-like, commanding the waves of fragmentation to recede. Such a posture would require a new perception of interest that would come only with a change of circumstance. Leffler thus reaches elsewhere the final logic of his argument:

Notwithstanding the desire of American officials in the 1920s and 1930s to expand markets, stabilize European affairs, pursue investment opportunities, and gain control over raw materials abroad, these goals did not become vital interests worth fighting for until changes in the international system impelled American officials to redefine them as core values. (Leffler 1991: 207)

And so it was changes in the international system that, through their impact on US policy, set the scene for the post-Second World War re-emergence of globalization, and that process remained hostage to state policies. But the influences of the international system cannot be divorced from their mediation through the play of domestic forces also. What additional insight is gained by bringing this dimension into perspective?

If one part of the explanation for the acceptance of fragmentation was the widespread perception of international circumstances which dictated it, the other was the unwillingness of governments to tolerate the costs of sustaining open multilateralism. Thus Aldcroft denies that the system was inherently defective and argues instead that it failed because 'the powers no longer accepted the costs of operating it' (1977: 4). At this point, the domestic situation becomes critical to the overall explanation. Why were the powers no longer prepared to accept the domestic costs of multilateralism?

It is in this specific sense that the approach adopted in this book, while not identical to, shares certain features in common with, corporatism. Thus far, the strategic and political notions of the period have been discussed, as has the globalization and fragmentation of economic, political, and social forces. It remains to trace the impact of the connections between state and society and between national systems and foreign policy. The key element here is the already identified unwillingness of national systems to bear the high political costs of sustaining commitments to multilateralism. The reason for this, at the most general of levels, was the heightened sense of vulnerability of the governments involved.

The reasons were palpably not the same in all cases. Arter argues that the collapse of liberal democracy in eastern Europe occurred before the slump and for largely domestic reasons: 'the challenges of integrating state and society,' he suggests, 'were not effectively met', and the growth of authoritarianism simply reflected the fact that they had become 'state-led societies' (Arter 1993: 46). Elsewhere, the victory of the radical right has been attributed by Hobsbawm to two main sources: the example of Bolshevism and the erosion of the old regimes. Nazism, on this account, was fostered by the fear of social revolution and, to this extent, Hobsbawm concedes 'Lenin engendered Mussolini and Hitler' (1994: 124). In other cases, fascism grew to take the place of previously weakened old ruling classes (Hobsbawm 1994: 126). Perhaps these analyses are too simplistic in detail, but in spirit they serve well to capture the essence of the domestic nervousness which did so much to shape the narrowly nationalistic foreign and economic policies of the period.

The approach is further corroborated by those historians who take a less ideological approach but regard the drift to *étatisme* and state interventionism as the pervasive tendency of the inter-war period *regardless of the specific political complexion of the government concerned*. Thus Charles S. Maier points to the historiographical inclination to look for commonality of approach and to regard fascism as being similar in intent (if not in style or scale) 'to the emerging interventions of the liberal capitalist states in the Depression'. On this reckoning, 'Fascism was just crisis capitalism with a cudgel' (Maier 1987: 71). Thus overdrawn, the comparison may conceal more than it reveals but, nevertheless, the emphasis upon similarity of response by governments to the crises of the inter-war period is instructive and suggests that all were, in some fundamentalist sense, facing similar problems and dilemmas. The more these governments sought to shore up their own domestic bases, the more they were driven to cut their national policies adrift from international commitments which threatened to pull them down. Thus the search for the sources of fragmentation leads us back to the style of national government at the time: the rise of the radical right and left, and the adoption of interventionism by many in the middle, would have served no purpose had national destinies remained in the hands of wider, and impersonal, internationalist forces which could not be controlled by acts of national will. By the 1930s, governments did not need to opt for fragmentation; they already, and quite literally, represented it.

5

STATES OF WAR, 1939–1945

As in the case of the Great War, the Second World War was simultaneously a unifying and fragmenting experience. It directly affected a greater number of human lives than any other single event and is hard to regard as anything other than a fully global experience. At the same time, the war deepened the divisions, and exacerbated some of the economic fragmentation, that had already become entrenched in the 1930s. Its global impact has been summed up in the following graphic terms:

Hitler's war brought the peoples of the world, hitherto still existing in fairly loose and abstract interdependence, into accelerating interaction. It was like a funnel into which was poured the turmoil of the inter-war years and all human diversity too. It was the most powerful common experience yet imposed upon humanity.

To be sure, the impact was not evenly felt. It is estimated that some 60 million people lost their lives in the war, of whom some 25 million were in the Soviet Union, 4 million from Germany, and 2 million from Japan. Britain and the United States lost 400,000 and 300,000 respectively (Weinberg 1994: 894). What these figures reflect is the duration, and the severity, of the fighting on the eastern front specifically where, it has been said, 'more people fought and died . . . than on all the other fronts of the war around the globe put together' (Weinberg 1994: 264).

How are we to assess the role of the war in stimulating or retarding globalization? To some, the war is not an independent cause but itself a symptom of a more deep-seated disease—be it the anarchy of the balance of power, the culmination of the era of nationalist imperialism, or the crisis of the capitalist system. However, if the war is not discarded as simply an epiphenomenon reflecting these other forces, then it becomes itself a major causal agent. In these terms, the effects of the war become important evidence for the formative influence of state policies and international relations: global war is the voluntaristic political act *par excellence* and an autonomous intrusion into other economically or technologically driven processes.

This chapter will depict the main phases and characteristics of the war. It will then assess, systematically, its impact upon fragmentationist and globalizing trends. In particular, it will take into account the effects of war upon the internal anatomy of the states directly or indirectly involved in the war. At one level, the war was a fight against totalitarian statism and yet, during the war, there was a substantial accretion of state power in all the belligerents. To this extent, the war contributed directly to the strengthening of state structures and coercive powers. At another level, the war seemed to have eroded the viability of the state: many states had failed to provide elementary security to their citizens and had not been able to protect them from aggression; states were helpless to defend civilians from direct forms of aerial attack; many state structures collapsed or capitulated; some states turned attacker upon their own citizens; the extension of European state power, in the form of colonial administration, was all but eliminated in large parts of Asia. To this extent, the war represented a crisis in the viability of the state.

The experience of war was to be filtered through these two antithetical developments. What they produced, in creative tension, was a new series of domestic political bargains concerning the nature and functions of the state and its relationship with its citizens—a bargain that was to be worked out during the early post-war years. However, states could not set their new domestic arrangements in place in isolation from the international context. What was thought desirable domestically could not always be delivered because of international constraints. And thus there had to be a separate series of bargains and compromises to set the new international order in place. In the longer term, these arrangements were to deliver a powerful stimulus to globalization. But this outcome was not immediate nor inevitable and was to depend upon a multiplicity of compromises both within and between states. What made such compromises possible was unprecedented American power, uniquely combined with an increasingly hostile international environment in which the 'West' was persuaded to tie its fortunes to that of the United States.

Beyond this, in what terms might the overall historical significance of the war be assessed? Traditionally conceived, such gross judgements have tended to focus upon the effect of war upon the balance of power. Accordingly, the great historical role of the war was finally to destroy the vestiges of a European-based balance system and replace it by a superpower-dominated bipolar order:

Germany's victory in 1940 swept away forever the shadowy remnants of the old European system; its defeat in 1945 opened the continent to an American–Soviet occupation and rivalry . . . and . . . brought into existence a bipolar set of relationships. (DePorte 1979: 116)

Thus viewed, the effect of war was to simplify the structure of international relations. However, simply to count the number of major players is to ignore the extent to which the watershed of war gave rise to a more complex set of international relationships. While power came to be concentrated in fewer hands, there was also a greater array of *types* of state involved in the international game after 1945. The point is well made by Iriye:

A remarkable development after 1939, and particularly after 1941, was that international politics came to embrace many different types of society, so that the more or less traditional rivalry between the great-power groups . . . was no longer confined to them. In fact, the very outcome of that rivalry seemed to hinge on events elsewhere: in the Soviet Union, China, and the largely underdeveloped regions of Asia, Africa, and Latin America. This totally novel situation created a sense of uncertainty about the shape of the postwar world. How could the underdeveloped, non-industrialized non-capitalist countries of the world contribute to postwar peace and security in cooperation with the advanced, industrialized West? That was one of the fundamental questions of the war. (Iriye 1981: 63)

In sum, if war simplified the pattern of international relations by reducing the number of states that could effectively resort to war, it also complicated international relations by multiplying the number and types of states that would have a role in the maintenance of peace.

Perhaps even more grandly, the war is often depicted as the turbulent storm which finally cleared the air and ushered in an unprecedented age of prosperity and stability. Thus viewed, the war is the architect of the long peace which followed. This perspective is cogently presented by Hobsbawm, who suggests that the war 'actually produced solutions, at least for decades' and was instrumental in resolving the profound antagonisms of the 'Age of Catastrophe', thereby setting the scene for the wondrous 'Golden Age' that was to succeed it (1994: 52). This heroic imagery is highly questionable but, to the extent that the war produced 'solutions', we must enquire more closely into their nature.

It will be the argument of this chapter that the war did not produce solutions in any automatic or mechanical sense. Rather, what it did was to create a constellation of political forces which might have led in a number of directions but from which one particular course became the basis of complex and interlocking bargains: this outcome was contingent and itself reflected the play of international politics. Crucially, the best way of comprehending this set of developments—and hence the historical significance of the war—is precisely in terms of the shifting of the balance between the forces of fragmentation and globalization.

This is the essence of the solution that was set in motion by the outcome of the war. Iriye is correct to describe the war, not simply as a clash between aggression and resistance or between militarism and peace, but as a profound contest between closed and open systems of international economic and political order (1981: 34). Others have also presented this as the 'central issue' of the war—the struggle between 'particularist nationalism' and 'global universalism' (Von Laue 1987: 133). If this is the real significance of the war, then it self-evidently becomes of cardinal importance in the history of globalization and international relations in the twentieth century.

The Shape of War

Before turning to a detailed survey of the impact of war, we require some overview of the war's broad characteristics and its course of development. This is necessary to create a frame of reference in terms of which assessments of the war's role can be made.

It is tempting, and possibly helpful, to think of the period 1939–41 as the war that Germany won. Although plans to invade Britain had been delayed, and subsequently evaporated, Germany otherwise reduced most of the remainder of continental Europe to submission or neutrality. By mid-1940, after successes in Poland, Scandinavia, the low countries, and France, Hitler's armies were in control of 'roughly the same geographical area as Napoleon at the height of his power' (Keylor 1984: 189). At this stage, the August 1939 Pact with Stalin was still operative and had critical effects. It ensured that, in contrast with the period 1914–17, Germany was not beset by a two-front war. It also had the consequence that economic blockade against Germany could not be effective, as the Soviet Union was a major source of raw materials for the German war economy and these supply routes were immune to British naval power. What had been set in place, militarily, on the ground by 1940 was largely to endure until 1944: in the words of the war's foremost recent historian, Gerhard L. Weinberg, it 'set the framework for the balance of the war' (1994: 186). There was a military stand-off and the various attempts to circumvent it, such as by the Mediterranean and North African campaigns, could only partially do so and had finally to await resolution by the turning of the tide on the eastern front and by the launching of the second front in the west in 1944.

Germany's victory in 1939–41 was then dissipated by the opening of the wars against the USSR and the United States in the second half of 1941. Militarily, Hobsbawm is certainly correct to describe the attack on the Soviet Union as 'senseless' and, given the resources that it was to tie down over the next three years, the launching of Operation Barbarossa on 22 June must be deemed 'the decisive date' of the war (1994: 39). Unhappily, even if senseless, Hitler's attack on the Soviet Union was an inescapable element of his ultimate purpose: the only issue for Hitler was the matter of its timing, and not whether it should take place.

Stalin's unwillingness to accept the reality of the danger reflected the profound dilemmas confronted by the Soviet state from the late 1930s onwards. The potential threat from German military power to its west was compounded by the traditional threat represented by Japanese imperial ambitions from the east: both materialized at a time when Stalin, by his own purges, had done much to undermine the effectiveness of the Red Army which would have to meet those threats. Faced with such critical choices, Stalin bought time where he could and hoped for the best. His Pact with Germany in August 1939, he believed, gave him tangible physical security which guarantees from the western powers could never credibly offer; this was supplemented by the Neutrality Treaty with Japan in the spring of 1941 which diminished, although it did not yet eliminate, the danger from the east. Ultimately, what saved the Soviet Union was Japan's own decisions to strike south, rather than to join Germany in opening a second front for the Soviet Union in June 1941. Not only did this allow the Soviet Union to survive the war, but also ensured that, after the war, it would re-emerge as an important Asiatic power (Iriye 1981: 83).

Another country looking both east and west was the United States. It too was confronted with challenges to its interests in both the Atlantic and the Pacific.

Roosevelt's policy was shaped by domestic constraints which sought to keep the country out of war, as in the revised Neutrality legislation: this domestic resistance was the legacy of participation in the First World War which many Americans regarded as a European machination into which the United States had been lured unwittingly, and after which the peace had been lost in any case. Even when Roosevelt's policy hardened against Japan during 1939–40, it adopted punitive commercial measures which in themselves were 'an expression of optimism that the United States could compel Japan to renounce regionalism and return to a framework of international cooperation' (Iriye 1981: 20): this was not the road to war, but an alternative to it. Meanwhile, in Europe, Roosevelt's policy remained that of keeping the British struggle alive, not that of becoming embroiled directly in war with Germany (Weinberg 1994: 239). But at least the United States' priorities had crystallized. Although the Japanese naval threat in the Pacific had been recognized throughout the 1930s, by the end of the decade the US Navy had come to accept the greater danger from across the Atlantic (Keylor 1984: 250). The Pacific was to be a secondary holding operation while the main resources were devoted to the European theatre.

However, the buildup of the US Navy, particularly from 1940, faced Japanese leaders with their own acute dilemmas. While the period 1940–1 remained one of uncertainty for Japanese strategy, with the competing logics of the 'strike north' and 'strike south' factions as yet unresolved, and a compromise with the United States not yet fully discounted, those committed to a strategy of war against the United States had an urgent timetable thrust upon them. If America was to be held aside while Japan consolidated its Asian sphere, then the window of opportunity for doing so was narrow: the accretion of US naval power would soon close it altogether (Weinberg 1994: 155).

Japanese troops began to occupy southern Indochina in July 1941, thus turning their backs on the alternative of war against the Soviet Union. Hitler's attack on the USSR in June gave Japan assurance that there would be no interference from that quarter. It remained only to shield its other (Pacific) flank from intervention by the United States. This was the logic of Pearl Harbor, an attempt not to 'defeat' the United States in any full sense of that term, but to give Japan a free hand in consolidating its new Asian order and then to dissuade the United States from any subsequent attempt to redress it. Unhappily, the means confounded the ends. Japan's goal was to convince the United States to accept a limited defeat but the manner of its execution ensured a total American response: 'an unprovoked attack in peacetime,' Weinberg observes, 'was guaranteed to unite the American people for war until Japan surrendered, thus destroying in the first minutes of war Japan's basic strategy' (Weinberg 1994: 155).

Driven by the experience of the First World War, the allies adopted policies of unconditional surrender in both theatres and the wars were prosecuted in terms of this remorseless logic. In part, the formula was a totem, reassuring wary partners that no separate peaces would be struck; in part, it reflected the judgement that with such enemy regimes, civilized states could negotiate no terms. And yet the key question that was to emerge, as allied armies converged on Germany and struck deep into its heart from both east and the west, was what was to become of Germany and Japan, and the liberated areas, after the war's end. If for the United States the war was being fought to replace closure with openness, then how was such openness to be achieved in a situation in which the sundry allies were already occupying their own separate 'spheres'. The logic of war thus gave rise to the contradiction of the peace: the war had been fought against closed blocs in Europe and Asia but the peace was now setting in place the emergence of new blocs dominated by the victors, and in jealous suspicion of each other.

A World Fragmented

The extent to which the war created, or aggravated, trends towards fragmentation can be examined in three areas: the international economy; developments in, and future ideas about, security; and the integrity of empires and relations with the underdeveloped world generally. In each of these areas there is ample evidence of the degree to which such a long-lasting and far-reaching war disrupted traditional patterns of life, intensified national feelings, and destabilized existing economic and political arrangements. It would have been astounding had it been otherwise.

Given the divisive, autarchic, and competitive nature of the world which slid into war, and that war is itself the ultimate test of self-interest and self-reliance, it was certainly to be expected that war would magnify those fractious characteristics already in existence. This was undoubtedly to prove the case in the economic domain:

some characteristics of the immediate pre-war economy were intensified for new reasons. The neglect of new investment at home continued in order to make more resources available for defence and destruction . . . Failure to invest abroad continued, and the realization of existing foreign assets accelerated under the same pressure to devote as much as possible to the prosecution of the war. Control over the use of foreign exchange became much more stringent and bilateral trading arrangements still more common. (Ashworth 1975: 264–5)

As in the case of the 1914–18 war, existing trading patterns were disrupted. Even if there was less import substitution than on that previous occasion, markets were lost and new sources of materials had to be found. In some cases, war's disruption to the flow of goods and materials was to be literally fatal. This was especially so with regard to food. Restrictions on supply, coupled with inflationary pressures, led to acute shortages in urban centres. Milward notes how this generalized disruption was likely to 'strike at its most vulnerable spot, India', and records that some one and a half million lives are believed to have been lost in the Bengal famine of 1943 (1977: 280–1).

What occurred as an incidental, and unintended, effect of war was also compounded by its avowed means and objectives. If the disintegration of the world economy into increasingly separate and autonomous regional blocs had been one of the war's formative conditions, the outbreak of war served only to reinforce this initial condition, the only difference being that these blocs sought now to strangle each other: there was a 'division of the world into two large opposed groups, whose economic relations with each other were merely those of mutual blockade' (Ashworth 1975: 264). Such blockade, as already noted, could not be greatly effective in the early stages of war since the Soviet Union offered an economic lifeline to Germany (Kennedy 1988: 339), even if it was to prove relatively more successful against Italy and Japan (Bond 1984: 194). But the degree of its effectiveness is less important, in this context, than the spirit of economic warfare in which the war was inevitably conducted.

If blockade was symptomatic of the fragmentation of warfare, even more central was the formation of the regional autarchies which were key objectives of Germany and Japan and against which the war was in large measure fought, certainly from the perspective of the United States. There was some similarity in the regional designs of both Germany and Japan: indeed, in some respects, Japan sought to replicate what Germany had already achieved by way of a 'manufacturing core supplied by a periphery of raw-material suppliers' (Milward 1977: 15). The German model had two principal features. These were the dominance of German economic interests within eastern Europe but, more importantly, the closing off of the area to other commercial contacts (Milward 1977: 153). However, Japan did not succeed in imposing as tight control over its satellites as had Germany (Milward 1977: 165).

Neither did Germany nor Japan succeed in developing a fully thought-out economic scheme for their respective new orders in Europe and Asia. Germany's New Order has been dismissed as being far from a 'coherent and efficient economic structure' (Aldcroft 1993: 98), and Iriye comments similarly of the 'superficiality' of Japanese thinking in that it 'failed almost completely to devise a coherent scheme' (1981: 66). However, what was achieved in practice was less important than what these autarchic schemes portended in theory: they suggested a future economic system riven between exclusive blocs, each vying to be self-sufficient and to harness regional resources as a basis for global power-political struggles. It was this lesson of the connection between economic and political fragmentation that was to preoccupy those who sought to devise an alternative post-war order.

By war's end, there was additional fragmentation in the extent of the economic dislocation, and the widespread occurrence of shortages, which the war had induced. In most countries within Europe, industrial and agricultural production was, at the end of the war, well below pre-war levels, in many cases by a margin of 50 per cent. In consequence, the world suffered an acute shortage of goods and foodstuffs (Aldcroft 1993: 112–13). Shortages of the latter were particularly difficult and 'cast a sombre shadow over the post-war years' (Milward 1977: 248). Indeed, in this respect, the war can be regarded as something of a negative watershed:

it became clear that the war had been the turning point between the apparent food surpluses of the 1930s and a new situation in which, in terms of human expectations, food shortage was to become a permanent feature of the post-war world. (Milward 1977: 293)

Finally, war gave rise to two potent new sources of fragmentation. Geopolitically, that part of eastern Europe that fell under the control of the Red Army found itself exposed to a new satellite status, transferred from servicing the needs of Germany to meeting those of the Soviet Union. It became first a source of reconstruction for the USSR's war-torn economy, and subsequently a closed area tied to the socialist economic system. For those countries in western Europe, and elsewhere, there was a different kind of problem but one which none the less set a premium on extricating national economies from the full effects of the international market. What created this situation was the dramatic 'division of the world into one great creditor and a host of impoverished debtors'. These vulnerable debtors were forced 'to protect themselves by the imposition of multitudinous stringent controls over trade and finance, in comparison with which those of the 1930s seemed slack and incomplete' (Ashworth 1975: 268–9). For both sets of reasons, the circumstances were scarcely auspicious for the triumph of an open and multilateral international order in the post-war period.

The omens were not appreciably more favourable on the security front. There was certainly, as will be seen below, a return to universalist language about collective security and international organization that betokened a globalist and integrated security design. But the imagery of universalism was only one of the legacies of war. What also endured, and was to some extent reinvigorated, was a model of security based on regional balances of power and spheres of influence: stability would thus be preserved less by a globalized security structure and more by the exercise of local preponderances. It would be peace in pieces, the archetypally fragmented security order, rather than a single and integrated system, as the rhetoric of collectivized security for the whole world seemed to imply.

This alternative to universalism emerged from the process of wartime bargaining and from the progress of the war on the ground. For the Soviet Union, given recent experience, post-war security could best be achieved by the establishment of direct physical control over territory and the creation of geographical space between itself and any future threat from Germany. This was a much more important objective than the nature of the international order itself and a necessary insurance to any reliance upon an international organization. It was with this set of demands during wartime that Roosevelt had to deal and to resist it would have jeopardized the continuation of the alliance. There was also the risk that if Stalin's goals were thwarted, he might achieve them by means of a separate peace with Germany, as he had in 1939 (Crockatt 1995: 45). Nor was Stalin alone in his preference for Great Power exercise of preponderance. Churchill readily acceded to Stalin's wishes in this regard and in 1944 reached his famous percentages agreement for post-war spheres of interest in south-east Europe. As early as 1943, Stalin's allies agreed in Moscow on the likely establishment of forms of government in eastern Europe that would symbolize Soviet predominance within the region. The Yalta meeting, in February 1945, confirmed the tendency towards recognition of a special Soviet sphere of influence. While the rhetoric of universalism, and faith in continuing allied cooperation, persisted, events on the ground were developing their own momentum towards what was eventually to become the most deep-seated fragmentation of the European continent in its modern history.

While much American rhetoric was hostile to such a development, United States policy elsewhere conformed to a similar type of practice. The pressures of war gave real substance to the Monroe doctrine by extending, and deepening, United States influence within its own hemisphere. All twenty Latin American republics followed the United States into the war, unlike in 1917 (Keylor 1984: 227). Economically and militarily, ties between the USA and Latin America were strengthened. The great American production effort during the war sucked in strategic materials from the south, leading to 'the almost total reorientation of the economies of the Latin American states toward the United States'. Bilateral military cooperation was also intensified (Keylor 1984: 228).

Whatever the rhetoric of multilateralism, the practice of regional preponderance was also shaping the future of post-war Asia. While the United States continued to support its client in nationalist China, which had been its strategy of countering exclusive Japanese designs in the region, it also asserted its own regional hegemony over the defeated Japan, the more effectively so because of the speed with which the A-bomb induced the Japanese surrender. Far from insisting on the destruction of the various manifestations of the closed door which had sprung up in China since the end of the last century, the United States acquiesced in the Soviet Union's retention of exclusive commercial interests in Manchuria. Most momentously of all, perhaps, the USA softened its traditional policy of opposition to the re-establishment of the old colonial structures in Asia and condoned, where it did not actively abet, the reinstatement of European power. As against open multilateralism, the United States seemed to promote a post-war Asian order that was based on competitive areas of exclusion. As Iriye remarked, 'the return of the European powers to Southeast Asia was to be part of the post war arrangements, just like the Soviet position in Northeast Asia and American predominance in Japan and the Pacific' (1981: 247–8).

The war had, in any case, profoundly destabilizing effects upon colonial systems and upon the role of the underdeveloped regions of the world. In some historical accounts, these peripheral regions are deemed always to have been integrated parts of the world capitalist system. From such a world system perspective, the war then represents no radical discontinuity. And yet, it seems much closer to the reality to depict the war as a major transitional phase which saw the periphery transferred either from colonial subservience, or from benign neglect, into a much more important part of the international system and of the world economy. This transition was one of the key developments of the post-1945 era.

The effects on empire were not unambiguous, and the war did not immediately lead to their fragmentation. On the contrary, it also produced a period of imperial revival, even if only short-lived (Holland 1985: 37). None the less, in the longer term, the war was corrosive of the imperial order (Betts 1985: 180) and it became America's policy, not to destroy 'Western' influence within these states but instead to encourage an accommodation which would induce them, when independent, to merge their economic activities more fully into an open world economic order.

In the meantime, however, the future integration of the underdeveloped world into a wider Western economic system could be but dimly perceived towards war's end. What was much more readily apparent at the time was both the stress within existing colonial arrangements but, equally, a determination on the part of the European powers to lay claim once more to what they regarded as their rightful patrimony: if this failed, the fragmentation of the old colonial order seemed a more likely outcome than its integration into a new and all-encompassing world economy.

As in the First World War, empires experienced the effects of militarization induced by a now genuinely global conflict. For example, the Indian armed forces which numbered some 193,000 in 1939 had swelled to over 2.5 million by 1945 (Prest 1948: 28). Again, as in the Great War, many colonial, and semi-colonial, territories suffered from the ravages of inflation: during the war, prices more than doubled in India and Palestine, almost tripled in Egypt, and increased more than fivefold in Syria and Lebanon (Prest 1948: 5). Such inflation 'broke the traditional balances of colonialism' and stored up new forces to be unleashed in the future (Holland 1985: 50). Throughout Africa, the economic impact stimulated wage-labour and urbanization, all with considerable socio-political implications (Holland 1985: 65). All in all, the war represented a 'massive boost to economic activity' in the non-Western world, even if the benefits were unevenly spread.

The most profound challenge to the European imperial order was, of course, experienced in Asia. It was here that Japanese power overthrew European control, with uncertain implications for its restoration in the war's aftermath. It was one thing for the Europeans to have to retain their colonial hold where it had been rendered more precarious by war; it was another to have to re-establish that influence where it had been physically overturned by Japanese occupation. The problem was aggravated not simply as an incidental by-product of the fighting but as part of a concerted Japanese policy of undermining Western influence through the instrumentality, however disingenuous, of pan-Asianism which had been promoted since the 1930s (Iriye 1981: 4–6). The exposure to Japanese wartime influences helped generate an 'Asian consciousness which, after 1945, could not be forced back into colonial containers' (Holland 1985: 40).

Assuredly, there were contradictions within the Japanese programme for Asia, and it was mostly self-serving. Iriye notes the paradox that the quest to liberate Asia from Western influence was itself based on Japan's 'infatuation with Germany' and was dependent upon German successes in Europe (1981: 10–11). Others note also that the practice of Japanese control tended to 'out-colonial' what was already in place, and its cultural policies were often little more than forms of Japanization (Goodman 1991: 3–4). Even so, there could be no doubting the extent to which the war fostered potent forms of anti-colonial nationalism, even if not pan-Asianism.

The Western allies indirectly conspired to encourage the same tendencies, even if Churchill was at some pains to assert the contrary. His Atlantic Charter agreement with Roosevelt in August 1941, before America's entry into the war, reiterated general principles of self-determination and independence, albeit that for

Churchill the relevant context for this was occupied Europe and certainly not the extra-European empires. Holland downplays the significance of this 'piece of windbaggery' but, even so, concedes that nationalist separatism was encouraged by seemingly having been accorded the 'touch of Anglo-American acceptability' (1985: 53).

More tangibly, the future balance of political forces within key Asian states was being shaped by the experience of nationalist resistance to Japanese occupation. The Chinese Communists benefited from this situation, so much so that it has been claimed that it 'was during the Second World War that the Communists won the civil war' and that it was the war that 'brought the Chinese peasantry and China to revolution' (Bianco 1971: 159, 155). Even if this is poetic licence, the general drift of the argument is supported by the similar empowerment of the Viet Minh, in Indochina, likewise by the combined effects of wartime rural hardship and the Viet Minh's successful harnessing of nationalist sentiment by its role in the resistance against the Japanese.

The war did not destroy Europe's will to empire. Indeed, in the case of France, it was if anything augmented as a psychological form of 'regeneration' from the humiliation of 1940 (Betts 1985: 190). For all that, the impact of war, even if not immediately revealed, represents an important turning point in the history of empire. But even more significantly for the theme of this book, it was to set in place the ingredients which would allow the United States to transform the final acts of imperial fragmentation into an important new stage in the process of globalization, by seeking to co-opt former empires into the Western economic system. Thus it has been said that while decolonization was a long and discontinuous process, it

reflected everywhere the shattering impact of World War II on the old structures of international order and the emergence of the United States as the dominant world power, able to provide a new definition of the character of the ties between North and South. (Smith 1981: 135)

The Integration of Global War

Almost by definition, a global war was bound to do more than pull things apart: in addition, it created new interactions and new forms of interdependence, just as it generated new conceptions about future international order and about the domestic purposes and responsibilities of states. Strategically, the war served as a reminder that all states were vulnerable to sudden attack, even those, like the United States, which had decided to stay out (Waters 1995: 115). From these sundry wartime experiences, in conjunction with the new international distribution of power, there emerged a powerful set of forces which were, even if not immediately, to unleash an era of globalization without historical precedent. This second face of war can be illustrated by examining the global strategy of the war, as well as its ideological and economic effects.

Was it a world war deserving of the name? Most historians are in no doubt about their judgement, whether it is made from the perspective of the dynamic causes of the war, the scope of its fighting, or the extent of its impact:

by 1939–40 the world was rapidly becoming one. Never had the chancelleries in London, Berlin, Moscow, Tokyo and Washington been so conscious of the effect of a decision taken by any one of their number upon the remainder. There had been interplay before . . . but never on the present scale. (Bartlett 1994: 226)

Aldcroft notes of its scope that it 'was far more global than World War I', engulfing as it did almost all Europe, North Africa and the Middle East, the Soviet Union and the United States, much of Asia and even Latin America. The United States was eventually involved in all campaigns and the war was thus 'the culminating point in the story of the steady globalization' of that country (Aldcroft 1993: 191). If there is a qualification in this regard, it is that Africa was mostly not a direct participant, apart from the desert wars in the north, and 'there was no East African front on the scale of 1914–18' (Holland 1985: 63): this did not, however, isolate it from the mobilization efforts of the empires, nor from the war's economic and social effects. With regard to the the extent of the physical impact, Ashworth reaches similar conclusions: 'The influence of physical destruction was far greater than in the First World War', he argues, because Asia could not make good the loss of production in Europe, and hence 'the rest of the world became still more dependent on supplies from the Americas, with serious effects upon international payments' (1975: 269).

Underneath the consensus of these general assessments, there remains a diversity of opinion about some of the finer nuances concerning the nature of the war. Was it a single and global war from the outset or did it develop into one? To the extent that it became global, were the reasons for this contingent or was this part of the war's essence fom the outset? These, and similiar, issues lurk behind the comments made about the relationship between the European and Pacific theatres, and about the various phases of the war identified by historians. For instance, many commentators discern a purely European war during the period 1939–41 (see Bond 1984: 169–70) and then speak of its 'transformation . . . into a veritable world war' from 1941 (Keylor 1984: 185). There is some ambiguity as to whether it was the German war against the Soviet Union, or the entry of the United States, which wrought this particular transformation (see Keylor 1984: 185, 193; Kennedy 1988: 341, 343).

However, rather than judge the war's global nature on the basis of the sequence and extent of the fighting, it may be more instructive to assess it on the basis of the interconnectedness of its causes. Iriye implicitly regards the origins of the Pacific war as being distinct from those in Europe when he suggests that in 1931 events in the Pacific were 'isolated from the rest of the world', whereas this had ceased to be so a decade later (1987: 1–2). Even if there were distinct and separate agendas at work in the European and Asian revisionism of the 1930s, it remains the case that from the perspective of several key players, the two interacted: as strategic problems, they were a seamless web rather than two issues to be dealt with separately and in sequence. This, as already suggested above, was the case for Great Britain, the Soviet Union, and the United States at the very least. Britain's problems of imperial strategy in East Asia and the Mediterranean ensured that Germany could not be treated as a self-contained threat: the multiplicity of sources of danger, in combination, predisposed governments in the 1930s to mutually reinforcing acts of appeasement. The Soviet Union faced the potential disaster of a two-front war and could not afford the luxury of treating Asian events in isolation from what was happening in Europe. Even if the challenge to the United States from both quarters was more remote, it still had to face painful choices about priorities and modes of engagement. In these interlocking ways, the war was a global whole in potentiality long before it became one in actuality.

Once underway, the war's reverberations in one theatre sounded distinctly in the other. German intentions and Soviet preoccupations were never far from the calculations of Japan's leaders, and fateful decisions in Asia followed from the course of events in Europe (Iriye 1981: 12). Indeed, Hitler himself saw the connections and deliberately planned on their bases: he saw his war against the Soviet Union giving Japan a freer hand in Asia and serving to distract the United States as a result (Weinberg 1994: 238). Even the United States operated within a framework of assumptions which shared these strategic interconnections: support for nationalist China was necessary to weaken Japan as an ally of Germany (Iriye 1981: 21–2).

There is one sense in which the issue might be resolved but it remains the most problematic: what was the scope of German ambitions? If German objectives were avowedly global from the outset, the discussion of phases and the expanding nature of the war becomes a matter of mere semantics. However, if Hitler had no plans, or if these changed over time, then the issue is harder to determine. This is not the place to rehearse the vexed debates about Hitler's goals and war aims, in so far as a rationale can be imposed on the seeemingly irrational in any event. Weinberg offers a categorical interpretation of the explicitly global scope of Hitler's ambitions from the very beginning, offering as evidence his programme of battleship construction for war with the United States which 'illuminates the world-wide ambitions of the Third Reich' (1994: 176). As against those, like A. J. P. Taylor, who have seen German actions as unplanned opportunism, Weinberg regards the phases of the war, and Germany's *ad hoc* mounting of campaigns, not as evidence of its limited and opportunistic intentions but simply as a determination to avoid the mistakes of 1914: 'If the last war had spread from a corner of Europe to the whole globe, drowning Germany in a flood of enemies,' he argues, 'Germany would so arrange the circumstances of its wars that they could be fought in isolation, one at a time, against enemies of its choice and with victory in each facilitating victory in the next' (1994: 22). Although it might seem then that the war expanded, and changed its original nature, this appearance is deceptive and was part of Germany's design for the best way of fighting a war for global supremacy.

Traditionally, the strongest evidence against such a point of view has been thought to lie in the nature of Germany's economic preparations for war. This, so it was believed, testified to the limited, and short-run, extent of its economic readiness: Germany was ready to support a few blitzkrieg campaigns and nothing more. Typically, material shortages by 1943–4 are attributed by some economic historians to 'Hitler's original conception of war' and particularly to his reluctance to 'sanction an all-out effort as far as mobilization was concerned' (Aldcroft 1993: 102; Milward 1977: 29). Accordingly, it was the very fact that Hitler came to be drawn into a global struggle *which he had not envisaged* that was to be his undoing.

This interpretation now seems doubtful in light of the powerful case against it made by Richard Overy. It is his argument that Hitler never intended limited blitzkrieg operations, supported only by half-hearted economic mobilization, but that his plans were overtaken by the premature outbreak of war in 1939 before he was in a position to mount his global challenge. Turning the conventional evidence from the German economy on its head, he contends that, far from supporting the view of Hitler's limited goals, it absolutely makes the case for his global aspirations:

Hitler's plans were large in scale, not limited, and were intended for a major war of conquest to be fought considerably later than 1939. The fact that the large armament failed to materialize was not due to any *Blitzkrieg* conception, but to the fact that economic preparations were out of step with the course of foreign policy . . . Hitler's object, in the long run, was European conquest and world hegemony. (Overy 1989: 209)

If this is accepted, Hitler was certainly operating on the basis of a globalized concept of strategy from the very beginning.

The war was also to be a potent influence upon the universalizing of political concepts and ideologies. This impact can be detected in two main areas. First, the very nature of the ideological challenge from Nazism and Fascism, portending as they did a completely new social and political order which undermined traditional liberal values, evoked its own response in the form of a universalistic programme of renewal: the threat from totalitarianism was regarded as potentially global in scale and its final defeat in 1945 was to be sanctified by the promulgation of a rival agenda for human affairs. Secondly, while all wars are destructive and tend to give rise in their aftermath to a profound questioning of social institutions, the Second World War was distinctive in the sheer scale of the human, and often civilian, suffering which it had inflicted. Unparalleled levels of human cruelty, and acts of wanton genocide, in turn gave rise to a reaffirmation of cosmopolitan human values, now to be more firmly codified as principles of human rights thought applicable to all humankind: here was a globalization of human value systems without historical precedent.

While after the First World War, President Wilson had represented the struggle as one against autocracy, for most of the European belligerents it had been conducted as a traditional struggle of national interests, even if the scale of the losses led some to question such a notion. In contrast, the Second World War was overtly ideological from the outset and was accepted not simply as a struggle for national security but rather as a clash of ultimate values and for the preservation of civilization. It was not just the German and Japanese armies which had to be turned back, but the forces of darkness itself.

Domestically, this ideological overlay helped induce the birth of a new post-war society, even more so than had been the case in 1919. Hobsbawm is surely correct to distinguish the post-First World War wish for a backward-looking return to normalcy from the forward-looking desire in 1945 for the creation of something new: 'For the Second World War was . . . not merely a struggle for military victory,' he suggests, 'but . . . for a better society. Nobody dreamed of a post-war return to 1939' (1994: 161). The international counterpart of such sentiments found expression in wartime statements about the new principles of international order and the systems of international organization, and collective security, which would underwrite them. An early such statement was the Atlantic Charter of 1941 which picked up the Wilsonian legacy and demonstrated that the 'older concepts of peace and stability through economic development, prosperity, and interdependence had survived the turmoil of the 1930s and would define the world order after the Axis menace had been removed' (Iriye 1981: 30). To be sure, there was equivocation as Roosevelt and Churchill took stock of the political realities (Keylor 1984: 201–2). Most surprisingly of all, perhaps, the Charter omitted any explicit endorsement of a post-war international organization as, at this stage, Roosevelt was far from persuaded of its merits and preferred to rely instead on a kind of international police force essentially provided by the United States and Britain (Divine 1967: 43–4). None the less, the Charter embodied an embryonic programme for a liberal and open international order that was to stand as a rallying cry to a world seeking escape from totalitarian suppression and divisiveness.

As noted above, the incarnation of such an ideological programme was adulterated by other political realities: spheres of influence jostled with the demands of universalism at war's end; and the UN Charter was itself an uncomfortable compromise between a reborn collective security, a reformulated Concert, and the vestiges of Roosevelt's concept of world policemen. Above all, the final victory of the internationalist vision in 1945 was tempered by the discovery of the A-bomb and the realization that the atomic scientists 'were the real architects of the brave new world' (Divine 1967: 314). But that universalism should have been adulterated in implementation does not detract from the symbolic importance of its articulation.

The war was also responsible for a revitalized, and cosmopolitan, doctrine of human rights in international affairs. It is certainly not the case that human rights were discovered in 1945, but the severity of the challenge to basic human decency and survival throughout the war years demanded a codified expression for their future protection. In part, the reason for this was the extent of civilian death and suffering during the war. In Europe, almost half the dead were civilians compared with one-twentieth in the First World War (Bond 1984: 197). The war was a 'global human catastrophe' which inaugurated an age in which 'killing, torture and mass exile have become everyday experiences' (Hobsbawm 1994: 52). As if to counterbalance this, the war also evoked a new-found concern on the part of the international community about how best to counter this trend. In a more limited sense, the development by the war-crime trials of a new category of crime—that of crimes against humanity—itself depended upon a generic and universal set of human rights which had been violated. This inducted what had hitherto been a merely philosophical issue into the mainstream practice of international law. Donnelly sums up the momentous breakthrough towards a universalized, and enforceable, doctrine of human rights which the war represented:

Before World War II, the issue of human rights rarely appeared on international political agendas . . . The catalyst that made human rights an issue in world politics was the Holocaust . . . Nuremberg was an important step toward international action against human rights violations . . . The Preamble of the Charter of the United Nations . . . includes a determination to 'reaffirm faith in fundamental human rights'. (Donnelly 1993: 5–6)

Finally, and paradoxically, the war also made a distinctive contribution to economic integration, notwithstanding the extent of the disruption and fragmentation which it also brought about. Never before in human history had the world as a whole, in so concerted a way, devoted such a high proportion of its economic reources and efforts to the prosecution of a single war: in this curious way, the world experienced a global interlocking of its economic activities without precedent:

By the winter of 1943–4 the world economy was far more mobilized for war than at any time in the past, including the period of the First World War. The planning and control of economic resources was far more extensive and detailed than it had been in 1914–18 while the proportion of output devoted to war purposes was also greater. At the peak of activity well over one-third of the world's net output was being devoted to war. (Aldcroft 1993: 104)

By any measure, this was a compression and intensification of the human experience on a world scale.

It must also be remembered that this was distinctively a war of resources and production in which victory was destined to pass to the side which could best command and produce the material necessities of war. In this sense, the Axis was doomed to failure: before the war, it accounted for 17 per cent of world manufacturing output, compared with 60 per cent for the USA, UK, and USSR combined (Aldcroft 1993: 101). This meant that the productive balance of power was much more disproportionate than it had been during the First World War (Kennedy 1988: 354). And in making such demands on the productive resources of the world, the war etched deeply its own characteristics as a powerful reminder for the post-war generation.

Of all the legacies of war, by far the most significant was the dramatic surge in the economic output of the United States. Between 1940 and 1944 the volume of industrial production in the USA increased by 15 per cent per annum, twice the rate that had occurred during the First World War (Milward 1977: 64–5). By war's end, more than half of all world manufacturing production was coming from the United States (Ashworth 1975: 268). Such was the outpouring of material from the country that it was able both to meet the needs of its own armed forces and also to provide equipment for its allies, principally Britain and the Soviet Union (Bond 1984: 178). But it was not only the salience of the American economy that was to be of such long-term importance: what was doubly significant was the overall impact that the war had on the very structure of the international economy and its division of labour. It was as part of this recast economic system that the United States was able to play its formative post-war role. In this respect, America's experience as the productive core of a combined anti-axis coalition was to be influential in shaping the post-war order.

The war saw the construction of an elaborate form of inter-allied coordination in the supply of raw material and economic resources. Alan S. Milward goes so far as to suggest that, with proper qualifications, 'the Allied economies could be considered as a common set of resources coupled to a common strategic plan' (1977: 51–2). In turn, this was to be of lasting importance because it was to the 'international system of economic supply' created by the allies during the war that 'the movement towards greater integration in the world system in the post-war period can be most directly traced' (Giddens 1985: 239–40).

What was created on the allied side was totally lacking within the Axis. Germany and Japan entered the war as autarchic economic systems and thus they continued for the duration of hostilities (Milward 1977: 42). In contrast, the allies created a system that was initially devised to solve the problems faced by Britain. This too was to be of long-lasting significance. Unable to meet its own needs, and also to export at pre-war levels, Britain had to draw materials from within the empire which were paid for by the building up of large sterling credit balances in favour of the suppliers. Additionally, Britain sucked in vast resources from the United States, financed by the provisions of the Lend-Lease arrangements, as British dollar reserves could not sustain the level of purchases from the United States of the first eighteen months of war. Thus Britain lay at the core of the coordinated system: 'British strategy,' Milward observes, 'opened the gates of supply to the whole world and ensured from the very start that the economic effects of the Second World War would be world-wide' (1977: 42).

Lend-Lease soon reached vast sums. By the end of the war, some US$43,615 million had been supplied under its terms, of which three-quarters went to the British empire and one-quarter to the Soviet Union (Ashworth 1975: 267). But American aid did not come without strings and has been regarded by some historians as a strategic device which contributed substantially to Britain's post-war economic dependence upon the United States: Britain had to divest itself of American assets; the run-down of its export sector was not to be readily retrieved at war's end; and the USA demanded from Britain commitments to post-war economic arrangements with which, in the event, it was to prove particularly onerous for Britain to comply (see Burk 1995: 47–8; Bond 1984: 176). But whatever its costs for Britain, it is important to stress that a coordinated system had been put in place and there was a commitment to implement its principles after the war had ended. For example, the wartime experience with food supply was to leave its imprint on post-war arrangements. As Milward contends, the lessons learned in dealing with wartime shortages were put to good use in coping with post-war lack of food, such that 'this thread of international collaboration and cooperation survived unbroken from the Second World War through the Marshall Plan and the United Nations Food and Agriculture Organization' (1977: 251–2).

Had inter-allied economic collaboration remained a self-contained sector of activity from which the Axis powers were to be permanently excluded, it would have served as a source of post-war economic fragmentation. What was especially significant about the American-centred economic system which emerged from the war was that it was one into which both Japan and Germany were to be speedily re-integrated. What Iriye says of the Japanese experience has a more general applicability. Suggesting a continuity between the 1920s and the late 1940s, he argues that post-war US–Japanese reconciliation became possible because of shared assumptions. Accordingly, 'Japan emerged as a symbol of the old order'— the order of the 1920s—and its main constituents were its orientation 'toward world interdependence and stability' and a balance between 'these objectives and domestic arrangements so that interest groups would have a stake in an open and stable world order' (Iriye 1981: 266). This raises the issue of the relationship between the war's economic legacy and the war's impact on the domestic political balance within the belligerent states. It is to this that we must finally turn.

Warring States

As with the case of the First World War, historians have argued about the instrumentality of war in bringing about domestic social reform. In particular, the war has been regarded as giving a stimulus to the adoption of social welfare policies, and to the application of planning techniques for social improvement. The first argument, which has been around for decades, is based either on the political assumption that 'the demands of total war forced government to make concessions to organised labour' (Stevenson 1986: 68) or on the sociological assumption that war fostered 'social solidarity and therefore social reform' (Smith 1986: viii–ix). The former emphasizes political reward for the contribution to the war effort, the latter the desire for a more egalitarian society for all those who had suffered 'equally'. Again, much of this is now contested and some regard the social effect of the war to be more pronounced in its traditionalism than in its radicalism, for instance in 'the revival of family life' (Winter 1986: 176).

The second area, that of economic planning, made a more durable impression and was harnessed to conceptions of a better society in which the ills of the 1930s could be averted by sensible economic management. The relative success of this had already been evidenced by the degree to which inflation, compared with the experience of the First World War, had been kept under control. This was a result of greater reliance on taxation as opposed to borrowing and also to more effective state performance in the realms of rationing and price controls (Aldcroft 1993: 107; Ashworth 1975: 270), all of which prefigured the positive role that the interventionist state could play in economic and social management. In Cox's terminology, the war saw the final flourishing of the 'welfare-nationalist' state within which government planning was a central element (1987: 184).

In sum, war experience seemed to embody the final triumph of the corporatist state, now even more technically expert than it had been in the 1920s. The war had forged ever closer links between government and labour. The latter could not be sacrificed as it had been in the inter-war period and the trade unions now enjoyed 'an entrenched position in the state' (Cox 1987: 185). Additionally, and possibly more importantly, was the axis now developed between government and industry throughout western Europe and also, to a degree, within the United States itself:

The relationship between government and industry in Western Europe underwent a decisive change as a result of these wartime developments and the two worlds of business and government administration were never again seen as the separate worlds they had still been in the thirties. The hope that the economy could be managed, and the political will that it should be managed, were greatly reinforced by the knowledge of the more detailed workings of business and industry which central governments were forced to acquire between 1939 and 1945. That is perhaps the most immediately obvious historical consequence of the changes in the direction of the economy during the Second World War. (Milward 1977: 131)

But here the war set in place the contradictory effects of its globalizing and fragmentationist tendencies, such that some resolution had to be found before the international system, and the international economy, could find a new post-war equilibrium. On the one hand, the allies had experienced a massive effort in organizing resources and production for the war by means of a world-wide system centred on the United States. In addition, many of the wartime arrangements had been contingent upon compliance with an open world economy in its aftermath, and Britain above all had been compelled to acquiesce in such undertakings. There was then in place a momentum towards an internationalized economy, driven from the United States. On the other hand, wartime political and social developments had engendered a more dynamic social consensus, underpinning the 'national-welfare' state. But how was this state to achieve its domestic goals while simultaneously acceding to the externally imposed disciplines of the international economic system? It certainly was not the case that there had been a selfless abandonment of national goals. As Milward remarks, war cosseted nationalism as much as internationalism and gave encouragement to the revival of the national state (1992: 16).

There was a possible solution in which the needs of the individual states could be reconciled with the international economy, although it would require adjustment on the part of states, as well as a new international economic order. The possibility was that 'Keynesianism, which had been tried with only limited effect on the national level, might not be more effective on the world level as a regulatory mechanism for a world economy' (Cox 1987: 188–9). In this way, national goals need not be abandoned while the imperatives of the wider system could also be recognized. But what bargains and compromises would be required before this could be brought about? How, in practice, was such a synthesis of state and system to be realized?

The solution, which did not emerge immediately at war's end, depended upon two intertwined sets of adjustments. The first related to domestic compromises and adaptations to international circumstances. The second related to a series of international deals which made adherence to the goals of the wider system acceptable, even if painful. It was in this latter respect that the play of international politics again became a major factor in the designing of what was to become the post-war *Pax Americana*, itself the midwife of a new and dynamic phase of globalization.

On the face of it, there was concordance between national and international needs. The move toward national planning was replicated at the international level in the secure knowledge that mastery of economic affairs could now be turned to beneficial effect in that realm as well. 'With a new consciousness of their power over the domestic economy,' Milward notes, 'governments turned eagerly to the task of building an international economic system' (1977: 131). Likewise, the same harmony of purpose is detected by other writers who conclude that 'as piecemeal planning evolved toward more comprehensive planning on the national plane, so did planned international integration proceed along with it' (Vatter 1985: 168). This is, however, a politically sanitized version and ignores the degree of tension between the *freedom* required for effective national programmes and the *constraints* needed to make a fully operative and stable international mechanism. Ultimately, it was only the phenomenal economic success of the system, and the sustained growth from the 1950s onwards, which helped to conceal this tension: in the few years after the war, it remained only too apparent.

The other necessary dimension of this transition was the international bargaining about the format of the post-war international economic order itself. Although the United States ended the war in a commanding position, and possibly able to impose its will on those dependent upon it, it soon became apparent that a diktat would be counter-productive: the United States might insist upon immediate currency convertibility, or upon the dismantling of trade protection, but to do so would fatally damage the European economies and so undermine the efficacy of the system as a whole. The United States thus was reliant upon a degree of compliance and this was something that had to be negotiated.

From the perspective of those states greatly weakened by the effects of war, the main objective was to negotiate deals that would maximize the possibility of protecting domestic priorities. In a country such as Britain, a consensus on this issue was to be found at opposite ends of the political spectrum, albeit with different motivations in mind. Milward detects resistance to any American-imposed dismantling of the imperial preference system in a right-wing sentiment that empire was the route to a restored national greatness, whilst on the left retention of national economic controls was regarded as the *sine qua non* of a just and egalitarian society (1977: 337). Both national visions were threatened by exposure to American economic might and both sought refuge in degrees of national, or imperial, protection. Thus British needs were centred on the maintenance of the sterling area, imperial preference, and general protection for its war-shrunk export industries.

The needs of the United States were scarcely identical. Given the vast wartime expansion of its productive base, the United States harboured concerns about the damage that would be done by a sudden collapse of export orders. Export markets had therefore to be sustained in the post-war period (Kennedy 1988: 359). There was in this a mixture of American motives. Manifestly, there was a degree of economic self-interest based on the need to consolidate the economic benefits the war had generated, but there was also a wider idealism which placed its faith in a multilateral trading order as the only way of averting a return to the economic rivalry, and concomitant political degeneration, of the 1930s (Milward 1977: 330–1). And even if Europe was acutely vulnerable to this economic programme, it had some incentive to cooperate as the price to be paid for avoiding an American reversion to isolationism (Cox 1987: 212–13). As will be seen below, compromises were struck which allowed the Europeans to retain currency and trading restrictions in the short term in return for commitments to dismantle them in the longer term. Thus were national and international policies to be harmonized.

One area of policy which neatly illustrates the process of mutual accommodation between the weakened powers of Europe, and the now preponderant power of the United States, is that of the future of the European colonies. During the course of the war, official American views on empire had undergone a gradual shift away from the traditional perception of them as unmitigated evils which American participation in the war must not be allowed to perpetuate. Even before 1945, this had been diluted by recognition that in a post-war world—exercise of control in which the United States would be involved—European empires might have some utility as 'a means of keeping the lid on Asian and African volatilities' (Holland 1985: 55).

This did not mean that European imperial control should be practised in the historical manner. The strong American preference was for an accommodation with colonial nationalism and gradual movement towards self-government, even if under continuing and benign Western tutelage. What America desired for a mixture of economic, ideological, and geopolitical reasons could also be presented as being in the best economic interests of the Europeans. As part of the transition to the post-war world, a new economic emphasis would be placed on the underdeveloped world as a whole, more fully integrating it into Western economic activities. This process had already begun during the war which, for much of Asia, Africa, and Latin America, had led to 'increasing integration within a consolidating global economy' (Giddens 1985: 240–1). To be sure, further moves in this direction would require the dismantling in the longer term of exclusive colonial economic networks which the United States had long opposed, and their replacement by the 'open door'. However, greater political independence, coupled with increased Western economic encouragement, would have the compensatory effect of stimulating the market for European industry throughout the Afro-Asian world. Accordingly, notions of 'colonial development'—as precursors of more general theories of development—began to exercise a powerful appeal. Holland places this in context:

Thus it was argued that the competitive power of the US economy could only be made bearable for other industrial producers if the world market as a whole was rapidly boosted, and that the most immediate scope for such accretions of consumer demand lay in Africa, Asia and Latin America. It was out of this school of thought, essentially concerned with industrial survival in the age of American hegemony, that the theme of 'colonial development' was articulated. (Holland 1985: 56)

But there is a still wider context in which this argument must be placed. In essence, the suggestion is that the fate of empire was one dimension of the wider accommodation between American and European interests as the war drew to a close. What the United States sought was a replacement of formal empire by a looser form of Western economic patronage from which all might benefit. The Europeans were to be persuaded to accept such a deal because it conformed with long-term economic imperatives, and in the absence of which no equilibrium could be found between European needs and American resources. Of course, in the event, empires were not to be given up by the Europeans in the straightforward and mechanical fashion which such an argument might suggest. None the less, there is a profound sense in which the ultimate fate of empire was bound up with the construction of the new political and economic arrangements emerging between the United States and Europe: what was to become the Third World was being given greater importance as part of this overall accommodation of interests. In short, the Third World was increasingly drawn into globalization as part of the deal over the future of Atlanticism.

What then was the overall significance of the Second World War? Paramount amongst its effects is the scale and the extent of the human tragedy which surpasses any accounting in terms of other, and more abstract, historical processes. But if the war marked some kind of turning point, or watershed, away from the fragmented and autarchic policies of the inter-war era, does its significance lie in its inauguration of a new era of Westernization, or of Americanization, or of globalization itself? It is perhaps futile to draw sharp distinctions between these overlapping categories. Although the centre of economic power lay firmly within the West, the cold war was soon to demonstrate that, ideologically at least, Westernization was not to have a clear run in the Third World: the Soviet Union would continue to promote its alternative blueprint. That said, and perhaps against all the odds, the Western political and value systems emerged from war regenerated and once more in the ascendant:

The American-led victory boosted the universalism of the Atlantic Charter and of Western aspirations generally. The Western model, now domiciled in North America, was restored to preeminence after the crisis of self-confidence in the inter-war years. The militaristic anti-universalism of fascism had been defeated. (Von Laue 1987: 146–7)

To this extent, America's victory was the West's victory and Westernization and Americanization defy convenient separation: the long-term process of Westernization was now simply 'domiciled' in the United States.

Similarly, there is a direct link between Americanization and globalization. Analysts have distinguished between the 'intensive' goals of the Soviet Union and the 'extensive' goals of the United States at the end of the war (Crockatt 1995: 40). By this is meant that the security threats to the former were much more direct and impinged upon national survival: the objective was to assert unilateral physical control over the likely sources of any future threat. In contrast, the United States had not been directly threatened but had been drawn into war, reluctantly, by the failure of global arrangements: its future security could thus be ensured by the construction of the appropriate international institutions, networks, and values which would prevent any such recurrence. Thus Americanization and globaliza-tion were to be intimately intertwined for this next phase of the century's history. As Iriye has remarked, 'the world was becoming Americanized just as America had become globalized' (1993: 215).

6

THE COLD WAR AND GLOBALIZATION, 1945–1969

This chapter will not offer a survey of the origins and development of the cold war but will, instead, concentrate upon the essential nature of the cold war and its integral relationship to the processes of globalization. It may seem odd to emphasize the contribution which the cold war made to globalization when, on the face of it, its most pronounced impact was a deep and pervasive fragmentation of the international system which led to unparalleled, if unconsummated, hostility between First and Second Worlds. The cold war, after all, rendered Europe 'much more divided than before' (Kennedy 1988: 377). However, the argument to be presented is that the cold war's ultimate effect has been one of integration, not disintegration, and although it created deep fissures between East and West, this served the purpose of integration within the West, stimulated an attempted incorporation of the Third World into the First, and may potentially contribute to a single global system in the cold war's aftermath.

The two post-war decades provide a striking test case of the relationship between globalization and the vagaries of international relations. Why was it that both the international security and economic orders which emerged after 1945 were to be so profoundly different from those of the inter-war period? Why did the phase of post-1919 reconstruction issue in a second round of global war within twenty years, whereas the post-1945 phase saw the creation of a 'long peace' that was set to endure throughout the remainder of the century? How, if at all, were these outcomes related to the predominant role of the two superpowers after 1945? The central issues raised by these reflections are whether globalization enjoys a relative autonomy from the international system and whether it has a capacity to survive the particularly favourable international circumstances which may have fostered it in the first place. Ultimately, this in turn poses questions about the long-term stability of, or potential for conflict within, the international system itself.

By the end of the 1960s, when the cold war seemed to have settled into a relationship of managed confrontation, theorists of international relations had become so preoccupied with explaining the long period of stability (in contrast with the inter-war period) that the focus of their attention was on stability and not on change (Lebow and Risse-Kappen 1995: 4). Out of this concern there emerged, by the end of the 1970s, a reformulation of traditional realism, inevitably dubbed neorealism, which offered an account of this stability in terms of the 'structure' of the international system. The main components of this structure were the 'anarchy' of the international system and the distribution of its power. It was the latter variable with held the analysts' attention as they elaborated theories about the essential stability of a bipolar world (Waltz 1979; Layne 1993: 40). Even if there was not an overriding logic of numbers alone, then the additional factor of nuclear deterrence would ensure that stability prevailed (Gaddis 1992*a*: 174).

An alternative interpretation to such rigidly structural accounts is that which takes cognizance of the 'texture' of international relations as well—included within which are measures of interdependence, multilateralism, institutionalization, and globalization. On this version, the stability of the international system is affected not only by the number of great-power players, but also by the textural environment in which they find themselves (see Keohane 1984).

What such an interpretive dichotomy fails to address, however, is the precise nature of the relationship between 'structural' and 'textural' forces. Is it the case that the latter can subdue the former and that there is a secular trend towards the restraining of classical great-power behaviour by their enmeshing in exogenously generated layers of interdependence and globalization? Or, as others would have it, is it the case that the 'structural', in the last resort, determines the 'textural', and that these layers of interdependence and globalization are but the workings of self-interested great-power action? These questions go to the heart of any understanding of the second half of the twentieth century and hold the key to what will ensue in the next.

That there is a direct relationship between political 'structure' and economic 'texture' has been given its classic exposition by Robert Gilpin:

although the economic and technical substructure partially determines and interacts with the political superstructure, political values and security interests are crucial determinants of international economic relations. Politics determines the framework of economic activity and channels it in directions which tend to serve the political objectives of dominant political groups and organizations. Throughout history each successive hegemonic power has organized economic space in terms of its own interests and purposes. (Gilpin 1971: 53)

If this is the case, it is reasonable to suppose that the contours of economic space will change in accordance with the hegemonic power structure. Moreover, if it can be shown that the major determinant of the economic space of the two post-war decades was the hegemonic power of the United States, locked in not-so-mortal combat with the Soviet Union, then it would follow also that any diminution in the hegemony of the United States, or in the structure of bipolarity, would, in turn, impinge upon the 'texture' of the international system. It is for that very reason that commentators have posited that the decline in the *Pax Americana* will issue in a concomitant decrease in the multilateral and globalized order to which it had given rise, since the latter was always contingent upon the former (Hirst 1995: 7).

But did the cold war so unidirectionally favour the forces of globalization? It has been noted that '[p]aradoxically, it was the Cold War system that also served the nation-state which had been weakened and delegitimised by the autarchic, militaristic nationalism which had led to the Second World War' (Cerny 1993: 33). What this reminds us is that, if the cold war saved the free world, what it was also saving was the individual states which fell within that system, and thus 'rescued' them from the disrepute into which they had fallen. Thus the cold war not only etched itself upon the 'texture' of international relations but also upon the fabric of the states themselves: cold-war induced globalization was a process that affected the internal politics of states as much as it affected their external relationships. In order to assess this claim, it will be necessary to locate both the cold war, and associated textures of globalization, within the framework of what was happening *within* states during this period. Initially, however, the discussion must begin with some conceptualization of the nature and development of the cold war itself; it will then move on to an examination of the relationship between the cold war and globalization; consider the place of the Soviet Union and of the Third World in the developing cold war; and finally, it will juxtapose the state of the international system with the state of the state.

Concepts of Cold War

This chapter will not rehearse the debates about the origins and causes of the cold war. These debates, and associated controversies about the dating of the cold war, eventually are based on competing conceptions of the cold war's essential nature—whether it was the product of a crisis in the balance of power, a clash of incompatible value systems, a response to Soviet expansionism, or the creation of rampant American capitalism. Each of these operates within a closed body of historical evidence, and each offers a narrative in terms of which certain dates become salient. Thus if the first dates the cold war from the consequences wrought by the ending of the Second World War, the second is much happier with the notion of a cold war that was at the very least latent from as early as 1917: once the operative concept has been selected, the chronology unfolds in accordance with it. In turn, these differing interpretations are important in understanding any causal relationship between the cold war and globalization, and hence it is with a basic understanding of the cold war that any analysis must commence.

'The analysis of what the cold war was,' Fred Halliday declaims, 'remains very much at the pre-theoretical level', and he endeavours to edge the analysis forward by distinguishing what seem to be the main (pre-)theories available: realist, subjectivist, internalist, and inter-systemic (1993: 21). The first three of these refer to conceptions of the cold war which focus, respectively, upon traditional interstate power politics, on ideologies and perceptions, and on the uses of external conflict for state or regime domestic goals. Halliday favours the fourth, the inter-systemic, which he presents as having three main features: the cold war as conflict between two distinct social systems; a competitive and universalizing dynamic; and a struggle that could only be ended, not in compromise, but by the victory of the one system over the other (1993: 23–4).

There is much that is appealing in this portrayal. It has the advantage of conceptualizing the significance of the cold war in terms much wider than that of a straightforward contest between two states: even if, as is undoubtedly the case, the superpowers were the two main protagonists, they were seeking to create patterns of international relations which had a wider systemic significance for most other states. Additionally, it has the principal virtue of highlighting the feature that, while the cold war was largely embodied in the Soviet–American antagonism, it was not exhausted by that relationship alone. This is a suggestion which has been pointedly made:

The driving force behind America's foreign policy has shown itself to be more basic than the containment of its cold war adversary . . . although the Soviet Union was the immediate focus of US security strategy, it was really quite incidental to America's liberal internationalist policy. (Layne and Schwarz 1993: 5)

Had the cold war been simply a rivalry between the United States and the Soviet Union, it would have been about the negative thwarting of each other's designs. What the inter-systemic perspective brings to the fore is that the cold war was more importantly about the positive goal of putting something in place—in America's case what we can for the moment refer to as a liberal internationalist sector of the world.

That said, we might make two refinements to Halliday's argument that help fit it into the framework of the present discussion. While the cold war surpassed Soviet–American rivalry in its significance, it was still located in that relationship in origin. This also reminds us that any such inter-systemic account cannot be divorced from the historic configuration of international power at the end of the Second World War. This was to be vital for at least two reasons. First, it provided the setting in which superpower conflict would stand out as the principal structural feature of the era. Secondly, and in consequence, only this configuration persuaded, and made it domestically possible for, the United States to take on its wider systemic role. Historians now emphasize the degree of 'political caution' and indecisiveness in United States policy, especially in the period 1945–7, and thus draw attention to the voluntaristic nature of the political decisions which led to the adoption of a new American role: things might have turned out otherwise (Crockatt 1995: 71). It was assuredly the structure of international power that made it possible for the United States to resolve its internal uncertainties.

The other refinement of Halliday's exposition is to shift the emphasis to a degree away from inter-systemic conflict and towards *intra-systemic* consolidation. This is not intended as a 'functionalist' argument that the cold war merely served the needs of a determining system, world capitalist or otherwise, and still less is it intended as a restatement of 'conspiracy' theories whereby the cold war was simply an invention to allow the United States, as well as the Soviet Union, to impose an order within its own sphere. The point is that the cold war was fought for something, not merely against an opponent, and the inter-systemic antagonism did, in practice, lend coherence to the intra-systemic design. For the purposes of this book, the intra-systemic effects of the cold war are, indeed, more important than the context of conflict in which they took place.

Manifestly, the cold war provided the latitude for each superpower to attempt to implement its own programme. Thus it has been remarked that what the cold war offered the USSR was 'a Soviet *chasse gardée* in Eastern Europe, within which the USSR could set the political, economic, and cultural rules' (Wallerstein 1991: 6–7). The cold war offered much the same to the United States. But if there was this initial symmetry, the main difference that was to emerge from the course of the cold war was that, historically, developments within the Western system became much more influential than those within the Soviet sphere. Moreover, America's rules extended well beyond keeping the Soviet Union at bay, or deterring a hot war with its protagonist. Hobsbawm has suggested that, given the black clouds still hanging over the capitalist system and liberal society in 1945, 'the post-war plans of the US government were far more concretely concerned with preventing another Great Slump than with preventing another war' (1994: 230). The distinction is artificial in that American officials saw an intimate connection between the two, but the comment is pertinent in so far as it directs our thinking to the positive content of America's international agenda. This might have existed without the cold war, but it could be more wholeheartedly pursued within the structural context of a seemingly direct threat to American national security.

Such a conception makes sense of other aspects of the cold-war literature. To some historians, the cold war lasted only for a short number of years, approximately until the Korean War in 1950. This was its acute phase when the risks of a breakdown into hot war were at their highest. According to such a view, the relationship thereafter stabilized, and while there were certainly to be important crises, over Berlin 1958–61 and over Cuba in 1962, these were part of the learning process whereby the superpowers developed their rules of mutual coexistence. What is wrong with such a periodization of the cold war is that it confuses a part of it—the Soviet–American antagonism—for its totality, and thus leaves out of the picture the important dimension of intra-systemic consolidation identified above. If viewed as an additional component of the cold war, then far from ending in 1950 or so, this dimension was only just getting under way at that point. It was from this period that the integration of cold-war blocs really began to take on its momentum. Crockatt notes that in terms of the institutionalization of the cold war, integration on the American side preceded that on the Soviet, the Marshall Plan, Federal Republic of Germany, and NATO all coming before their counterparts—COMECON, the German Democratic Republic, and the Warsaw Pact (1995: 80). Be that as it may, the significant point for the present discussion is that the process of intra-systemic consolidation and integration lasted long beyond the phase of acute danger of Soviet–American hostilities.

In these terms, then, this chapter will treat the cold war as a phase which endured through until the late 1960s or beginning of the 1970s. Conventionally, again, the reason for accepting any kind of terminal break at this point is that it is associated with a relaxation in the superpower relationship, that of the Nixon–Kissinger *détente*. Thus many commentators are happy to adhere to a chronology of the cold war in which some kind of watershed is achieved around 1969 or 1971. But there are two different, albeit intertwined, reasons for attributing significance to these dates. The one, and the most common, is that *détente* marked a diminution in the intensity of Soviet–American competition, to be replaced by the institutionalization of this rivalry within such frameworks as the Strategic Arms Limitation Treaty (SALT). The other, and less often remarked, is to regard this as a turning point in relations *within* the two competing systems. As regards the United States, then, 1969 becomes a watershed, less importantly in its relations with the Soviet Union and more so from the point of view of its relations with its 'Western' allies.

Hobsbawm typically argues that the period 1945–90 should not be viewed as a 'single homogenous period' but considered instead as falling into two halves broken in the early 1970s (1994: 225). Atypically, rather than describe the first half as one of tension and conflict, he is more impressed by the characteristic of stability which it displayed. Throughout that period he contends 'the tacit agreement to treat the Cold War as a Cold Peace held good' (1994: 228). What then might have brought this period of stability to an end? Here Hobsbawm forms part of a wide, and heterogeneous school, the one unifying feature of which is its tendency to write the subsequent history of the cold war after the early 1970s in terms of what was happening in the Western system, rather than in terms of Soviet–American relations *per se*, although the latter served as some kind of barometer of what was occurring elsewhere. Expressions of this view are as diverse as those of Gilpin and Wallerstein. For Gilpin, the erosion of America's commanding position within the Western system was the product of the economic challenges from Germany and Japan, coupled with the stresses of maintaining Western security against the Soviet Union (1981: 173–4). For Wallerstein, the period is part of the world system crisis represented by a 'revolt against US hegemony', although like Gilpin he sees this as expressing itself in the form of a decline in American political power (1991: 125). However formulated, the ending of the first phase of the cold war is to be understood as deriving from a set of changes, and problems, within the Western system itself.

Finally, a modified inter-systemic interpretation makes sense of the variety of historical opinion as to where the geographical core of the cold war was to be found. Traditionally, the epicentre of the cold war has been thought to lie in Europe, and in Germany specifically. Thus Martin Walker most recently insists that the cold war 'was fought about the fate of Europe . . . It was thus the last and greatest of Europe's civil wars' (1993: 5). It is then commonly asserted that the conjunction of the Chinese Communist revolutionary success in 1949, and the outbreak of the Korean War in 1950, helped transform the cold war into a global rivalry. Alternatively, for others, the cold war was a global contest both by its very nature and from the outset. Walker, somewhat inconsistently with his other claim, is also adamant that the 'Cold War was truly a global conflict, more so than either of the century's two world wars' (1993: 1).

What these various arguments have in common is their tendency to make judgements about the geographical scope of the cold war simply on the basis of the dimensions of Soviet–American geopolitical rivalry. In turn, what they ignore is that the cold war could not but be other than global when regarded both as a contest between two systems and, more particularly, as an attempt by the United States to consolidate a Western system that included as much of the globe as lay outside the Soviet sphere. Admittedly, such a Western system could not be constructed globally in a single stage, and so it had to establish priorities—western Europe and Japan. But to regard these as the only areas of cold war conflict is to confuse the negative aspects of Soviet–American contest and the wider, and more positive, objective of Western systemic integration. Before examining in greater detail the connections between the cold war, and what was to happen within the Western system, we need first to look at the evidence for globalization in the first post-war decades.

A Fast Globalizing World?

Many analysts draw a contrast between a world economy and an international economy, the latter relating to exchange between separate national economies whereas the former denotes the creation of 'transnational production organizations whose component elements are located in different territorial jurisdictions'. In these terms, according to Cox, the *Pax Americana* began, from the 1950s, to forge a world economy (1987: 244). In fact, this world economy did not displace the international economy, as multilateral economic exchange accelerated apace during the 1950s and 1960s; instead it developed alongside this burgeoning international economy. What both forms of economic organization sought was economic growth and the record of achievement on this score was outstanding. Over the period 1950 to 1973 the real annual growth of GDP of the major industrialized economies averaged 4.8 per cent (Kenwood and Lougheed 1992: 245).

Whether measured in terms of openness, multilateralism, internationalization, or globalization, economic activities expanded rapidly in all of those areas:

Between the end of the Korean War and the oil crisis of the 1970s, the world economy bounced. Never before or since have so many economies shared such extraordinary and sustained expansion. Restrictions on cross-border transactions and travel were progressively relaxed. Economic integration surpassed the levels attained under the pre-1914 gold standard. (Foreman-Peck 1995: 258)

At the heart of this growth lay the dynamic effects of the US economy and of the ubiquitous American dollar which contributed both to the reconstruction of overseas economies and to US corporate expansion. Once again, by the late 1950s, the institutions of multilateralism prevailed as currency convertibility was finally resumed by most countries and the mechanisms were in place to maintain exchange rate stability, pegged to the dollar at a fixed price in gold.

The measures of these various economic developments in the fields of trade, capital movements, and production organization are all equally impressive. Those for the acceleration in international trade are the most widely cited and trade is normally regarded as the key sector which encouraged the dramatic growth of these decades. Broadly speaking, merchandise trade grew at an annual average rate of 6 per cent between 1948 and 1960, and even faster—at some 8 per cent—between 1960 and 1973 (Kenwood and Lougheed 1992: 286). Significantly, this growth in trade outstripped growth in GDP and achieved approximately twice the rate over this period (Gilpin 1987: 190). From this, the following conclusion has been drawn:

A particularly important feature of the postwar period was that *trade increased more rapidly than production*, a clear indicator of the *increased internationalization* of economic activities and of the greater *interconnectedness* which has come to characterize the world economy. (Dicken 1992: 16)

This growth in trade was encouraged by a general liberalization of tariffs and by the increased effectiveness of the system of international payments (Panic 1988: 165).

Unlike the 1930s, there was once again a surge in international capital movements throughout the period, the major source of private capital being the United States. By 1960, total private US investment abroad stood at almost three times the level of 1938 and the outflow during the 1950s reached an annual level of some US$2,000 million (Kenwood and Lougheed 1992: 250).

Much of this was associated with changes in the organization of industrial production. The creation of the European Common Market, for instance, encouraged the setting up of production units within Europe. This spread of corporate activities across the world was a major feature of the 1950s and 1960s. Dicken sees this as initiating a qualitative change in the nature of the international economy 'into a highly complex, kaleidoscopic structure involving the *fragmentation* of many production processes and their *geographical location* on a global scale in ways which slice through national boundaries' (1992: 4). He supports his claim with statistics about the number of overseas subsidiaries set up by the major TNCs during the 1950s and 1960s. During the period 1946–52, these were being established at a rate 50 per cent higher than the previous peak in the 1920s, and this accelerated further at the end of the decade. By the mid-1960s, they were being set up at ten times the rate of the 1920s (Dicken 1992: 51).

Globalization and Cold War

Merely to cite similar statistics would tell us very little about the driving forces behind such developments. In this section, a more purposeful attempt will be made to review the interpretive links between the nature of the cold war and the trends towards internationalization and globalization of international political and economic activities.

There are various ways in which the connection can be, and has been, drawn. Three might be suggested which, although distinct in the emphasis each brings to bear, are by no means exclusive and tend, if anything, to reinforce each other. These are that globalization was encouraged: (1) because of the bipolar nature of the cold war; (2) because of the peculiarly universalistic nature of American goals and ideology; and (3) as a result of the unique hegemonic power and leadership enjoyed by the United States after 1945. The outlines of each will be reviewed in turn.

The first emphasizes the particular structural properties of the bipolar cold-war order, the interaction between the two blocs and the spur which this gave to intra-systemic consolidation.[1] In starkest form, and paradoxically, it was the very fragmentation of the world into two cold-war camps which generated a new impetus to a globalization which, if at first limited in geographic scope, was universalist in final ambition. The point is hinted at by Leffler: 'Simply stated,' he suggests, 'the cold war and the division of Europe were regrettable prospects but not nearly so ominous as the dangers that inhered in economic contraction, autarkical trends, communist gains, and the prospective erosion of US influence throughout the industrial core of western Eurasia' (1992: 504). On this logic, partial fragmentation was the price that had to be paid for long-term globalization. In that sense, and more trenchantly, the cold war was actually about the fate of globalization.

How did this come about? That there was a link, in the European case, Mastny is in no doubt. He says of the creation of a modern form of capitalism and of European integration that they were 'so closely linked with the Cold War' that it is hard to imagine them having occurred in any other circumstances (1995: 78). That the European fragmentation ran so deep, he attributes to foreign policy mistakes on Stalin's part which hastened the institutionalization of the West (1995: 79). Whatever the cause, the sense of an irrevocable split between East and West certainly had the effect of simplifying Washington's own policy choices. Hitherto Moscow's preferences had to be taken into account; thereafter they could be largely ignored, and certainly subordinated to the priorities of systemic construction within the West. As Leffler notes, Washington's attempts to reconstruct Europe and reintegrate Germany, while at the same time not offending Stalin, had placed too many conflicting demands on policy-makers (1992: 121). In summary, the creation of a Western institutional and security structure required a prior acceptance of the division of Europe (Maier 1993: 393). From about 1948, the US could concentrate on developing its own order within the non-Soviet world.

Precisely because of the bipolar split, the United States felt that it had to tighten its hold on its allies: cold-war conditions, at the same time, facilitated this end. Thus it was the cold-war divisions which both required intra-systemic integration

---

[1] Halliday (1986: 31) notes the distinctive quality of the cold-war competition in that it was 'a rivalry that is *globalised*'.

and which made it possible. The objective for the United States was to 'integrate these areas into an American-led orbit before they could gravitate to the East' (Leffler 1992: 16–17).

Such an analysis carries with it certain clear implications: closer interdependence within the Western system is functionally related to the cold war and this suggests that it may not necessarily be sustainable outside such a context. Thus John Mearsheimer regards the interdependence that has been generated in western Europe since the war not as an independent source of more cooperative relations within that region but as being, in turn, dependent upon the international relations environment established by the cold war. 'It is more likely,' is his considered judgement, 'that the prime cause was the Cold War' (Mearsheimer 1990: 46). Cerny likewise testifies to the symbiotic relationship between cold-war divisions and intensified multilateralism within the Western industrialized world:

such multilateral processes did become viable where they operated in conformity with the parameters of the Cold War system. Furthermore, those limited forms of multilateralism were crucial to the development and maintenance of the Cold War system itself, both as a kind of legitimation . . . and as a set of institutional mechanisms within the capitalist world. (Cerny 1993: 32–3)

Presumably, on this reckoning, the erosion of the cold-war system could be expected to undercut the network of multilateralism within the Western system itself.

The second type of connection drawn is that between globalization and the specific content of American programmes and ideology: above all, the emphasis is placed upon the uniquely universalist content of American thinking. Specific manifestations of this will be considered in detail below. At this point, the argument need only be presented in general terms. The distinctiveness of American thinking lies in its proclamation of universal principles in combination with its 'economic and cultural dynamism' which have 'helped to revolutionize social and economic conditions around the world' (Crockatt 1995: 33).

What, in general terms, was the content of this universalist programme? Its origins lay in deep-seated domestic experiences which, in turn, the United States wished to replicate elsewhere. This has been described as a design for projecting 'the experience of the New Deal regulatory state into the international arena'. The powerful impetus of what were regarded as burgeoning economic successes at home, coupled with appropriate political adaptations, led to a programme for their replication on an international scale—an 'effort to institutionalize a multilateral international economic and social order' (Ruggie 1993: 25). In particular, American thinking continued to be beset by concerns about the revival of the closed and bilateral economic relationships which had proved so disastrous in the 1930s, and sought to choke off any such threat. State-controlled trade and currency movements were thought likely to find appeal in the Soviet Union and might forge a community of politico-economic interest between western Europe and the USSR which would be deeply damaging to the American economy and might corrode free-enterprise values within the United States itself (Leffler 1992: 8).

At that point, the closing off of western Europe would become more than an economic setback for the United States and, in so far as this allowed the Soviet Union to command Europe's resources, also become a threat to the very safety of the United States. Leffler thus depicts the fusion which occurred in American cold-war thinking when 'geopolitical, economic, ideological, and strategic considerations' all came together in such a way as to be operationalized as policy: 'traditional foreign policy goals were transformed into national security imperatives' (1992: 24). Concomitantly, universalism moved from being a set of values to underwriting national security policy.

Finally, the connection with globalization can be made more directly to general theories of hegemonic leadership. As previously indicated, these argue that it is the predominance of the most powerful political actor which allows the establishment of the framework of economic activity. In the post-1945 period, the United States favoured a highly transnational order and the growth of TNCs reflected the environment in which they now found themselves. Accordingly, Robert Gilpin has made his general assertion that the multinational corporation 'exists as a transnational actor today because it is consistent with the political interest of the world's dominant power'. Economic and technological factors then become secondary in shaping the modes of production because they come into play only as 'the United States . . . has created the necessary political framework' (Gilpin 1971: 54).

The system put in place by the United States eventually worked so effectively that it appeared as something which had evolved naturally. But this was an illusion: it operated because it was a work of political artifice. It resulted from a period of 'intense negotiations' during which the international economic order was 'worked out politically', precisely because it was not an 'outgrowth' (Maier 1993: 392). Of course, theories of hegemonic leadership tell us that the leading power sets the rules: they do not tell us about the substance of these rules. At this point, the political framework that the United States chose to establish has to be explained by reference back to the intra-systemic development associated with the cold war, and the particular values and experiences which the United States brought to its leadership. As John Ruggie has pointed out, 'all hegemonies are not alike' and the fact that the American one is associated with multilateralism, transnationalism, and globalization is a reflection of that country's distinctive political and economic beliefs (Ruggie 1993: 25).

There is obviously much overlap between these three versions of the relationship but the nuances set them slightly apart. This is readily illustrated in terms of the change of circumstance which, it follows, might lead to a diminution in globalization. In terms of bipolarity and the cold war, any change in the basic structure of international power, and removal of this central antagonism, might then be expected to have the spillover effect of a lessening of integration within the rival systems themselves. In the case of America's universalist ideology, a change in American values, political priorities, and national security perceptions could lead to a rethinking of the United States' attachment to an open and multilateral international order. Finally, if it was hegemonic leadership which allowed the order to be established, any decline in the United States' capacity to sustain its leadership role would entail the decay of its preferred order, just as Britain's system had eroded with the passing of its power.

The New Security and Economic Orders

What was the substance of the new order that was progressively to be set in place after 1945 and what were the landmarks in its attainment? In both the security and economic spheres, there was a blueprint in existence by 1945 which, in the event, was to be substantially modified in practice: neither the United Nations nor Bretton Woods delivered the promised results in the anticipated way. While multilateralism was to survive in both areas, it was not quite the multilateralism that had been envisaged in much of the wartime planning and discussions.

With regard to security, the transition which took place was from the multilateralism of universalist collective security to the multilateralism of bloc security structures. The United Nations Charter was a complex blend of internationalist and power-political principles. While the effective operation of a genuine collective security system depended primarily upon great-power cooperation, the organization was worldly enough to realize that if such cooperation was not forthcoming it would be better for the system to be incapacitated. The Security Council was the hub of this compromise. If the Permanent Members so agreed, the organization was a potent one and could take all kinds of action both against, and in support of, its members; if they did not, the veto ensured that it would remain quiescent. Of course, the drift of international politics in the late 1940s rapidly ensured that the United Nations would succumb to the latter role and, *pari passu*, the practitioners of international security turned to other institutional forms.

In the case of United States policy-makers, the drift to containment took several years. During 1945–7, there remained the belief that the restoration of British power would serve as some kind of check on the Soviet Union, both in Europe and in the Middle East. From 1947, that belief quickly dissipated and the United States found itself as the architect of a series of multilateral alliances which constituted a new, and unanticipated, collective security system. NATO, ANZUS, and the Treaty with Japan paved the way for similar arrangements in the Middle East and South-east Asia which eventually constituted an interlocking network of security arrangments extending across much of the globe. It is clear, however, that the United States expected others to make their own contribution to this system. The whole purpose of reconstruction was to enhance security as much as it was to contribute to prosperity. None the less, here was a clear demonstration of the general tendency, remarked above, for the cold-war induced disintegration of the whole to encourage the integration of its resulting parts.

If there was one compelling consideration at work during war-time planning for the future it was that security would depend on the construction of a viable international economic order. To the United States, the measure of that viability would be the extent to which the principles of openness and multilateralism would take the place of the autarchy, bilateralism, and competitiveness of the inter-war period. It is perhaps some indication of Washington's priorities that the meeting at Bretton Woods to agree the post-war economic institutions was held in 1944, the year before the meeting at San Francisco to ratify the United Nations.

The Bretton Woods agreements were to establish both a set of international economic institutions and also, and just as importantly, a set of economic principles. There was recognition of the differences of opinion held by the various states—particularly between the United States' preference for extensive liberalism and those weakened economies which saw no alternative to the retention of controls and protection. Necessarily, then, what was finally agreed was a series of compromises (Brett 1985: 105).[2] However, it was the American hope and expectation that these tensions and conflicts could be overcome, in the international domain just as they had been in the domestic, by abundant economic growth: in a climate of expansion, redistributive questions could be addressed less painfully (Maier 1987: 128).

The institutions of the new international economic order were the International Monetary Fund (IMF), the World Bank, and, eventually, the General Agreement on Tariffs and Trade (GATT), which was to serve in place of the failed International Trade Organization. The IMF would operate to secure a stable scheme of international settlement by means of minimizing national controls, encouraging convertibility, and stabilizing exchange rates. This last would be accomplished by committing members' central banks to defend their currencies to within one per cent of par rates and allowing them to draw on IMF funds in order to do so. The World Bank would provide a source of capital lending, although in the early years it was pushed into the background by the Marshall Plan. The GATT embodied the goals of free and equal trade. Collectively, these were to provide the lubricants which would induce post-war recovery and a substantially increased role for international exchanges of goods and capital in the international economy as a whole.

The stability of the exchange and payments system, and the ability of the war-torn economies to participate in international trade, depended critically on the US dollar. It was the pegging of the dollar to a fixed price of gold that was to ensure stability of the international exchange rate system and a supply of US dollars that would be necessary to tide the Europeans through balance of payments difficulties. It was the severity of the latter problem that was to be considerably underestimated in 1945. More importantly, in the longer term, these two elements of the system were in conflict with each other: the more the rest of the world depended upon an outward flow of dollars from the United States, eventually the less confidence there would be in the stability of the dollar. It was the confluence of these two trends which finally disrupted the Bretton Woods system by

---

[2] So much was this so that Bretton Woods, contrary to its popular reputation, accepted a non-liberal approach to international financial movements to safeguard the welfare state. See Helleiner (1994: 164).

the early 1970s (Gilpin 1987: 140). None the less, if a liberalization of trade and internationalization of economic activity were the objectives, the system provided handsome returns. Between 1950 and 1980, world exports as a percentage of world GNP increased from 11.7 per cent to 21.2 per cent (Gill and Law 1988: 145).

Not all the principles of this system could be implemented immediately and, just as in the security realm principle was tempered by expedient practice, so the timetable for full achievement of the Bretton Woods principles was to be extended and short-term compromises reached. The process has been characterized as a series of trade-offs in which the United States 'used its economic strength to provide short-term inducements to the weaker countries to co-operate, in exchange for a willingness to build a long-term commitment to liberalisation into the structure of the institutions themselves' (Brett 1985: 63–4). The Anglo-American loan discussions of 1945–6 were symptomatic of what was to happen more generally. Britain suffered an acute payments crisis immediately at war's end and a $3.75 billion US loan was arranged. However, the agreement simply papered over the cracks of Anglo-American differences. Britain sought autonomy, protection, leadership of a Commonwealth bloc, and dealings with Europe on its own terms. American loans came with strings attached which threatened these British priorities (Hogan 1987: 20). In particular, in return for the loan Britain had to undertake commitments to the convertibility of sterling and to trade liberalization which would undermine the sterling area and a privileged British trading zone (Foreman-Peck 1995: 256). In the event, there was compromise and the USA's geopolitical imperatives overturned its own economic principles, at least for the shorter term. Leffler describes the process whereby the US came to tolerate British restrictive practices in both the currency and trading fields (1992: 63).

Much the same was to occur on the broader economic front with the United States having to accept infringement of economic principle in order to achieve an accommodating economic practice with its would-be partners. The extreme version of this argument is to be found in Alan S. Milward, where the idea of compromise is discarded: what happened was that an alternative European system took the place of the American-preferred Bretton Woods programme. Thus Milward claims that 'the success of Western Europe's reconstruction came from creating its own pattern of institutionalized, international economic interdependence', and that what emerged was not what 'has erroneously been labelled "the Bretton Woods system" ' (1984: xvi). But this goes too far in marginalizing American power and preferences, even if concessions had to be made. It is certainly the case that American strictures could not immediately and effectively be implemented, so much so that by 1947 some two-thirds of western Europe's trade remained organized on a bilateral basis and through various state controls (Leffler 1992: 8), and currency convertibility took much longer to realize than had been expected (Cohen 1993: 6). For all that, the United States enjoyed a pre-eminent economic position and, geopolitically, became increasingly important to the needs of western Europe and Japan. To the extent that the western European countries came up with solutions not designed in Washington, they did so within parameters that the United States could tolerate.

The reason for this tolerance was that America's objectives located economic principles in a real world of emerging cold-war rivalry, and also of a careful scrutiny of domestic balances of political power. It would not have served any US interests had scrupulous adherence to Bretton Woods been observed at a cost to the international balance of power or to domestic stability within the countries that were forming the emerging Western system. Indeed, it has been suggested that this domestic dimension was so important that the Bretton Woods system encouraged a role for the state as intermediary between international and national economic interests (Cox 1987: 254–5). Only thus could a fully stable and effective Western system be developed. This domestic dimension will be addressed at the end of the chapter, for no discussion of the new international security and economic order would be complete which did not take account of it.

The Road to Globalization

Intra-systemic consolidation and integration took more than a decade after 1945 to complete and it was the implementation of this design which set the framework within which forces of globalization were to be released. The Marshall Plan, unveiled in 1947, was a prominent landmark on this road and deserves a more detailed discussion. In fact, the Marshall Plan can be regarded as part of the bargaining process over the terms on which other countries could be induced to participate in an open and multilateral economic system. 'The Marshall Plan,' it has been contended, 'provided the incentive to join the new economic order and allowed time, as well as funds, through which the adjustments could be made' (Cox 1987: 215).

That the Marshall Plan was a complex and multi-faceted programme is abundantly clear. It was a compound of geopolitical, economic, and social goals and its mainstays were the attempts to exclude Soviet influence by European reconstruction and integration, to circulate US dollars with which American products might be bought and international trade stimulated, and to induce social stabilization in which the appeal of left-wing doctrines would be diminished. If successful, all this would be achieved at minimum cost to the United States. Above all, the Plan 'epitomized the American commitment to sustaining a transnational economy' and was the key element in securing adherence to the principles so entailed (Maier 1993: 394). Even if considerable compromises had to be made, it was an endeavour to replicate the world economy in America's own image—'an international projection of the corporative political economy that had evolved in the United States' (Hogan 1987: xii).

The need for any programme on such a scale was not apparent to US policymakers in 1945. It required both the deterioration of Europe's economic circumstances, and a worsening of the perceived balance of power in Europe, for initiatives of this kind to be taken. In 1947, western Europe drew 45 per cent of its imports from the United States but was incapable of earning the foreign exchange necessary to pay for them (Leffler 1992: 163). As Europe's material circumstances failed to improve, the United States more clearly understood the threat to its wider interests. Only through genuine economic recovery might the new international economic order be attained:

They wanted European countries to boost their productivity and efficiency, compete effectively in international markets, and find sources of supply outside the Western Hemisphere. If these countries succeeded, they would cut their deficits, overcome the dollar gap, free themselves of US subsidies and be able to adopt multilateral trade arrangements. (Leffler 1992: 158)

This economic crisis threatened a wider political challenge to US interests. In the absence of recovery and European participation in an open international economy, the danger was that these countries would return to closed-off economic arrangements and that communist parties would benefit from high levels of social discontent. What was feared then was not a direct Soviet military threat but western European drift into autarchy or into the Soviet orbit (Leffler 1992: 163). It was this combination of circumstances that triggered the adoption of the Marshall programme. Between 1948 and 1952, some US$13 billion was transferred to western Europe of which more than $3 billion went to the UK, $2.7 billion to France, and $1.4 billion to West Germany (Foreman-Peck 1995: 246). However, before this could be put in place, there was a lengthy period of cajoling and bargaining as US and European priorities clashed, and differences between countries like Britain and France quickly rose to the surface.

In summary, what were the main motivations behind the programme? It was every bit as much political as economic, and emphasized the necessity of encouraging European integration both as a means of nudging the Europeans away from bilateralism, and as a more effective counter to Soviet influence. 'The United States,' Milward observes, 'did not only intend to reconstruct Western Europe economically, but also politically' (1984: 56). In turn, this political architecture of European integration, initially embodied in the Organization for European Economic Cooperation (OEEC), was the corollary of, and part counterpoint to, an exclusive emphasis on free enterprise solutions. As Michael J. Hogan, the foremost historian of the Plan, has argued, it was a blend of the free traders' and the planners' approaches. The former 'aimed to reduce barriers to the free flow of goods, services, and capital, put intra-European trade and payments on a multilateral basis, and permit natural market mechanisms to promote a rational integration'. But as an insurance against market failure, political institutions were to be created which could transcend national sovereignties, break down barriers, and provide the political framework for transnational economic activities (Hogan 1987: 191). This was the new world economy in embryo.

It has been suggested that, far from being enhanced and driven by the cold war, this vision was abandoned precisely because of the exacerbation of superpower relations. Gilpin argues that as the geopolitical clash with Soviet power sharpened, American plans for the international economic order underwent 'a drastic reversal'. His point is that the strengthening of western Europe became the major priority and economic principles of multilateralism and non-discrimination had to be sacrificed on this altar (Gilpin 1971: 59). There is something to this but the claim is overstated. To be sure, and as noted, the US was prepared to make concessions to the short-term economic needs of its partners, but this scarcely amounts to a total abandonment of the multilateralist programme. What emerges from Hogan's detailed study is that, from time to time, US tactics over the Marshall Plan did change, but the long-term strategic goals remained constant: multilateralism in payments, trade, and production persisted as key American objectives (Hogan 1987: 198).

The considerations which underpinned the Marshall Plan can be found equally in American thinking about the post-war reintegration of Germany and Japan into the Western system. On these issues, there was some tempering of original intentions to adjust to cold-war pressures but there was also a consistent determination to incorporate both countries into the kind of economic sphere which best reflected American principles. At the war's end, the realities of occupation and the pressures to eliminate all vestiges of the old political order in both countries distracted attention away from economic reconstruction as the top priority. By 1947, however, the realization that German economic recovery was essential for wider European recovery and indeed integration, and the growing imperative of Soviet containment, led to adjustment in allied thinking.

Similar changes took place in attitudes towards Japan and this was reflected in a redirection of occupation policy (Crockatt 1995: 99). The emphasis shifted away from extirpating what was believed to be the cultural bases of militarism and political extremism and towards economic and political revival to create an anti-communist counterweight within the Asia-Pacific region. Such recovery entailed access for Japan to regional sources of raw materials and to neighbouring markets. Since any spectre of a recovery of Japanese power also had profound implications for the security of neighbouring countries, the shift in emphasis also involved the United States in policies of regional reassurance which had significant long-term consequences for the region.

Within Europe equally, German recovery entailed regional reassurance but in this case the solution took on a much more explicitly integrationist form. A revival of German economic power was needed in the interests of the international economy and as part of the cold-war pattern of counteracting Soviet influence: European integration was the vehicle chosen to reconcile these various objectives (Hogan 1987: 198). The most sensitive area in which this issue was raised was the military: an effective NATO, especially after the outbreak of the Korean War, required German armed forces, and the whole saga of the failed European Defence Community (EDC) was about an attempt to find the appropriate wider institutional setting in which German remilitarization might be made acceptable to its European neighbours.

In both cases, a softening of the terms of occupation was an essential precondition of securing compliance within Germany and Japan. The costs of long-term embitterment had been exemplified in inter-war Germany and the US became pro-gressively more committed to a strategy of rewards in which greater local autonomy was the pay-off for increased integration within the Western system. 'The goal was to co-opt German and Japanese power,' Leffler comments, 'by demonstrating to local elites that their national aspirations could be fulfilled within a US-led orbit' (1992: 500). If this was the chosen means, the end sought was precisely the intra-systemic consolidation which the unfolding of the cold war both required and made possible. Above all, it was to be the economic contribution which both Germany and Japan could make to this grand design that would facilitate the adop-tion of a widespread multilateral economic order. Just as economic growth was believed to have reduced domestic tensions within the United States, so regional economic growth, promoted by these two motors, would entice both western Europe and Pacific Asia into an open economic order by reducing their domestic political costs in doing so. To achieve this, Germany and Japan had to be recon-structed as special kinds of states in which the political was subordinated to the eco-nomic. In the words of Maier, they would be reformed as 'nexuses of economic transactions' rather than as 'centers of political power'. In this way, he concludes, 'America most completely carried out its postwar economic postulates' and the foundations for progressive globalization had been laid (Maier 1987: 146).

Although America's policy for European integration was closely related to its German policy, it also had a more general philosophy and dynamic. Nor was European integration to be entirely wrought in accordance with American pref-erences: just as in the case of the Marshall Plan, projects for European integration were underpinned by a variety of considerations and a mixture of European and American concerns. These related principally to the solution of European eco-nomic and security problems and to Europe's future political identity and status in the world.

Economically, Europe was struggling to recover, not only from the after-effects of global war, but from the triple assault on its economic fortunes represented by the two wars and the depression in their midst. The result of these had been the breakdown of an effective international economy and their 'international trans-actions remained largely bilateral in nature' (Maier 1993: 404). From this per-spective, European economic integration was the preferred solution to the progressive fragmentation of the European economy that had been occurring since 1914 (Milward 1984: 463).

What was desirable in the economic sphere also made doubly good sense in terms of strategy. A degree of European unity was widely seen as an antidote to the internecine fragmentation that had characterized European international life since the First World War and would have the happy effect of strengthening west-ern Europe's potential for resisting Soviet political encroachment. At the same time, it would offer the best solution to Europe's troubled internal balance of power by harmonizing German recovery with the needs of French security (Hogan 1987: 22). Thus the strategic case for European integration was very much strengthened when the need for German economic and military rehabili-tation became paramount in the late 1940s and early 1950s.

But lest it be thought that all schemes for European integration were exercises in the abnegation of power and in the forswearing of a power-political past, it must be insisted that integration was also widely perceived as a means by which a weakened Europe might compete effectively with the new world powers and was thus in itself a new form of power politics: only by some form of unification could Europe count for something against the superpowers (Melandri 1995: 103). Even within this ambit, not all recidivism had been pushed aside and there remained power-political motivations that were as much national as European-wide in nature. Thus the project of European integration was seen by some national play-ers as the best means of projecting national power in the straitened circumstances of the post-war period. European integration was, in this perspective, not a wholly new departure but rather the continuation of national policy by other means and, to some extent, a 'diplomatic manœuvre' (Milward 1992: 17).

None the less, whatever its indigenous characteristics, this was a force that the United States sought to direct to meet its own objectives. While initially sceptical about the idea of a regional economic bloc, as this might constitute an impedi-ment to a wider multilateral trading order, the United States was won round to its support because of the interaction between cold-war rivalry and the dynamics of intra-Atlantic relations, especially so from 1947 (Hogan 1987: 28). The attraction of the policy resided in its neat combination of both the economic (European cooperation for reconstruction as the basis of the Marshall Plan) and the strate-gic (containment of the Soviet Union from without and of Germany from within) dimensions of American thinking. As Hogan suggests, 'integration operated as an interlocking concept in the minds of American policymakers, the link that con-nected the economic and strategic goals' (1987: 429).

While the cold war as Soviet–American rivalry provided the necessary context for European integration—and in this sense Hobsbawm is correct to claim that the cold war 'created the "European Community" ' (1994: 239)—it was also the cold war as intra-systemic consolidation that accounts for the precise form that the integration was to take. In part, the process reflected tensions between the United States and its European partners, not to mention that tensions between the European partners themselves, and the dynamics of these various relation-ships shaped the style of European cooperation. In turn, this explains the paradox that the 'Community' was 'created both by and against the USA' (Hobsbawm 1994: 240). It was in the context of Soviet–American antagonism that the American imperative for European integration was born, but out of the complex dynamics of intra-systemic relations that Europe found its precise shape.

The Failure of the Soviet Challenge

If globalization emerged from the successful creation of an expanding Western system, then a necessary part of its explanation must lie in the failure of the Soviet Union to provide an effective challenge to that political and economic framework: the fate of globalization was contingent upon, not only the fact of the cold war, but also its actual course. Why then was the Soviet Union unable to advance its alternative programme or to resist the economic space being set in place by the American-led design? If Hobsbawm wishes to associate the Short Twentieth Century with the lifetime of the Soviet state, how is it that that state should have been so marginal to one of the century's key trends, the development of globalization after 1945?

To a degree, the early failures might be attributed to Stalin's adoption of counter-productive policies. Far from resisting the consolidation of the West, Stalin's initiatives served only to hasten them. Thus Mastny questions Stalin's reputation for shrewdness given that a series of his 'foreign policy disasters' helped Western integration, nurtured a strong West German state, and encouraged the formation of NATO (1995: 79). Ironically, Stalin's overt challenges succeeded only in resolving America's domestic uncertainties and in providing the west Europeans with the incentive to secure deals with Washington. On the same kind of logic, Stalin's successors might be criticized for their pursuit of a modified policy of confrontation, within the newly defined limits of peaceful coexistence, since this in turn fostered greater international pluralism. As was to become apparent, this pluralism proved a much greater threat to Soviet, than to American, interests. 'A plural diffusion of strategic power,' Calleo correctly claimed, 'means, in actual substance, the rise of those very Eurasian neighbours who are historically the principal threats to Russian security and ambition' (1987: 122–3). Thus pluralism exercised an asymmetrical impact on the development of the cold war, and ultimately favoured the United States.

But to analyse the cold war simply in terms of personalities and Soviet policy mistakes seems misplaced: it confuses the adverse effects of policy choices with the more basic sources of systemic weakness which would have asserted themselves regardless of the specific actions of the Soviet leadership. The endemic problem for the Soviet state was its stifling system of political control and the absolute priority it assigned to military strength. Whether the latter was deemed necessary as a form of international status and influence, or is understandable as a sensible requirement of national security as others have claimed (MccGwire (1991: 8) accounts for these capabilities in the light of 'legitimate security concerns'), its negative impact on the Soviet economy is undeniable in either case.

The militarism of the Soviet state was reinforced in its limited appeal to the Third World and hence military aid and sales figured disproportionately in its quest for influence in that quarter. Its reliance on military means reflected its inadequacies in other areas: the Soviet challenge in the developing world was set against the background of its trade with that area representing a bare 6 per cent of that of the capitalist world (Nogee 1981: 449). Its economic aid programme tended also to be concentrated upon large show-case projects of often doubtful economic merit. While it might be true that the Soviet Union could offer 'a totalitarian mechanism of domestic control to authoritarian Third World elites' (Whelan and Dixon 1986: 463–4), this was a flimsy basis from which to mount a serious global ideological challenge. Unsurprisingly, one survey of the cold-war period concluded that 'Soviet influence in the Third World remains limited' (Nogee 1981: 450).

The Soviet Union was unable to break out of these endemic contradictions: the weaker its challenge in other areas, the more Soviet leaders sought to lend credibility to their superpower status by further militarization through the Brezhnev era; the more they did so, the greater was the damage to the long-term viability of the country's economic infrastructure. This paradox, in Bialer's terms, between the semblance of external expansion and the reality of internal weakness, was a structural condition of the Soviet system that finally proved its undoing (Bialer 1986: 2).

This brings us closer to identifying the reasons for the Soviet Union's inability to prevent the consolidation of the Western system, or to circumscribe its potential for expansion. In the 1980s, Paul Dibb presciently described the Soviet Union as 'an incomplete Superpower' in that it lacked 'major global economic, technological and ideological influence' (1986: xix). Without these resources, the Soviet Union had no mechanisms for globalizing its own system or for effectively incorporating newcomers within it: those few exceptions that were drawn in—such as Cuba and Vietnam—proved to be liabilities, not assets, to Soviet power.

In short, the Soviet challenge to the Western system faltered for two principal reasons. First, for all its quest to subvert and overthrow the west, the Soviet state discovered that it progressively *needed* its competitor both to justify its own domestic system and to legitimize its hold over eastern Europe. Secondly, the narrow basis of the Soviet claim to superpower status is but another way of saying that its challenge was unidimensional. For the United States, the cold war had two dimensions—inter-systemic competition and intra-systemic consolidation (Crockatt 1995: 12). In contrast, the Soviet Union was a player in the clash of Soviet and American power, and less effectively in the wider rivalry between the two opposed systems: but it was not a player in that vital, and ultimately telling, intra-systemic game where the dynamic of globalization had now come to be located.

The Emergence of the Third World

Finally, and as previously argued, what was to emerge as the Third World was a crucial ingredient in that intra-systemic accommodation within the West. It was always likely to be the case that the cold war and the Third World would interact at this historical juncture. The emergence of the superpowers with increasingly global interests, at precisely the time that large tracts of the underdeveloped world were moving towards post-colonial political independence, meant that the two forces would become caught up in the vortex of each other. As Paul Kennedy was to phrase it, '[w]hat was happening, in fact, was that one major trend in twentieth-century power politics, the rise of the superpowers, was beginning to interact with another, newer trend—the political fragmentation of the globe' (1988: 392).

The importance of this lay both in the short-term requirements of the stabilization of United States economic relations with its core allies, and also in the longer-term project of constituting a global multilateral economy. The connection has been drawn as follows:

European countries had to save dollars by developing alternative sources of supply outside of North America. They also had to earn dollars by increasing exports to the United States or to countries that had a favourable balance of trade with the United States.

All these solutions placed heavy stress on the overseas colonies and territories of the European powers as well as on other raw-material-producing areas in the Third World. (Leffler 1992: 164)

If European reconstruction demanded that the United States help create the political framework in the Third World which would enable Europe to pay its own way, then the reintegration of Japan into a wider international economy also required a framework which would provide Japanese access to raw materials and markets. The Asia–Pacific region thus took on substantial importance for United States policy and that policy had to strike a fine balance between indigenous pressures for self-determination, worries about economic nationalism and communist penetration, and finding a new imperial equilibrium which would safeguard Western (and Japanese) interests throughout the region.

These cumulative pressures were to draw the United States into military commitments in the Third World as the only way of protecting the political framework, and hence the economic space, of multilateralism. Although unintended in the late 1940s, by the 1950s active military engagement had been found necessary to support the US-preferred economic order. In part, this became necessary as a consequence of the rapid atrophy of European colonial power (Leffler 1992: 498).

All of this ensued from the post-war onset of decolonization and from its accompanying change of philosophical temper: the mood shifted gradually away from colonial paternalism not least because it was hard to reconcile the persistence of the imperial order with the reaffirmation of freedom and self-government which had seemed to be the *raison d'être* of the recent struggle against the totalitarian powers. Ironically, the principle of racial equality—one of the solvents of the colonial system—was itself boosted by the Nazi outrages and the resultant 'abhorrence felt at the working-out of a noxious doctrine of racial superiority' (Vincent 1984: 252). Thus was it that a primarily European experience fed into, and became itself a dynamic constituent of, that great theme of the twentieth century—the revolt against the West (Barraclough 1967: 153–4). But decolonization was never a straightforward zero-sum contest between the old imperialism and the new colonial nationalist movements. Colonial historiography now recognizes as commonplace that the two, usually cast as 'inveterate opponents', were part of a more complex reality in which they were 'often wary, suspicious partners' in dealing with both popular radicalism and the vestiges of the old political hierarchies (Darwin 1991: 101). None the less, domestic stabilities had been eroded by wartime turmoil and continued to be so by the new dynamism of post-war colonial administration, responding to the economic and commercial demands emanating from the metropolitan centres.

How did the Third World, as it finally became known, relate to the cold war? Symbolically, of course, it embodied the quest for autonomous development, outside the structured choices of alignment which the cold war sought to impose. And yet the cold war retained its imperious hold in both indirect and direct ways. Indirectly, the formation of the Western bloc ensured that American economic and political succour would be made available for the residual imperial aspirations of its European allies and, in this sense, the cold war if anything retarded some parts of the decolonization process (see the analysis of British policy in Darwin (1991: 67–8)), despite the erstwhile anti-colonial credentials of the United States. More directly, and once the cold war and the Third World had become engaged in systematic interactions from the mid-1950s onwards, the cold war imposed its constraints by its preoccupation (either positively or negatively) with domestic social change and revolution in Third World countries, by superimposing an East–West dimension onto all Third World interstate conflicts, and by the direct engagement of the superpowers themselves (Halliday 1989: 27–8).

The role of the Third World in post-1945 processes of globalization and fragmentation can now be considered in summary form. Thus far, it has been suggested that it became organically linked to the cold war as part of the essential task of intra-systemic consolidation. In the longer term, this was to ensure that capital flows to the underdeveloped regions, economic aid, and programmes of economic development would themselves become integral elements of what was happening within the Western system itself: an extension of the system was part of the bargain over its acceptance by its core members.

In wider historical perspective, decolonization and the emergence of the Third World can be seen to have contributed to other aspects of globalization as well. Most notably, it ensured the universalization of Western political practice through the institutional spread of the nation-state which now progressively enveloped the globe. These state structures were 'built from the outside in, and from the top down' and were derived from Western models by western-educated élites (Von Laue 1987: 307). The cold-war period thus coincided with a further extension of Western influence and, incidentally, with the further erosion of indigenous cultures and political arrangements: the two processes merged in the superimposition of ideas of modernization and development which, in turn, generated a 'fateful disorientation' within much of the non-Western world (Von Laue 1994: 190–1). Curiously, the West itself remained deeply troubled about its own globalizing legacy, recognizing the political reality of the spread of Western state practice and nationalist doctrines, but at another level resenting the extension, and feeling that what were essentially Western ideals had somehow been misappropriated by 'foreign' peoples. What has been a unifying and homogenizing process has, at the same time, constituted new points of global division (see Said 1993: 261).

In short, the emergence of the Third World also created fragmentationist effects. It did so most obviously by the stress on powerful state structures which was the inevitable result of the absence of any organic link between the new states and their constituent societies. Many Third World states opted for a coercive *étatisme* that has been their most distinctive institutional form (Mayall 1990: 49; Bull and Watson 1984: 224). They did so, of course, often because of their own perceived weakness and as a means of keeping the intrusive international system, forever identified with imperial domination, at bay. Such tendencies were further reinforced by the willingness of the cold-war international system to supply military equipment and expertise with the result that the Third World military, like the state itself, became a creation from the outside (Tilly 1985: 185–6). State-directed development was a reflection of the economic weakness of these states and of their determination to escape the old forms of colonial dependence. Thus conceived, Third World economic strategy tended to emphasize state management and control as a conscious de-linking from threatening global economic forces and, to this extent, to be proactively 'deglobalizing' (Parkins 1996: 70–1).

The likelihood is that, in the longer term and for all their superficial globalizing effects, imperialism and decolonization will come to be seen as fragmentationist. The reason for this is that there was never any deep-seated accommodation or synthesis between the two worlds. '[I]mperialism juxtaposed two worlds' is one historian's confident judgement: 'it did not integrate them' (Betts 1985: xv). To the extent that imperialism has created a legacy of globalization, it is most marked in the continuity of opposed cultural forms—'a general world-wide pattern of imperial culture' and a 'historical experience of resistance against empire' in Edward W. Said's words (Said 1993: xii)—which has taken on a universalized, rather than localized, significance. Whatever the scope of its symbolism, this scarcely represents a move towards a homogenous global society.

States, Cold War, and Globalization

Finally, these various international developments both between and within systems need to be located in the context of what was also happening within the domestic polities of the states themselves. Manifestly, the combined effects of depression, ideological polarization, totalitarian experience, and protracted war left a profound impression upon the states which emerged from those ordeals in 1945. They generated what has been termed 'a much wider political consensus' within the post-war European political systems (Milward 1992: 27). Keynesian and welfarist principles formed part of this powerful political consensus within western Europe, and of which the United States would have to take account (Brett 1985: 65). But within the United States itself the New Deal represented the striking of political and economic bargains.

Accordingly, there is a widespread view within disparate bodies of literature that the political framework sponsored by the United States within which globalization was encouraged was not simply an *international* but also a *domestic* one: changes in the international order were inextricably interwoven with changes in the nature of state performance and, hence, globalization describes something happening to states as well as between them. In terms of the argument of this chapter, the changing nature of the state was itself a necessary part of the process of intra-systemic consolidation associated with the cold war.

Precisely what was happening to the state has been explained in a number of distinct ways, but all accounts agree in presenting it as a shift in terms of the state's brokerage role between domestic and international constituencies. This is a convenient mode of analysis and the issue can be reviewed along these lines. The general framework is conveniently captured by the following description of the post-1945 shift in state responsibilites:

Whereas the nineteenth-century gold standard and the ideology of laissez faire had subordinated domestic stability to international norms and the interwar period had reversed these objectives, the postwar regime tried to achieve both. The state assumed a greater role in the economy to guarantee full employment and other goals, but its actions became subject to international rules. In this way it would be possible for domestic interventionism and international stability to co-exist. (Gilpin 1987: 132–3)

For many analysts, this expresses the central issue, although the manner in which it is elaborated varies thereafter. The following summary will focus on the points of agreement to be found within these accounts as a broad measure of the areas of historical consensus. Ruggie, like Gilpin after him, presents the case for an 'embedded liberalism', whereby the post-war order was a compromise between the two periods which had gone before, and sought to combine the multilateralism of the pre-1914 period with acceptance of 'domestic interventionism' (Ruggie 1991: 203). This presentation of the argument suggests a disjunction between domestic and international trends whereas many historians tend to emphasize instead their complementarity. Thus one commentary on Ruggie's position records the alternative view that 'international regimes grew out of the same transformation in the philosophy of government that spawned new domestic regimes' (Burley 1993: 129). This interpretation is especially associated with the work of Hogan in which the theme of the new international order being a projection of US domestic experience is paramount. Hogan constantly reiterates his notion of a 'New Deal synthesis' lying at the heart of US policy, its goal being the establishment of 'networks of corporative collaboration' whereby the US could forge internationally a 'neo-capitalist order similar to the one in the United States' (Hogan 1987: 136). Maier likewise takes the view that the post-war system was an amalgamation of new international and domestic political orders and shares Hogan's notion of the powerful influence upon these processes exercised by 'a transnational élite' engaged in the same kind of corporative collaboration internationally as had taken place domestically within the United States (Maier 1993: 409, 391).

One of the most powerful expressions of this line of argument is that developed by Robert W. Cox which embraces the corporatist elements in Hogan and Maier but renders them in a more distinctively world capitalist and materialist perspective. As with the foregoing, Cox is at pains to describe the necessary interconnection between changes in the international order and domestic transformation within the state itself: indeed, this was essential to the international project. He thus writes of programmes like the Marshall Plan as being designed to penetrate into 'the conscious shaping of the balance among social forces within states' and as engineering a 'center-right' orientation which supported a new style of state performance (Cox 1987: 215–16). The new model of the state he terms the 'neoliberal' and he depicts it as serving a mixture of national and world economy needs. It differs from the welfare-nationalist state in that, instead of pursuing national goals above all, the neoliberal state is configured to 'adjust the national economy to the growth of the world economy'. Moreover, rather than seek security and economic welfare as a stand-alone entity, the neoliberal state seeks 'security as a member of a stable alliance system and its economic growth as a participant in an open world economy' (Cox 1987: 219–20). If the real measure of globalization is the transition from an international to a world economy, then this domestic transformation could be seen as an essential stage in the inauguration of a process of mature globalization since it presages a single integrated world economy rather than the interaction of separately recognizable and interacting national economies. Whether this transition occurred as fully at this time as Cox would have us believe is open to serious question, and the premise is further weakened by his own admission that there is nothing in its 'appearance' to distinguish the neoliberal state, only in its 'goals' (1987: 220). But the general thrust of the analysis remains suggestive.

The argument loses force when it reverts to a kind of economic determinism in which 'the internationalizing of the state' is described as a response to 'the world economy of international production' (Cox 1987: 253). It is impoverished by its neglect of the facts of state power, American predominance, and the vagaries of international relations. None the less, it serves as a useful reminder that the fillip to globalization that occurred during the cold-war era was given by the new international order associated with American power but also through some adjustment of state policies and practices to this order (if by no means to the degree that Cox's argument implies). This association between international and domestic transformation is important for an understanding of globalization. What it also suggests is that if the process of globalization is hostage to the rise and fall of hegemonic power, as also to the general play of international relations, it is equally hostage to developments in domestic politics which have a tendency to take unanticipated, and in a sense counter-systemic, turns. For this reason, the projection of secular trends towards globalization becomes additionally problematic and hazardous.

The distinctive traits of late twentieth-century globalization—transnational corporations (TNCs), the territorial segmentation of production, financial integration, structured choices between universalist ideologies, the envelopment of the world by the nation-state, unilinear concepts of development and modernization, and the zenith of Westernization—were all directly associated with the specific configuration of cold-war international politics in the 1950s and 1960s. Moreover, they were encouraged by the twin dimensions of the cold war—an inter-systemic rivalry and an intra-systemic growth. Would these traits be sustained after 1970, when the cold war seemed to suffer an acute split in its personality, and East-West competition diminished at the very same time as West-West consolidation began to falter?

7

ERAS OF NEGOTIATION AND CONFRONTATION, 1970–1989

There is a fair case to be made for regarding the beginning of the 1970s as another of the significant 'punctuation' points of the twentieth century because the period was witness both to the end of the post-war Golden Age of economic growth—to be replaced by a much more uncertain phase in which inflation, unemployment, and environmental concerns perceptibly changed the economic mood—and also to marked relaxation in the confrontational policies of the superpowers, even if this was to be relatively short-lived and soon succeeded by the so-called second cold war. Such major upheavals in both international economic and security relations are significant in their own right, but the function of this chapter is to explore their interconnections from the distinctive perspective of their association with trends towards globalization and fragmentation in the international system. Did the period mark the end of that post-war phase wherein a particular configuration of military and political power had sustained a liberal capitalist international economy, and did this portend a return to a more unstable, closed, regionalized, and protectionist economic system? And was this the result of a wider diffusion of power and a more fragmented political order in which the cold-war blocs lost cohesion, at the same time as Third World nationalism became more assertive against both First and Second World controls?

Alternatively, does this period signify the beginning of an ongoing disjunction between economic and political trends—the former showing remarkable resilience in a globalizing direction whatever the vagaries of cold war or *détente*, and associated degrees of bloc cohesion, in the international political sphere? The answer to this question depends upon the explanation offered for the more unsettled economic conditions from 1970 onwards. If seen as the consequence of the passing of American hegemony, they may be taken as a kind of confirmation of the continuing political determination of economic activity; if regarded as the result of autonomous changes in the nature of the international financial system itself, they might indicate a bifurcation between economic and political trends. However, such a stark choice is clouded by the intervention of related debates about whether US power was in fact in decline, whether it persisted in a new structural form, and whether the very essence of power in international relations was not in any case changing in such a way as to question the relevance of traditional hegemonial theories.

The Security and Economic Orders

In particular, we need to explore the relationship between *détente* and globalization. If, as argued in the previous chapter, the cold war happily generated and sustained processes of globalization, does it follow that *détente* would entail economic and political fragmentation? Or is this counter-intuitive? To answer these questions, the nature and significance of *détente* will need to be examined. In particular, and following again from the previous chapter, the argument will be developed that *détente*'s importance for an understanding of globalization lies less in it as an aspect of Soviet–American relations and more so for what it reveals about *intra-systemic relations within the Western sphere*: *détente* is significant for globalization because it tells us something important about developments within the Western camp.

Such a framework of analysis links up closely with the many arguments about the supposed passing of American hegemony—the demise of the *Pax Americana*—and about its impact on the international economy. In terms of hegemonic stability theory, the suggestion is that the breakdown in the international economic order was a consequence of the loss of American leadership (see generally, for example, Gilpin 1987; Keohane 1989*a*, 1989*b*; Nye 1990; Walter 1991). It is not the intention here to enter directly into such debates but their implications do touch upon the nature of our understanding of the dynamic interrelationship between the international economic and political systems in the 1970s and 1980s.

The identification of these twin watersheds, one in the economy and the other in international security, immediately invites reflection upon the possibility of connection between the two. In turn, this leads us to confront once again the choice between the primarily political theories which regard the economy as a function of the prevailing political framework, as against the primarily economic theories which contend that profound, and autonomous, changes in economic organization took place in the latter half of the twentieth century and that these changes are the driving force behind emerging patterns of economic activity (Shonfield 1976: 93–4).

What changes occurred in the realm of international security? The most pronounced shift which took place was from an era of confrontation to an era of negotiation. The latter was the characteristic feature of the relaxation in superpower tensions of the early 1970s but, in turn, this relaxation was rooted in wider changes in the distribution of international power. If Kenneth Waltz is correct in his claim that the 'Cold War could not end until the structure that sustained it began to erode' (1993: 49), then the major element of that structure—bipolarity—seemed to falter in the late 1960s and early 1970s in such a way as to imply the cold war's imminent demise. Paradoxically, *détente* itself had the contrary effect of reinforcing bipolarity and thus, in the short term at any rate, of undermining its own prospects of success. As Robert Litwak has suggested, the focus on superpower relations and on the Soviet Union's equality conferred 'an ostensible new legitimacy to the image of bipolarity during a period in which its relevance across a spectrum of issues was clearly waning' (1984: 3). At the time, however, the widespread perception was that bipolarity was coming to be replaced by a shadowy multipolarity and that the principal structural consequences of the Second World War were finally working their way out of the system: the new distribution of power was thereby identified with the final passing of the post-war era (Buchan 1974: 4).

The era of negotiation was characterized by formalized dialogue between the superpowers. This covered the management of their strategic relationship through the Strategic Arms Limitation Treaty (SALT) in 1972 and the initiation of conventional arms control negotiations in the Mutual and Balanced Force Reductions (MBFR) framework. With regard to formal recognition of the *status quo* in Europe, agreements over Berlin and the two Germanies set the scene for the wider Conference on Security and Cooperation in Europe (CSCE), which culminated in the agreements reached in Helsinki in 1975, and regarded by many as the nearest the powers had come to reaching a post-war peace settlement. The United States and Soviet Union also sought to improve their bilateral economic relations with agreements about trade and sharing of technology. More generally, they endorsed various sets of principles for the prevention of crises or for their management should they occur, and for the avoidance of nuclear war. Much of this was little more than rhetorical but reflected the improved atmosphere none the less (see Garthoff 1985; Bowker and Williams 1988).

This era of negotiation was initiated in the context of what was widely understood to be a diffusion of international power and some loosening of the existing two cold-war blocs. The image of an incipient multipolarity took hold and was popularized by President Richard Nixon in his formulation of a pentagonal balance in which the United States, Soviet Union, China, Japan, and western Europe were cast for the leading roles. Such an image was at best premature but fostered the impression of an era of rapid movement in which new opportunities were emerging for accommodation with former enemies at precisely the same time as new challenges from erstwhile allies were developing. It was in this sense that Nixon's geopolitical vision was an attempt 'unsuccessfully to extend traditional realist concepts to apply to the economic challenges posed by America's postwar allies' (Keohane and Nye 1977: 7).

In brief, the era of negotiation combined two main sets of dynamics: the first was a formalization of the relationship between the superpower adversaries and the second was a defensive monitoring of relations within the respective cold-war blocs. In the words of one analyst, *détente* was 'an effort to arrest developments which threatened to displace superpower dominance of the cold war system' (Crockatt 1995: 205), an effort in which the two superpowers had a shared interest and in which they might act as 'partners' even while continuing as adversaries (Bell 1971: ch. 4). The full import of this suggestion will be examined below.

If overall the watershed in security relations was cause for some limited optimism, changes in the international economy seemed much more negative and regressive. If there was volatility in both areas, this was welcome in unfreezing a security relationship which had been locked into dangerous confrontation but less so in disrupting the settled conditions which had produced the surge of economic growth enjoyed in the 1950s and 1960s:

The first half of the 1970s will probably come to be regarded as a watershed in the development of Western capitalist economies. Effectively the period marked the end of the 'super-growth' phase of the post-war period . . . Indeed, compared with the relatively placid and successful decades of the 1950s and 1960s, that of the 1970s was an extremely turbulent period, reminiscent in some respects of the inter-war years. (Aldcroft 1993: 195)

This new volatility, and associated fall in rates of growth, was significant in itself, but also for its creation of a more fractious political mood. In a sense, the growth of the previous two decades had created an illusory depoliticization of economic affairs whereas the clashes of interest which emerged in the 1970s brought the political disagreements into high relief. Above all, this growth had concealed the political costs incurred in maintaining a liberal and multilateral international economy (Walter 1991: 13). As the growth curve slackened, these political costs became more apparent. As regards the theme of this book, it might then be said that encouragement had been given to processes of globalization in a hitherto politically cost-free environment, but it remained to be seen, after 1970, whether this momentum would be sustained in the more adverse political context.

The international economy faced a number of sources of dislocation by the beginning of the 1970s—falling rates of growth, monetary and exchange rate instability, widespread inflation and unemployment, anxieties about a return to protectionism, and concerns about access to critical raw materials. Within the Organization for Economic Cooperation and Development (OECD) group, rates of growth fell back from an average 5 per cent per annum in the 1960s to 3.5 per cent in the 1970s (Aldcroft 1993: 196). Of course, by historical standards even this figure remained impressive: in the context of the time, however, the even higher rate had come to be regarded as the norm, rather than as the exception which it is now seen to be (Aldcroft 1993: 200). The onset of the twin domestic problems of inflation and unemployment created the spectre of a return to national controls to counteract these trends. Already, by the late 1960s, the GATT principle of non-discrimination was under strain and over the next decade there was widespread resort to non-tariff barriers, such as quotas and voluntary restraints (Keohane 1989*b*: 81–3). So gloomy was the economic outlook that it became fashionable to depict the last quarter of the twentieth century as the beginning of a generalized world economic crisis (see e.g. Cox 1987: 275; Hobsbawm 1994).

What was happening to the world economy generally was closely associated with, and to a significant degree influenced by, what was happening to the

American economy specifically. The relative standing of the US economy internationally was thought to be falling, inflation was regarded as an American export, and the stability of the world's monetary arrangements was eroded by fears about the value of the US dollar. The relative decline in the US share of world economic activity was perceptible, if understandable: it fell as a share of the aggregate GDP of the US, Germany, Britain, France, and Japan combined, from some two-thirds to one-half between 1960 and 1975 (Keohane 1989b: 85). Taken in isolation this might not have been troubling, but in conjunction with other problems it became a source of profound disquiet: in 1971, the US experienced its first balance-of-trade deficit of the century (Cohen 1993: 200); its overall balance-of-payments deficit reached US$29.7 billion in the same year (Buchan 1974: 121–2); American gold reserves had fallen from $26 billion in 1949 to $12.1 billion by 1971 (Buchan 1974: 73); and domestically, export industries and labour unions called for protection (Calleo 1987: 89; Shonfield 1976: 75). In August of that year, the United States lashed out at its own offspring, the liberal economy, when it imposed a 10 per cent import surcharge and terminated what had become the increasingly hypothetical gold-convertibility of the dollar. Revealingly, commentators pointed to the paradox that it was the United States which was leading the national rebellion against the constraints of international interdependence of which it was itself the principal post-war architect (Shonfield 1976: 61).

The disturbance caused by these events was experienced most fully within the international monetary system and it is from this period that historians date the collapse, or erosion, of Bretton Woods. Inflationary pressures increased in the United States in the late 1960s, intensified by the fiscal consequences of the Vietnam War. At the same time, holdings of vast amounts of dollars offshore inaugurated a volatile Eurodollar market which called into question the nominal value of the dollar (Nye 1990: 183–4). The fixed exchange rate system seemed to function merely as a transmission belt whereby American inflationary pressures were spread world-wide, and those countries which sought to impose tighter domestic financial controls contributed to speculation against the dollar (Aldcroft 1993: 205). In the end, the strains within the system became unsustainable and the pegged-rate system of the 1960s was progressively abandoned in favour of a variable-rate system by the mid-1970s, under cover of which many currencies were devalued, including the dollar itself. It is widely considered that the prodigious growth of private capital markets during this period helped to undermine the Bretton Woods system but also to soften the effects of the transition to a floating regime. Equally, many economists regard this development of capital markets—one of the principal motors and indicators of subsequent economic globalization—as itself a key turning point in the demise of the political determination of economic activity (Foreman-Peck 1995: 311).

To repeat the question, how if at all are these security and economic watersheds interconnected? One answer is that they were explicitly brought together in the substance of United States foreign policy. In the context of East–West relations, President Nixon and his Secretary of State, Henry Kissinger, applied the policy of linkage in which economic rewards were made conditional upon Soviet good behaviour in the security sphere. In the context of intra-Western relations, it is equally the case that the United States consciously drew a connection between security and economic agendas in a way which it had hitherto avoided. Indeed, in a sense, the symbolic significance of the period was the United States' abandonment of its own erstwhile self-denying ordinance whereby it had explicitly delinked the two domains: European and Japanese economic recalcitrance had been accepted by Washington as the price that had to be paid for the greater good of a secure balance of power (Shonfield 1976: 2; Garthoff 1985: 321; Calleo 1987: 16; Nye 1990: 90–3). Now, by raising the issue of alliance burden-sharing, the United States was serving notice of its unwillingness to continue to provide public security goods without a greater economic contribution from its allies. There is then the interesting parallel that the United States was using exchange rate flexibility, and economic levies upon its allies, to reattain for itself 'more scope for the autonomy of domestic policies' (Pinder 1983: 75), at the same time that the Nixon Doctrine and *détente* were trying to secure for the United States greater freedom of action in the geopolitical domain. The danger was that others might follow Washington's example, resulting in repetition of the 'beggar-my-neighbour' cycle of the 1930s.

Such linkages between economy and security may be dismissed as being merely tactical and the question can then be explored at a more profound level of interconnection. Was the return to 'unilateralism' by the United States in both security and economic affairs symptomatic of a deeper structural change in the international system as a whole which fostered an interplay between the two? There are various ways in which such a connection might then plausibly be analysed. It could be simply that the lessening of security tensions between East and West permitted a raising of economic agendas previously stifled: in the diminished concerns about security in the early 1970s, statesmen could afford to address economic problems.[1] But even more profound connections have been drawn. Hobsbawm links together the demise of the economic Golden Age with the tectonic shifts which have finally caused the cold-war political order to crumble and presents them as combined elements in a single global crisis (1994: 403). And yet there are problems in drawing together and reconciling the economic evidence for a final crisis of capitalism with what appeared to be the geopolitical evidence for the final triumph of capitalism in 1989 and this suggests that such all-embracing analytical schemes obscure as much as they clarify.

Short of such 'world crisis' imagery, is there a median position between this and the view that they were connected only by the temporary tactics of American foreign policy? The argument of this chapter is that both watersheds reflect important transitions in post-war conditions and both reveal the growing tensions that had been created within the Western economic system over the preceding two decades: *détente* in the political sphere was both a cause and a consequence of the disruption that afflicted the international economic system. As indicated, *détente* must then be understood to be as much about relations

---

[1] This is how Cohen (1993: 191) explains changes in the Japanese–American relationship.

within the Western bloc as about the antagonistic relationship between the two superpowers.

Before this argument is developed in detail, its relevance to the theme of this book needs to be established. How, in general terms, did this period relate to globalization and fragmentation? The answer is that it had ambivalent effects. On the side of globalization, it might be argued that *détente* encouraged the process in a number of ways. It did so by eroding one of the key fissures of the cold war, namely that between First and Second Worlds, and by permitting the very small beginnings of increased contact and trade between the two. This opening up of the East potentially set it on course, in the longer term, to be drawn into the currents of globalization that had thus far passed it by. It did so also by facilitating the free movement of peoples, on however small a relative scale, and thus by expanding the degree of social contact between East and West. And finally, the injection of the agenda of human rights into the Helsinki process once again encouraged notions of cosmopolitan values cutting across time and space, however much the centre of gravity of such human rights' conceptions remained firmly within the Western orbit. The very style and substance of Kissingerian policy—summits, linkage, new openings, the structure of peace, legitimate international orders— drew attention to the interacting totality of events and encouraged the impression of an age when 'diplomacy had indeed become truly global' (Litwak 1984: 79).

But events did not move in this direction alone. Litwak himself drew attention to the counterpoint, as expressed in the pluralism that was to be orchestrated through the Nixon Doctrine:

These pivotal, locally preponderant states were to be the recipients, as it were, of American devolution and become increasingly responsible for the promotion amd maintenance of regional stability. Paradoxically, the emergence of these new centers of different kinds of power resulted in a certain *fragmentation* of the international system as a whole. (Litwak 1984: 135)

This fragmentation expressed itself in a number of ways. To the extent that the cold war had imposed a single fault line of difference across the globe, it had been a powerful source of ideological uniformity and rigidity. This now began to dissipate and a hundred different flowers were permitted to bloom. Even United States foreign policy lost its apocalyptic vision. One of its foremost practitioners speaks of Nixon's foreign policy being a challenge to 'American exceptionalism', replacing it by a view of the world in which 'no clear-cut terminal point beckoned' (Kissinger 1995: 742). Strategically, the cold war had similarly constituted a point of compelling linkage, attaching global significance to any regional event: regional rivalries and balances of power—India versus Pakistan, Arabs versus Israel—had become functionally integrated with the global contest between the superpowers. Again, the weakening of the cold-war antagonism suggested the possibility of a greater disaggregation of political and strategic developments at the centre from those on the periphery: the sum no longer had a significance greater than its parts. 'Detente was marked,' it has been argued, 'by the attempt to separate or disentangle the different international tensions which are in periods of Cold War bound together by the conflict of east and west' (Halliday 1986: 10–11; see also Bowker and Williams 1988: 265–6). Although in practice *détente* failed to make this separation, it could be regarded as the logical extension of reduced antagonism at the centre. Moreover, the role played by actors like China, France, and not least by the United States itself, bore witness not only to an abstract pluralism in the international system but to the more tangible national-istic basis of foreign policy: national interests once again became discernible under the systemic overlay which had concealed them during the heights of the cold war.

Finally, the international system experienced what can only be described as a kind of functional fragmentation. As analysts struggled to discern the emerging balance of power in this more pluralistic world, they noted that it was made up of a number of seemingly disparate games played on distinct political, strategic, and economic boards, and that power was itself, in consequence, becoming more dif-fuse in its application: there was no single balance of power but multiple balances within separate issue areas, and possibly in various regional settings. It is in this respect that writers have noted that 'the fragmented structure of world politics among different issues has made power resources less fungible, that is, less trans-ferable from one issue to another' (Nye 1990: 189).

In summary, the political consequences of the easing of the cold war were mixed as far as globalization and fragmentation were concerned. While it might be thought that the reduced salience of the iron curtain amounted to the over-coming of the most potent source of fragmentation in the international system, the results were to be more ambivalent than such a confident assertion would lead us to believe. While the diminution of the cold war blurred the lines of this con-frontation, it also had the secondary effect of loosening cohesion within the sys-tem as a whole. Globalization was promoted to the extent that it provided selective opportunites for the Second World to opt into wider systemic activities, but fragmentation was also the result of the increased freedom for alliance mem-bers to opt out of their respective spheres. It is less than clear in which net direc-tion the balance moved. A similarly mixed verdict must be returned with regard to the upheavals within the international economic system: while on the one hand, there was the prospect of more effective integration of eastern Europe into parts of the world economy, this was counterbalanced by the fissures developing between the core members of the Western system itself.

Détente and the Western System

If the cold war manifested itself in two ways, as an antagonistic relationship between East and West and as the consolidation of a network of relations within the West, then likewise *détente* may be understood as having two dimensions, a relaxation of tension between East and West and an attempt to reach a new bar-gain within the Western bloc. Most of the historical accounts tend to focus upon the former of these but a full understanding of *détente* requires us to see the nexus between the two.

Détente did not represent a sharp break with the past in either sphere. It is thus misleading, as Bowker and Williams have pointed out, to think in terms of *détente* and cold war as being two distinct forms of relationship. Each is, in fact, a combination of elements of cooperation and conflict and within *détente* there is some shift of emphasis towards the former (Bowker and Williams 1988: 11; Garthoff 1985: 2). There had been earlier relaxations of this kind in 1953–5, 1959–60 and after the Cuban missile crisis, raising the question whether the shift from cold war to *détente* was simply a cyclical phenomenon, or whether there had been a linear development towards a more positive and broadly based *détente* across the entire post-war period (Stevenson 1985: 15).[2] Such a question is prompted by a focus upon East–West relations but demands a slightly different perspective to accommodate the West–West dimension as well. When the latter is incorporated into the concept of *détente*, we discover that while the issues which were to unsettle the Western system in the early 1970s were to continue to be of concern over the following two decades, only at this juncture, and again with the onset of the new cold war at the end of the decade, was there such a stark connection between the state of intra-bloc relations and the trajectory of superpower relations.

As soon as any notion of a radical discontinuity between cold war and *détente* is rejected, it becomes easier to see the East–West dimension of *détente* as a continuation of the cold war by other means. Kissinger's notion of a legitimate international order, which he believed had so successfully stabilized the post-Napoleonic world in 1815, would be instituted by giving the Soviet Union a stake in the existing *status quo*, thereby conscripting it as a guardian of the system, rather than leaving it on the outside as a revolutionary power bent on its overthrow. The expectation was that as the Soviet Union became 'more extensively engaged in an organic network of relations with the existing world order', it would have an interest in maintaining that order (Garthoff 1985: 1070). This clearly meant that the United States had not rejected containment. As with the adoption of the Nixon Doctrine, the emphasis was upon containment by means less costly to the United States:

Yet the objective of preventing Soviet expansion was not abandoned. Instead of accomplishing this through deterrence and military intervention, the United States would now encourage the Soviet Union to observe a policy of self-restraint, or what Stanley Hoffmann has termed 'self-containment'. The means had changed, but the ends remained what they had been. (Bowker and Williams 1988: 55)

In East–West terms, *détente* in the early 1970s was driven by a particular congruence of factors on each side. For the Soviet Union, the *détente* process promised recognition of status as a superpower equal and as co-director of the international system; it held out the prospect of some alleviation of pressure on a faltering economy and access for it to Western technology; given the sharp

---

[2] Stevenson (1985: 201) subscribes to the latter point of view, arguing that each attempt at *détente* 'has in fact left a legacy' on which the next could build.

deterioration in Sino-Soviet relations, it was a prudent measure of geopolitical reinsurance; and it would serve as a vehicle for legitimization of its position in eastern Europe. For the United States, as indicated, *détente* offered a less burdensome containment; this, in turn, seemed more urgent given the stresses experienced by the US economy; above all, Soviet acquiescence was necessary to allow America to extricate itself from Vietnam with any vestige of honour. Juxtaposing these various elements, Litwak presents *détente* as a coherent overall strategy for diminishing the communist challenge to the point where it could be restrained by the devolution of power to regional co-optees, via the Nixon Doctrine:

The central thesis of this study is that American post-Vietnam foreign policy was premised upon the belief that the establishment of a new relationship with the United States' Communist great-power rivals would create the favorable political atmosphere so as to facilitate the orderly devolution of American power to incipient regional powers. The resulting stability along the periphery would, in turn, feed back into the central balance and thereby sustain the momentum of *détente*. (Litwak 1984: 54)

That *détente* should ultimately fail is readily accountable within the foregoing framework. Clearly, each superpower had a different set of objectives in shifting the emphasis from conflict to cooperation and, eventually, these objectives proved incompatible: American policy required Soviet restraint whereas Soviet policy acted on the premise of a legitimized role as a world power (Bowker and Williams 1988: 79). These misconceptions revealed themselves in the course of Third World challenges to American interests throughtout the 1970s (Halliday 1986: 209–10). At the same time, *détente* became the victim of American domestic politics and the mood-swing away from post-Vietnam self-doubt and recrimination and towards a perceived need to reassert American leadership to prevent the precipitate erosion of Western interests.[3]

Such an account is persuasive in dealing with one aspect of *détente* and its decline, namely the relationship between the two superpowers. Its inadequacy lies in its failure to address the relationship between *détente* and the intra-systemic consolidation which has been identified as an equally important aspect of the cold war. To the extent that this dimension is recognized at all in the literature, it tends to be relegated simply to one of the factors predisposing the United States to seek a working accommodation with the Soviet Union: prospective disintegration within the Western bloc, and the emerging economic challenges from within it, dictated that the United States divert energy and resources from its confrontation with the East in order the more effectively to manage its relations with the West (Bowker and Williams 1988: 48–9). While this is indeed consistent with the present argument, the point goes beyond such claims. What is being suggested here is that the priority attached by the USA to maintenance of its core relations within its own bloc was not merely a *motivation* for *détente* but rather an integral part of it, just as it had been an integral part of the cold war: if *détente* sought a less costly form of rivalry with the Soviet Union then a reconfiguration of the Western

---

[3] Garthoff (1985: 13) traces the failure of *détente* to 'domestic political considerations in the United States as much as any other factor'.

system was a necessary means to that end. At the same time, the potential fragmentation within the Western system produced its own incentive for dampening the rivalry with the Soviet Union: this was necessary to prevent a spillover of uncontrolled conflict, anywhere in the world including the two spheres of influence, from drawing the superpowers into confrontation with each other (Stevenson 1985: 186–7), as President Sadat of Egypt had tried to do in launching his war with Israel in the Middle East in October 1973. In short, if the United States was prepared to negotiate over the terms of its confrontation with the East, it was likewise compelled to renegotiate over the terms of its cooperation with the West.

At this point, a problem emerges with the preceding line of argument. It has been asserted above that the onset of *détente* and the emergence of the new cold war demonstrate a peculiar conjunction between the dynamics of East–West relations and the dynamics of West–West relations. The problem lies in explaining why 'management' of the Western system should have been associated with relaxation in East–West relations in the former instance but with a return to cold-war policies in the latter. The tentative answer which will be offered is that the attempt to renegotiate the terms of the intra-Western contract in the early 1970s reinforced rather than quelled the centrifugal tendencies within it, since East–West *détente* gave allies more freedom of manœuvre (Bowker and Williams 1988: 25), and it was this which led finally to an attempted reassertion of American leadership within a cold-war contoured world by the end of the decade. To this extent, the second cold war, as far as West–West relations were concerned, was the necessary consequence of the failures to deal with bloc cohesion during the first phase of *détente*.

The connection between West–West and East–West relations is most readily acknowledged in discussions of the separate tracks of intra-European and superpower *détente*, in so far as the former was recognized as a potential threat to superpower interests. European initiatives towards the east had already encouraged NATO to adopt the Harmel Report in December 1967 in which continuing defence and containment was to be accompanied by contact and dialogue. The policy of *Ostpolitik* pursued by West Germany's chancellor Willy Brandt in 1969 gave great momentum to this intra-European dialogue (see Garton Ash 1994 for the background to these issues) . However, this created a dilemma for the United States, as indeed for the USSR, in that it was faced with the seeming choice of 'either a managed *détente* in which the United States played the central role or an unmanaged situation in which the Soviet Union . . . would be able to drive wedges between the members of NATO' (Bowker and Williams 1988: 48). Kissinger has admitted the early misgivings about Brandt's *Ostpolitik* felt by the Nixon administration, based on a fear that the two Germanies might come together on a 'nationalist, neutralist program', but maintains that Washington chose to support the policy because the 'alternative was riskier still' (Kissinger 1995: 735; see also Garthoff 1985: 109). The US endorsement of European *détente* and its policy of incorporating it within a wider superpower-driven process of East–West accommodation were, in that respect, a strategy both for improving Soviet–American relations and for containing intra-bloc initiatives within parameters which did not threaten vital superpower interests. This offers a good illustration of the more general comment that has been made elsewhere:

Broadly, then, the shifts within Eastern and Western blocs meant that East–West relations were subject to currents of West–West and East–East tension, inclining both superpowers to pursue *détente* with one eye firmly on their own friends. To put it another way, the success of superpower *détente* was heavily dependent upon containment of their respective alliance partners. (Crockatt 1995: 212)

The irony was that this solution simply created an additional problem for the superpowers elsewhere: having squeezed out the dent in one part of the ping-pong ball (Europe), it was a matter of some consternation to discover that it reappeared in a new position (the Third World). Moreover, this new indentation had particular qualities which exacerbated the problems of cohesion within the Western camp. Since many of the achievements of *détente* served to stabilize the European situation, a side-effect was to displace tension to elsewhere. This took the form of what appeared to be a new Soviet challenge in the Third World in the second half of the 1970s. For the Europeans, taking a more parochial point of view, this was a net benefit; but for the United States it meant coping with the Soviet Union in areas where its allies were prepared to lend Washington little support (Garthoff 1985: 1084), and over which they would periodically defect, as in the Middle East War in 1973. If *détente* in West–West terms was about a new distribution of intra-systemic burdens, it turned out to be palpably counterproductive as far as Washington was concerned. Kissinger's abortive Year of Europe initiative in 1973 compounded the damage that had already been done. In short, if Europe had, however reluctantly, acceded to the American programme for incorporation of the Third World into the liberal economic order, and this had been a fundamental ingredient in the original trans-Atlantic bargain, then this aspect of US–Japanese and US–European relations found itself under increasing stress as a result of superpower *détente* policies at the centre. Far from *détente* serving to restore cohesion to the Western system, it put pressure on its weakest link—the slender basis of Western commonality of interest in the Third World. In part, the reason for this was the European and Japanese perception that American Third World policies 'seemed to be serving a narrower definition of its own national interest, less identified with the welfare of its allies or the health of the global system in general' (Calleo 1987: 8). From Washington's perspective, this was simply cant disguising the allies' reluctance to take a fair share of the global burden. This failure, and the additional damage which it caused, ensured that the problems of Western cohesion were not then resolved and would have to be returned to at a later date.

These tensions were made all the more apparent as *détente* stalled and retreated in the second half of the decade. In most respects, the Europeans had gained more from the process than had the United States itself. Not surprisingly, when Washington shifted the emphasis away from negotiation and back to confrontation, its allies were reluctant to follow suit and clung tenaciously to their own *détente* with the East: an intra-European momentum had developed which the superpowers would find difficult to halt (Kennedy 1988: 402). When the United States in the late 1970s 'denounced *détente* and turned to a new cycle of rearmament' (Calleo 1987: 54–5), it then became inevitable that this change of direction would have a further disruptive effect upon intra-Western relations. By the time of the Soviet invasion of Afghanistan in December 1979, Europe's continuing commitment to *détente*, it has been suggested, ensured that 'the crisis in East–West relations' would also generate 'a crisis in Atlantic relations' (Bowker and Williams 1988: 2–3).

Such a perspective permits us to resolve one last remaining puzzle. If one half of *détente* was actually about a readjustment in intra-systemic relations, and if as part of that the Nixon Doctrine sought geopolitical devolution to regional 'champions', why was there not a more sustained American attempt to promote devolution to the core members of the Western system, namely Japan and western Europe? Many commentators have drawn attention to this seeming anomaly (Calleo 1987: 61; Litwak 1984: 136). Although there was assuredly an American quest for economic burden-sharing within the alliance, there was no serious attempt to move beyond this and encourage the emergence of indigenous defence structures in Europe or Japan which might serve as *substitutes* for American power. Kissinger had written a paper in 1968 which held that 'a more pluralistic world—especially in relationships with friends—is profoundly in our long-term interest' (quoted in Bowker and Williams 1988: 50). In practice, such an option was eschewed. The reason for this must surely be that ultimately *détente* did not represent the end of the cold war but simply an alternative strategy for its prosecution. This being so, the maintenance of intra-bloc cohesion was as important in the 1970s as it had been in the 1950s. Indeed, even the Soviet Union shared an interest in the West's cohesion as an essential legitimation of its own hegemonic position.

It remained the American calculation that this cohesion was itself dependent upon a tightly knit and integrated community of states within which the United States exercised considerable leadership and leverage. At the end of the day, even United States efforts to secure a rebalancing within its alliances were circumscribed by this enduring and vital concern. Thus were the two elements of *détente* intertwined, just as had been the twin elements of the cold war. If the resolution of East–West tensions could not move beyond the constraints of West–West relations, so the readjustment of West–West relations remained hostage to the needs of the persisting geopolitical rivalry with the Soviet Union.

US Decline and the End of Globalization?

It is implicit in much of the foregoing discussion that, if processes of globalization had been heavily dependent upon the political framework created by American power, and upon the intra-systemic networks of the cold-war period, then we might expect a decline of the cold war and of American leadership to be associated with a reversal of globalizing trends. Are such assumptions borne out by the historical evidence?

The strongest assertions of this style of argument are those associated with hegemonic stability theory. As already suggested, these posit a direct link between the power of a hegemon, the elaboration of a political framework which is conducive to a certain style of economic activity, and the encouragement of certain forms of economic organization. In the particular application of this theory to American power, it is contended that American post-war dominance created an economic space (characterized by openness and multilateralism) which was conducive to the formation of transnational modes of production and to the mobility of capital. The most powerful indicators of economic globalization are thereby related back to the specific effects of American power and the policies which it has pursued: geopolitically, globalization has been an almost unintended side-effect of the onset of the cold war and of America's need to foster an integrated system on its 'side' of the iron curtain. Put in these terms, the erosion of the cold war, disintegration within the Western bloc and, above all, the decline of American hegemony must, in combination, be thought likely to be inimical to the further progress of globalization.

The central idea of the theory, as Andrew Walter explains it, is simply the adaptation of Adam Smith's insight to the international context. By analogy with the role of government in a national system, which provides the minimum infrastructural and regulatory mechanisms for economic activity, so hegemony in the international system is the functional substitute for government and the 'means by which the minimal political preconditions of an open world economic order could be established and maintained' (Walter 1991: 22).

There are two ways in which the analysis of globalization can be related to this type of discussion. First, and more directly, analysis within such a theory attaches significance to the decline of American power for the reason stated. American decline has been interpreted by some as the specific, and inevitable, consequence of the costs of maintaining this hegemony (Cox 1987: 277), or more broadly, and historically, as symptomatic of imperial overstretch, the 'fact that the sum total of the United States global interests and obligations is nowadays far larger than the country's power to defend them all simultaneously' (Kennedy 1988: 515). Either way, the impact is the same: according to the theory, 'the decline of hegemonic structures of power can be expected to presage a decline in the strength of corresponding international economic regimes' (Keohane 1989*b*: 74–5).

Less directly, the issue becomes caught up in wider reflections upon the changing nature of international power wrought by the development of interdependence (Keohane and Nye 1977). Within such debates, it is argued that military power is less usable and that many problems are no longer susceptible to the exercise of this kind of power (Buchan 1974: 128). In these terms, the very meaning of hegemonic power is open to serious challenge. Can any state again play this role, whatever the historical precedents? If this be so, what is happening is less the erosion of American power *per se* and more the changing nature of power itself as a result of which the very notion of a hegemonic stabilizer becomes increasingly suspect:

Some trends in world politics suggest that it will be more difficult in the future for *any* great power to control the political environment and to achieve what it wants from others. The problem for the United States will be less the rising challenge of another major power than a general diffusion of power. (Nye 1990: 175)

This, in turn, is part of a more general disagreement about the persuasiveness of the evidence for American decline in the first place. Paul Kennedy's *The Rise and Fall of the Great Powers* captured a public mood in the United States in the late 1980s which readily accepted the proposition that American power had declined, both relatively and absolutely, since the Golden Age of the immediate post-war period, but these contentions have not been allowed to go unchallenged. While this debate is tangential to the present discussion, the implications of the argument are not. Joseph S. Nye has emphasized the confusions introduced into the discussion by the anomalous Second World War factor which had created an unnatural situation of American economic preponderance, given the weakness and incapacity of its potential competitors. By 1970, the artificial precedence of the American post-war economy had worked its way through the system and a more natural equilibrium was reached in which America's share of world GDP returned to its pre-war norm of some 23–5 per cent, a share that has been essentially maintained since. From this perspective, there has not been secular decline but simply a return to normalcy after the egregious circumstances of 1945 and their aftermath (Nye 1990: introduction). Moreover, looked at in this light, the period of sharpest US 'decline' was that between 1950 and 1973, the period typically regarded as that of unquestioned hegemony (Nye 1990: 73). Of course, while Nye's claim in this regard might be thought to counter perceptions of decline in the late 1980s, it does little to detract from the notion of American decline by 1971, thereby precipitating a destabilization of the economic and political orders in the early 1970s. Even here, however, Nye insists that the evidence of American weakness is far from convincing. Indeed, on the contrary, American behaviour in 1971 tends to support the opposite case in that the United States was sufficiently dominant to act unilaterally in overthrowing the rules of the international monetary game. 'If hegemonic economic behaviour is the ability to change the rules of the international game,' Nye reminds us, 'then 1971 did not mark the end of US economic hegemony' (1990: 94). The United States was still able to act unilaterally in this way because, relatively speaking, the US remained cushioned from world economic conditions in that its own domestic market continued to be paramount for its economic well-being (Britton 1983: 119).

More pertinently, there is also a point of view which holds that, whatever America's role in first creating the conditions favourable for a transnational world economy, it thereafter developed sufficient momentum of its own to be able to survive without American leadership (Keohane 1984). Indeed, according to one interpretation, the political values and market economy beliefs which were once injected by the United States are now sustained, hegemonially, by the system itself. Such a Gramscian perspective is presented by Gill and Law:

The centrality of the United States and the regimes it has created can be seen as facilitating an emerging transnational historic bloc, in which the leadership of the more dynamic transnational corporations has come increasingly to the fore. These developments are associated with the growing mobility of capital, the revival and spread of market forces, and the ideological hegemony of associated liberal 'frameworks of thought' . . .

In consequence, fears that a decline in American dominance will lead to a breakdown in the liberal international economic order are largely misplaced. (Gill and Law 1988: 357–8)

Thus interpreted, transnationalism continued to be fostered by the 'invisible hand' of American power long after 1970. At this point, two divergent lines of argument meet each other on common ground. Gill and Law's point is that American power is now so entrenched in forms of structural power that the economic space for transnationalism is safeguarded, even without overt American political leadership. A second line of argument, meanwhile, locates the economic changes of the 1970s in the separate development of intense international mobility of capital: it thereby suggests that there are other, and better, explanations for the disruption of the Bretton Woods system, and for the disappearance of the stable economic conditions of the 1950s and 1960s, apart from the demise of American leadership. While analytically separate, both of these positions share some common ground in emphasizing the role of other factors, either in sustaining the liberal economic order without direct American leadership, in the first case, or in explaining the degree of destabilization which has occurred to it, in the second. Moreover, the substance of the explanation is similar in both cases. The forces that now serve as a functional substitute for American power are the very ones that helped overturn the Bretton Woods system in the first place, rather than American decline: both, in related ways, give a diminished role to ostensible American power, either in sustaining a liberal framework or in accounting for the threats to it, and emphasize instead the role of dynamic economic forces. Even more critically, both modes of analysis allow us to resolve the apparent paradox that significant measures of economic globalization have continued apace since 1970, regardless of the seemingly less supportive condition of interstate relations.

What the evidence suggests is that a transnational economic order has been sustained since 1970—despite the appearance of American decline—because the economic forces released during the cold-war period have now themselves become a kind of self-reinforcing structural political condition. The idea that politics and economics have gone their separate ways is, in this respect, superficial. This is a complex argument and is best presented in logical stages.

To be sure, the demise of the Bretton Woods system, followed quickly by other damaging set-backs to Western economies, generated more dismal economic prognoses and fears of a return to 1930s-style protectionism. Typically, there were voluble demands for protection from within the United States itself. There is no denying that the liberal GATT regime found itself under pressure in the face of various neo-mercantilist practices (Cox 1987: 303). And yet the appearances and the perceptions of the death of the open economic order belied much of the economic reality. 'Public mood shifted more than power resources' notes Nye, drawing attention to the basic continuities in levels of economic interdependence (1990: 176).

Moreover, neo-mercantilism did not lead to less trade (Cox 1987: 303). If one of the fears was that the political framework after 1971 would be less supportive of a liberal trading order, then the actual evidence contradicted the perception. By the early 1970s, the volume of international trade had almost doubled compared with the level of 1960 (Shonfield 1976: 105–6). Analysts have spoken of the 'remarkable growth of trade interdependence in the 1970s' and note that, even in the case of the United States, exports as a percentage of GDP increased from 5.4 per cent to 9.8 per cent over the decade, while in the case of the EC the percentage rose from 10.6 per cent to 12.7 per cent (Pinder 1983: 76). Much of this performance was sustained in the 1980s. Nye's figures document that foreign trade doubled its share in the US economy over the 1970s and 1980s (1990: 183). Admittedly, much of this increase was in trade *within* the industrialized West, giving it the appearance of an 'enclave inside the world system' (Shonfield 1976: 102–3). But even in the case of the developing countries, exports of manufactured goods had, by the end of the 1970s, exceeded for the first time their exports of raw materials (Dicken 1992: 27). There is at least enough evidence in all of this to cast doubt upon any simple causal link between a purported decline of American power and any weakening in the international trade in goods.

The evidence about the international mobility of capital is even more compelling. Rather than the 1970s representing a watershed in which liberal financial arrangements collapsed with American power, Walter points to the *continuity* in the international monetary system since the 1950s and, in particular, to the dramatic growth in private capital markets since the 1970s (1991: 190). This leads him to question the significance of the passing of American hegemony as expounded by hegemonic stability theory:

Although it suggests that American decline has resulted in increasing mercantilism and the erosion of the postwar 'liberal regimes', in fact the recent evolution of international money and finance has been decidedly in the direction of *liberalisation*: increasing freedom of capital flows, financial deregulation in the major countries and an unprecedented degree of financial market integration between them. (Walter 1991: 196)

For Walter, this suggests not only that the putative effects of American decline are less significant than supposed, but also that capital liberalization is a more likely cause of international monetary instability than is the end of American hegemony. Others note that, whatever the rhetoric, the experience of the 1970s revealed that any return to national economic management was itself now constrained by the very transnationalism that had been created, and which was to prove difficult to overturn. To an extent, the greater equalization between the United States and its economic partners made this interdependence more politically acceptable than hitherto in places like western Europe (Pinder 1983: 76, 73–4).

This is not to deny that there was less stability in the international economy than during its post-war Golden Age. However, if these arguments are accepted, they suggest that the explanation for this is to be found in factors other than America's fall from economic and political grace. There are other explanations for that instability and, more importantly for the present argument, these very forces help explain why economic trends did not slavishly follow the movements in international politics in the 1970s.

Those who account for the increased instability in international economic regimes in the 1970s for reasons other than American decline tend to do so by some combination of the following three factors: the general development of economic interdependence; the specific effects of private capital movements; and the tensions generated between the former two and the domestic political pressures to follow more autonomous national economic policies.

The first of these has already been discussed. The view became popularized in the 1970s that the consequence of interdependence was diminished governmental control. If hitherto there had been a pervasive and optimistic liberal belief that interdependence bred cooperation and harmony, it now became apparent that it could equally be a source of instability in that it unleashed activities that could not be regulated by national governments (Buchan 1974: 121). In the Nye version, so much was this the case that proponents of American decline had seriously mistaken the generalized effects of interdependence for a specific weakening of American power: not only could the United States no longer guarantee stability but no government could.

Secondly, much of the discussion focused upon the impact of the growth of private capital as a transnational source of instability. Andrew Shonfield was insistent that the 'international market in short-term capital made a spectacular comeback during the 1960s', having played a relatively minor role since the late 1920s (1976: 110). This had been stimulated by the growth of the Eurodollar market from the 1960s and was given a further boost in the 1970s by the injection of recycled petrodollars into the Western financial system after the 1973 hike in oil prices. This provided a source of prodigious international lending over the succeeding decade (Britton 1983: 106). So important was this development that some have detected in it the real beginnings of an integrated capital market that might be described as globalized: 'The capital markets of Europe and America have been so closely integrated that it no longer seems right to think of a plurality of related markets in different countries. What we observe now is better described as a single international market for capital' (Britton 1983: 105).

Thirdly, there is the factor of domestic resistance to this growing interdependence, a widening incongruity between the economic realities and the political imperatives of the period. This mixture acted as a potent source of instability as governments, including that of the United States, sought to exercise autonomous control over their economic destinies. Indeed, the United States overthrow of the fixed-rate exchange regime was nothing if not an act of such political unilateralism, intended to give it greater freedom of domestic economic action. In part, it was a response to demands for protectionism which were emerging internally, rather than to international currents. 'Protectionism,' Keohane noted, 'is largely a grass-roots phenomenon' (1989*b*: 92). In short, what eventually placed such strain on the Bretton Woods system was that while its regulatory mechanisms sat comfortably with the national welfare state, there was a more overt conflict between national control and complex interdependence in the 1970s, given the freedom with which capital markets could now undermine national economic policies. If this tension was experienced throughout the Western industrialized world, it was, as Walter observes, 'felt most acutely in the US itself' (Walter 1991: 242–3).

So what was cause and what was effect in this complex circularity? Analytically, no clear-cut answer can be given as changes in the international distribution of power, in the technicalities of economic and financial organization, and in domestic political balances interacted with each other in ways that were both cross-cutting and mutually reinforcing. The ambivalence is neatly captured in the mixed verdicts returned about the role of American power which serve as a barometer of these wider issues. To some, the expansion of an internationalized capital market was itself the effect of diminished American power. It was 'an effect of weakening hegemony' and a response to the policy vacuum left in its wake. In the absence of an agreed post-Bretton Woods regulatory framework, private capital found its own natural levels (Cox 1987: 302). To others, like Walter, the causal sequence is seemingly reversed in that burgeoning capital mobility is presented as the cause of the demise of the old regulatory system. To the structuralists, American power has not declined but has simply found expression in less overt, and often economic, forms. To yet others again, the theorists of complex interdependence, American power is as much victim as architect of uncontrollable economic forces. But these interpretive differences are never as sharp as they appear at first glance. Walter completes the vicious circularity:

Rather than American decline, international monetary disorder can be attributed more fundamentally to the ongoing process of domestic and international financial liberalisation, *a process in which the US has played a crucial role.* (Walter 1991: 4, emphasis added)

On this reckoning, if there was a strange death of liberal America, it was as much an act of suicide as of homicide by non-governmental economic agents.

Détente and the Third World

The period of *détente* was seemingly auspicious for the Third World in allowing it to make its demands for a revision of the prevailing international economic order. Numerically, it was predominant in most international forums, its economic muscle was about to be flexed by OPEC, and there was widespread optimism that a New International Economic Order (NIEO) might be generated. The very quiescence of the cold war was itself suggestive that other issues might find a place on the international agenda. All things considered, the early 1970s represented 'a unique window of opportunity for the Third World' (Krasner 1985: 11). And yet, if Halliday's account is accepted, it was precisely in the area of the Third World that superpower relations were to slide back into confrontation: a wave of revolutionary change in the Third World precipitated the new US containment policy introduced towards the end of President Carter's term of office and implemented vigorously under its successor Reagan administration (Halliday 1989: 34–5).

In terms of political globalization, the 1970s witnessed a short flowering of awareness of a new set of 'global' political issues. The efforts of the Third World in the 1960s to promote development through the United Nations Conference on Trade and Development (UNCTAD) were now joined by the emerging concerns about global population, scarcity of resources, and widening North–South gaps. This awareness was to be short-lived, at least as far as substantial and serious international political dialogue was concerned. It was followed by a return to a more conventional security agenda, as well as by the onset of widespread Western disillusionment with, and disengagement from, those very international organizations in which the new agenda had been briefly promoted.[4] The reason for this stand-off was patently, as Stephen Krasner's account demonstrates, that Third World demands were not confined to economic and development issues but went to the heart of the very international political order. What the Third World demanded was a shift in the international balance of political power, reflected in new regimes such as the NIEO, and it was this that the West collectively refused to countenance. The Third World wanted 'power and control as much as wealth' and its agenda was 'fundamentally political' (Krasner 1985: 3, 27). It is hardly to be wondered at that this generated a new confrontational attitude between the haves and have-nots. If James Mayall is correct in his assessment that the long campaign for the NIEO was largely 'the continuation of anti-colonial nationalism by other means' (1990: 49), it is hardly surprising that the West should have chosen to respond in kind and that any embryonic global consensus on the new agenda should have proved abortive.

For all the high hopes of the early 1970s, the sad irony was to be that further Third World integration into the world economic system was to be postponed until the 1980s and onwards, and was to be the direct consequence of Third World *weakness*, not of *strength*. Its integration was to occur, not on its own terms, but on those set by the West and its panoply of international financial institutions. Far from being an expression of the autonomy of the Third World, in which state control and national development were the top priorities, the terms of engagement denoted the final capitulation of the Third World's struggle for separate national development in the face of a more competitive, and importunate, international economic system. Instead of the NIEO symbolizing the new political order, the old political order managed to thwart the NIEO.

---

[4] Cox (1996*a*: 498), notes the cleavage between the continuing US support for economic multilateralism and its disillusionment with political multilateralism, especially the UN General Assembly.

Nor should this outcome have been a surprise. As already noted, the emphasis on national sovereignty and national autarchy in Third World political and economic practice was born out of inherent weakness. The very acceptance by the international community of these states, lacking as they did many of the resources and appurtenances of genuine statehood, was a 'courtesy' granted to 'pseudo-states or quasi-states' (Bull and Watson 1984: 430; the argument was later developed at length in Jackson 1990). This weakness undermined effective, and concerted, international action on their part. It also ensured that both between North and South, and within the South itself, processes of fragmentation would be as salient as any superficial globalization (Halliday 1989: 1–2).

The disempowerment of the Third World, and its own loss of internal cohesion, culminated in doubts as to whether the Third World continued as a meaningful entity at all. The oil shocks of the 1970s further fragmented the developing world into the oil producers, who benefited, and the non-oil producers, who suffered most. In any case, some developing countries and particularly those in East Asia, were making their own dash for growth and seemed scarcely to fit the criteria of a uniform developing world. As the cold war faltered, the Non-Aligned Movement lost direction, and this had been one of the most important points of political identity that had held disparate countries within some kind of common ideological bond (these tensions are described in Halliday 1989: 21–2). In one famous obituary, the Third World was said to be 'disappearing' and its 'leading protagonists either dead, defeated or satisfied to settle simply for national power' (Harris 1986: 200).[5] Both politically and economically, the world had become too complex, and variegated, for such simplistic categories as that of the Third World to retain their hold.

From Negotiation back to Confrontation

If the rhetoric of a return to national economic management was more persuasive than the record of its achievement during the 1970s and 1980s, might the same be said about the politico-strategic sphere during this same period? Was a return to cold-war confrontation more rhetorical than real, more a matter of atmospherics than of substance? Historians continue to debate the reasons for the downturn in East–West relations in the late 1970s, as well as the degree of its severity. Was it really a reversion to cold war, a second cold war as Fred Halliday has claimed? Again, this issue will be reviewed with the sole objective of shedding light on the connection between the state of East–West relations and the state of West–West relations.

Hobsbawm, for one, seems largely persuaded that the superpower confrontations of the Reagan period were more rhetorical than real, the product of a kind of US psychosis resulting from the 'traumas of defeat, impotence and public

[5] The argument is implicitly rejected in the defence of the category of the Third World found in Thomas (1987: 1–4).

ignominy which had lacerated the US political establishment in the 1970s'. Thus seen, he feels entitled to dismiss the 'bizarre' American behaviour as little more than an externalized 'therapy' (Hobsbawm 1994: 244, 247). And yet elsewhere, he tantalizingly locates the second cold war in the context of major change within, and crisis of, the world economy, although he does not commit himself to more than the suggestion that the one 'coincided' with the other (Hobsbawm 1994: 244).

Such validity as there is in speaking of a second cold war derives from the context of structural continuity in which it took place. Thus although the balance between cooperation and conflict has shifted repeatedly across the post-war period, these shifts have taken place within the structure of a divided international system characterized by rivalry and based on the unusual balance of power which emerged from the Second World War. In these terms, it is appropriate to distinguish between the *détente* of the 1970s and the 'genuine' end of the cold war in the 1990s, just as it is legitimate to characterize the retreat into ideological polemics, and nuclear recidivism of the early 1980s, as a return to cold war (Crockatt 1995: 6).

To say this is not to deny differences between the circumstances of the late 1940s and early 1980s, as Halliday, the foremost proponent of the 'second cold war' thesis, is happy to concede. Amongst these, he notes that while the first cold war took the form of a generalized struggle against communism, the second was quite specifically fought against Soviet power. He also accepts that, whereas there was very little direct political contact between East and West in the former, various negotiations, including some over arms control, persisted throughout the deterioration of relations in the 1980s. But whereas others conclude from these differences that there was no second round of the cold war, properly called, Halliday is adamant that these differences can be accounted for simply by the shift in the balance of power. Negotiations continued in the 1980s because they had to, whereas in the 1940s 'the USSR was too weak to negotiate; the USA too strong to need to' (Halliday 1986: 20).

These debates may seem semantic. Halliday assuredly does not set enough store by the changes of context that had occurred by the 1980s, including the vast network of contacts between East and West, as well as mutual expectations about each other's behaviour based on several decades of experience. These changes marked the 1980s off from the 1940s, and arguably lent the former greater assurance of stability. But he is surely correct to insist on the potentially heightened levels of disaster that flowed from the vast nuclear armouries in place by this stage: the risks of hot war may have been reduced but the costs of mishap had been magnified beyond all sensible calculation. Be that as it may, the point of significance for this discussion is that the terminology of second cold war is appropriate because, just as with its predecessor, this draws our attention not to the inter-systemic competition alone, but also to the intra-systemic developments which accompanied it. It is to this feature that we must finally turn.

It was argued above that the failed attempt to renegotiate the basis of intra-Western cooperation in the early 1970s—riven as it was by economic differences, by diverging interests in *détente,* and by increasingly vocal disagreements about Third-World affairs—left a residual problem of bloc cohesion for the latter part of the decade. In some respects, it would have to be said that centrifugal tendencies had been intensified, rather than reduced, certainly within the Atlantic alliance. The United States felt that it had been deserted by its allies on a range of global issues, Vietnam and the Middle East foremost amongst these. At the same time, the European allies increasingly questioned the efficacy of the American nuclear guarantee in a setting of superpower nuclear parity which SALT had seemingly ratified, while remaining largely dependent on that American military protection. The NATO decision of 1979 to deploy a new generation of American intermediate-range nuclear weapons to European bases drew attention to these misgivings and sought to 'recouple' the American deterrent to European security. On their side, the allies had agreed in 1977 to increase their financial contributions through NATO to their own conventional defence. David Calleo usefully sums up the fissures left as a legacy by the *détente* period:

Failure to achieve devolution in Europe during the superpower détente of the 1970s had one particularly unfortunate consequence. It encouraged European détente policies that, although they had quite different goals from those of the Americans, counted on an indefinite continuation of American military protection . . . The United States was thus left with the task of protecting a Europe whose geopolitical interests were growing ever more divergent from its own. (Calleo 1987: 61)

The onset of another severe recession at the end of the decade did nothing to alleviate this situation.

How then does the revival of the cold war relate to these problems? It is tempting to slide into the easy reply that the exacerbation of superpower relations was but a means to bringing recalcitrant allies to heel: the icy blast of cold war, and threats of Soviet nuclear intimidation, would soon convince wayward associates of the practical limits of Western pluralism and ensure that divisive economic and political questions were subordinated to the more pressing agenda of geostrategic competition. Halliday comes close to saying as much:

The USA and the USSR sought to accompany the heightened level of confrontation with each other by greater controls on dissent within their own ranks . . . The reassertion of internal unity and hegemony was, however, but a concomitant of the re-establishment of a new international unity, with in this case the reassertion by Washington of US hegemony as forcefully as circumstances allowed. This reinforcement of the US position was most evident in military matters . . . But it was also extended to encompass inter-capitalist economic policy. (Halliday 1986: 16–17)

Halliday presents this tightening of the US grip on its bloc as part of the necessary 'mobilization' for the new cold war. Of course, this runs perilously close to the conspiracy theory that the cold war was no more than a superpower invention designed for the sole purpose of keeping allies in line. The argument here is somewhat different: the second cold war was not *about* intra-systemic cohesion, in the sense that a return to East–West confrontation was a mere pretext for this objective. None the less, just as in the case of the original phase of the cold war, any recrudescence of inter-systemic conflict was bound to have an effect on relations within each system *since that was part of what the cold war was*: a change in one half of the cold war could not but impinge on the other. In any event, if the second cold war was *intended* to remove intra-bloc dissension, on economic and other matters, it was singularly counter-productive. Divisions between Washington and its allies over such matters as economic sanctions against the Soviet Union, and whether or not to proceed with a gas pipeline project from the USSR to western Europe, became deeper than ever. To that extent, the revival of the cold war emphasized, rather than diminished, the disparities of interest within the Western bloc.

The second cold war was too short-lived to have had any lasting impact, one way or the other, on the process of globalization. It was soon overtaken by dramatic changes in the Soviet leadership, breakthroughs in arms control with the signing of the Intermediate Nuclear Forces (INF) Treaty in December 1987, and new political thinking within the USSR. Mikhail Gorbachev was fêted in the West and the recent spat in superpower relations rapidly receded into the shadows of history. In turn, this new *détente* was overwhelmed by the very forces which it itself had unleashed. The old order was swept away in the Soviet Union and eastern Europe. At this point, *détente* gave way to the collapse of the cold-war structure altogether. Whether this would inaugurate the final apotheosis of globalization—with the obliteration of the cold-war lines of division, and the incorporation of the entire globe in a single world capitalist system—or whether it would usher in a new era of fragmentation—with the removal of the geopolitical constraints of the cold war—remained to be seen. In the event, it was to do both.

8

BEYOND THE COLD WAR, 1990–2000

There are two broad perspectives which might be adopted in an attempt to understand the significance of the end of the cold war. The first is to regard it as the central factor in unleashing a new historical period predominantly characterized by fragmentation. In turn, the reasons for it having done so are apparently twofold: first, the end of the cold war signified the beginning of the end of the systemic coherence which lay at the core of the cold war and, by definition, resulted in the dissipation of intra-systemic integration (Wyatt-Walter 1995: 92); secondly, the cold war acted as a structural control on pre-existing ethnic and sub-national aspirations and these have now, no longer suppressed, burst to the foreground. Cumulatively, observers felt that since 'the cold war was a stable system, they could envision only instability resulting from its end' (Crockatt 1995: 372). The other perspective is that the end of the cold war remains essentially irrelevant to the processes of globalization, particularly in its economic incarnation. Economic globalization, it is claimed, continues apace, leading a life of its own now radically divorced from the international political framework which first nurtured it. In turn, these issues are tangled up with deep-seated disagreements as to whether the cold-war period was the cause of international integration or whether this integration is a symptom of other, and deeper, changes in international relations.

It seems self-evident that the end of the cold war wrought dramatic changes in the visible landscape of international relations: prominent amongst these were the demise of the Soviet Union, collapse of the Warsaw Pact, the unification of Germany, and the removal of the constraining effects of superpower bloc leadership. The search has since been underway to identify the new axes of conflict that will replace that between East and West. The key issue for the historian of the twentieth century, however, is how these short-term consequences of the end of the cold war relate to longer-term trends in international relations: even if the post-cold war order represents a 'fundamental transformation' and is a change 'of kind', it may still be the case that these transformations had roots in the period before the cold war's end (Cerny 1993: 27). In particular, this poses the question: were some of the deeper security patterns that became established during the cold war a creation of the cold war itself (and doomed to disappear with its passing) (see e.g. Mastny 1994: 55–6), or were they autonomous of the cold war and a reflection of more general, and ongoing, processes of change in international rela-

tions (see e.g. Alder and Crawford 1991: 141)? Thus it has been claimed that
'many of the subnational and transnational material and ideational forces that
were exploited by the Cold War superpowers . . . antedated the Cold War and are
flourishing in its aftermath' (Brown 1994: 130). If we regard the cold war, not as
a single event but as a series of ongoing developments, we can reach a nuanced
judgement as to how its ending fits into the wider story of the twentieth century:
the objective then is to regard the passing of the cold war, not as the termination
of a unique and anomalous phase of history, but as part of a continuing interplay
between the forces of globalization and fragmentation. Thus viewed, the most
likely outcome is not a relapse to a pre-1939 world but a rebalancing, if in uncertain proportions, of both these trends.

The debate about the significance of the end of the cold war may serve, for purposes of introduction, to delineate this wider historical issue and to demonstrate
how this raises vital questions about the future. What has changed with the end
of the cold war? The question has been answered in a number of different ways,
ranging from the judgement that it is 'merely a new form of the existing order', to
that of 'a wholly new order' which is marked by 'the diminished competence of
states, the globalization of national economies' and the 'fragmentation of societies' (Rosenau and Czempiel 1992: 23).

Within one strand of analysis, the main impact of the cold war's end is upon
the interstate distribution of power and, in particular, upon the structure of the
international system. From this point of view, it brought to an end the bipolar distribution, although imprecision reigns as to what has taken its place. The mixed
verdict ranges from the hybrid, a 'configuration so odd' that it cannot be defined
(Jervis 1991/2: 41), to one in which 'bipolarity endures, but in an altered state'
(Waltz 1993: 52), to multipolarity (Mearsheimer 1990), and to unipolarity (Layne
1993: 5). Whatever the emerging distribution, it is within such power-political
terms that the eclipse of the cold war should be understood.

From a second perspective, the cold war was characterized by an increasingly
dominant liberal international economy in dynamic interaction with its rival.
This was predicated upon the expanding group of democratic capitalist states,
wedded to open international economic principles. In turn, this configuration is
believed to have fostered an association between domestic structures of democracy and international peace and stability. In close proximity to this argument are
subsidiary claims of the growing obsolescence of war as an instrument of national
policy, and of the greater opportunities for international cooperation created by
the pervasive interdependence of the second half of the century (see e.g. Buzan
1994: 96). The key historical question, however, is whether these processes are
causally autonomous of the cold war, and therefore independently capable of sur-
viving its end, or whether they are in some sense an artifact of cold-war international policies and doomed to decline with the passing of its beneficent
conditions.

Thirdly, one might draw attention to a historical materialist, or world system,
depiction of the cold war. Taking as its point of departure the gradual evolution
of the capitalist mode of production, and its distinctive forms of exchange

relations, this would analyse the cold war in terms of social and economic formations. Accordingly, Halliday views its end as the victory of one social system over
another: 'if pop music and tee-shirts are the gunboats of the late twentieth century,' he remarks, 'there is an underlying continuity in the multi-layered and
aggressive drive of capitalism to destroy all rival socio-economic systems'
(Halliday 1993: 31). This might imply a resurgence of American power as the
leading state within the victorious capitalist system. And yet to a cognate world
system theorist, the significance of the end of the cold war appears to be quite different: 'The Cold war was the Pax Americana', Wallerstein declaims. 'The Cold
War is over,' and so he concludes syllogistically 'thus the Pax Americana has now
ended' (1991: 2).

From yet another, and fourth, perspective, the end of the cold war coincides
with salient trends in the development of a global society. International relations
cannot now be understood as the autonomous realm of interstate security relations, nor as the passive domain of benign spillover effects from the international
economy, nor yet as the mere epiphenomena of an economic substructure.
Instead, multi-dimensional social relations are changing both the context, and
the substance, of the 'international', which itself becomes an increasingly problematic category. The preferred framework of analysis becomes instead 'global
society' or 'global civil society' (Shaw 1994*a*, 1994*b*; Cerny 1993; Lipschutz 1992).

There remains, even across such disparate accounts, considerable consensus
that future world politics will be shaped by the contradictory, but interrelated,
forces of globalization and fragmentation. The first trend emphasizes the expansion of integrated functional activities—particularly in the economy, communications, and aspects of socialization—towards a genuinely global system. The
second trend, and at least in part as a reaction to the other, reasserts claims to
national and ethnic identities, individual cultures, regional trading blocs, and
smaller forms of political association. There is a surprisingly wide recognition of
the existence of these integrative and disintegrative forces: transnationalism versus ethno-nationalism; political federalism and intergovernmentalism versus
separatism; cosmopolitan culture versus multi-faceted individual identities; and
modernism versus its resisters.

It is not simply that an understanding of these forces is essential for any general
interpretation of the dynamics of the future international system but, more
specifically, it helps place the significance of the end of the cold-war order in historical perspective. Whatever its polarizing effects in inter-bloc terms, it is
assuredly the case, as argued above, that the cold war contributed to globalizing
and integrative tendencies: the liberal world economy was unquestionably
enhanced as an adjunct of American cold-war strategy and most historians
accept, for example, that European integration was at least partly the creation of
the cold war. The key question at century's end is what effect the end of the cold
war will have on these tendencies, and some authors incline to the pessimistic
view that the second half of the twentieth century will reveal itself as the anomalous period during which nuclear-armed bipolarity, the cold war, and the effects
of two World Wars conspired to produce an exceptional phase of international

integration: with the erosion of these special contextual conditions, the disintegrative forces of the first half of the century will reassert themselves: 'The next decades in a Europe without the superpowers,' Mearsheimer controversially suggested, 'would probably not be as violent as the first 45 years of this century, but would probably be substantially more prone to violence than the past 45 years' (1990: 6). On this view, the period 1945–89 will, in retrospect, be seen as an oasis of stability sandwiched between the instabilities of the periods which preceded and succeeded it.

Others take the more optimistic view that the integrationist policies of the past fifty years have by now become so entrenched that they are self-sustaining and will survive the passing of the cold war: whatever their original causes, they have now established a dynamic of their own and there will be no recurrence of the autarchic nationalism and totalitarianism of the previous era:

These dramatic breaks from the past and the general peacefulness of the West are to be explained by increases in the costs of war, decreases in its benefits and, linked to this, changes in domestic regimes and values . . . [T]hese changes in the developed world are so deep, powerful, and interlocked that they cannot readily be reversed by any foreseeable event. (Jervis 1991/2: 47)

How are we to select from this multiplicity of perspectives? In order to do so, we need to dissect the nature of the cold war's ending; examine the ambiguous evidence about the trends towards globalization and fragmentation in its aftermath; and, finally, base our judgement on the analysis that most effectively accounts for these trends by integrating developments in international relations with changes in the internal composition of states.

The End of Which Cold War?[1]

It should already be apparent that the debate about the consequences of the *end* of the cold war is intimately bound up with the debate about the *nature* of the cold war, and what it signified. Indeed, there is almost a happy symmetry, the explanations for the ending of the cold war providing a sharp mirror image of the interpretations of its origins, both deriving from a shared set of assumptions about what the cold war *was*. The early debate about cold-war origins might be classified into balance-of-power, ideological, orthodox, revisionist, and post-revisionist schools of thought. These, in turn, were predicated on notions of the cold war as embodying, respectively: a radical crisis in the distribution of power; a clash of incompatible world views; an expansionist Soviet foreign policy; an aggressively capitalist American globalism; and a synthetic combination of elements of each spiced up with mistakes and misperceptions. Conforming to this, the end of the cold war has provoked interpretations which replicate the same

---

[1] This general issue is discussed in Cox (1994); LaFeber (1992).

format: the return to a more 'natural' balance of power; the ideological victory of liberal capitalism; the loss of the cold war by a congenitally weak Soviet state; the winning of the cold war by robust American strategic policies; and the passing of the cold war by a mixture of domestic change, people power, wise diplomacy, and good fortune.

The point is not to become involved in these scholarly wrangles for their own sake, nor to investigate these various positions in detail. Their importance for the present argument is that the relevance of the end of the cold war for contingent processes of globalization and fragmentation depends very much on one's assessment of the cold war itself. More pointedly, the answer that is given to this question will determine the wider issue at stake: are the processes of globalization and fragmentation still largely shaped by the events of the international political world, such as the end of the cold war, or is there now a greater disjunction between them? Or, to reverse the causal relationship, is there evidence that it was not the end of the cold war which engendered renewed globalization and fragmentation but, instead, that it was a shift in the balance between these two trends that brought the cold war to an end?

These issues have lurked, like shadows, in the background of the debates about the end of the cold war. It is the present intention to give them greater prominence. The argument will be set out by developing three related sets of binary interpretive oppositions. These sets are: accounts of the end of the cold war 'from above' versus accounts 'from below'; the notion that the end of the cold war represented a resolution versus the notion that it was a circumvention; and the view that the peaceful nature of the end of the cold war testifies to embedded changes, versus the view that fragmentationist forces have rebelled against the globalizing remnants of the cold war. When brought together cumulatively, these three disputed perspectives help us to capture the centrality of globalization and fragmentation to the debates about the end of the cold war.

The view that the end of the cold war was delivered 'from above' encapsulates a number of separate claims: what they have in common is that the termination of the cold war can be understood as a policy choice adopted by national leaders. This would include the sundry suggestions that the United States won the cold war by deliberately seeking to push the Soviet Union over the economic edge, or by incidentally sparking off reform in the Soviet Union through programmes such as the Strategic Defense Initiative (Gaddis 1992*a*: 43–4).[2] It would include also those accounts which maintain that revolutionary change and economic collapse were an *effect*, not a *cause*, of Soviet leadership choices: thus it is commonly argued that 'the catastrophic decline [of the Soviet economy] of the late 1980s was a direct result of Gorbachev's policies' (Crockatt 1995: 341; see also Wohlforth 1994/5: 108). Above all, this perspective incorporates all versions which stress the successful diplomacy whereby Soviet–American relations were normalized, even if the trade-off was the West's stake in the personal survival as leaders, first of

---

[2] Hobsbawm (1994: 249) dismisses all such versions 'There is no sign that the US government expected or envisaged the impending collapse of the USSR or was in any way prepared for it when it happened.'

Gorbachev and then of Yeltsin (the best of this genre is Beschloss and Talbott 1993).

The view 'from below' emphasizes the dynamic impact of social forces operating outwith policy choices and equally has many variants. Within the contours of his global society perspective, Martin Shaw, for instance, directs attention to the wider impact of 'global economic and cultural relations' which directly influenced the societies of the USSR and eastern Europe 'independently' of the specific actions of Western states (1994*a*: 67). This argument stresses that what happened in the East was not unique but reflected the growing influence of transnational civil movements elsewhere as well:

The 1980s began with one kind of social movement, the peace campaigners, on the streets of Western European capitals, and ended with another, the movement for democracy, on the streets of Eastern European capitals. These two movements, together, represented important moments in the complex processes . . . which unravelled the Cold War system. (Shaw 1994*b*: 662–3)

While sharing the focus on 'people power', this interpretation is different from that, for instance, of Gaddis. He too gives pride of place to the 'spontaneous but collective actions' of the people of eastern Europe but does so in so far as this reminds us that the cold war was 'really about the imposition of autocracy and the denial of freedom'. The cold war came to an end when the people had demonstrated that 'authoritarianism could no longer be imposed' (1992*b*: 24). This was tantamount to a unilateral change in the East, as opposed to Shaw's insistence on change in the global social system as a whole. Both, however, are compatible with the notion that the relatively free transmission of ideas and social goods between East and West was critical to this process and had been undermining systemic closure for a long time: economic contacts and attractions; penetrative communications (such as FRG television watched by millions of citizens of the GDR); and 'twenty years of better relations between the two parts of Europe' (Cox 1994: 188–9). On this analysis, we might accept Hobsbawm's quip: 'The paradox of the Cold War was that what defeated and in the end wrecked the USSR was not confrontation but détente' (1994: 251). But is there not a danger here that we end up in the tautological position that what caused the end of the cold war was the end of the cold war?

The second issue is the nature, or the extent, of the resolution embodied in the end of the cold war. On the one hand, there are the various proponents of complete victory and resolution. Extending the imagery of cold war, some versions of this naturally are expressed in terms of its being 'the functional equivalent of World War III', issuing in a new *post bellum* order (Mueller 1992: 39). Embellishing the metaphor, some depict the end of the cold war as a form of 'unconditional surrender' by the Soviet Union (Gaddis 1992*a*: 26). These accounts are couched in terms of the interstate rivalry between the two superpowers. An alternative version is that proffered in Halliday's inter-systemic competition: 'the form in which the Cold War ended was not that of a balance of power, or of a mutual exhaustion, but of the prevailing of one bloc over the other, in other words a systemic victory' (1993: 32). This view is shared by others who reject attempts to portray the cold war as having ended earlier than 1989. For them the critical definition of the 'end' is not various *détentes* and accommodations but 'the final collapse of the communist project and the re-entry of Eastern Europe into the world system' (Cox 1994: 200). For others again, the resolution is so complete that all ideological life forms, apart from liberal capitalism, have become extinct and history itself brought to an end (Fukuyama 1992).

Set against these various proclamations of finality, there is the opposed suggestion that the cold war was not so much resolved as became progressively irrelevant or superfluous. The clearest statement of this is that provided by Crockatt: 'the cold war system,' he writes, 'was subject to a dynamic—the growth of the capitalist system—which was tangential to the cold war itself. The cold war did not so much collapse as it was bypassed' (1995: 371). Here we have the interesting—and hybrid—suggestion that the cold war increasingly became a story separate from developments within the Western system—such as growing economic interdependence and regimes to govern it—and that eventually the latter story became the more important: it became the only game in town. But whereas the theories of victory posit a resolution from within the cold war itself, this 'bypass' notion argues that the cold war was diminished in importance by dynamic developments from without. The problem here is whether those dynamic developments in capitalism can be accepted as a different story from the cold war or whether, as argued throughout this book, they are not better understood as an integral aspect of that intra-systemic cohesion which was itself a defining attribute of the cold war. Thus conceived, one dimension of the cold war—its intra-systemic dynamic—finally became much more important than the other—the inter-systemic competition: what ended the cold war was a form of fratricide between its twin organisms.

Thirdly, we need to account not simply for the end of the cold war but additionally for the peculiar manner of its passing. In particular, and as frequently noted, what is most striking is that this moment of historical punctuation was achieved peacefully. Using this as a means to criticize realist theory, Lebow demonstrates the apparent anomaly. 'Instead of launching a preventive war,' he notes quizzically, 'the Soviet Union sought an accommodation with the United States, its principal adversary and rival hegemon, and made concessions that greatly enhanced the relative power of the United States' (Lebow and Risse-Kappen 1995: 36). Gaddis himself insists that there is no historical precedent for 'how *peacefully* the Soviet Union would relinquish its position as a superpower, indeed its own existence as a state' (1992/3: 51–2). How are we to explain this? Again, there are two opposed interpretations. The first relates back to the view 'from above', suggesting that the transition was managed by skilful diplomacy or, as Gaddis hints, that at the very least we were simply 'extraordinarily lucky' (1992/3: 51–2). A quite different variant, but sharing an 'internalist' frame of analysis, is that the transition has not been as peaceful as is claimed. On this interpretation, the spate of ethnic and sub-nationalist wars of the 1990s are not to be considered as the coincidental aftermath of the end of the cold war but as an essential part of that termination. The cold war was overpowered from within by separatist forces which cumulatively rendered the Soviet–American antagonism unsustainable. Thus viewed, the peaceful transition was peaceful only at the superpower core and embodied a new bargain between Russia and the United States to maintain the central peace, even at the expense of intra-systemic conflict. However viewed, 'peace' was maintained by dynamics from within the cold war relationship itself.

The second interpretation—the 'externalist'—shifts the focus of analysis away from the cold war relationship to the pervasive changes in the international context in which its demise was to take place. It might be labelled that of 'embedded multilateralism', following its most eloquent exponent:

In 1989, peaceful change . . . accommodated the most fundamental geopolitical shift of the postwar era and perhaps of the entire twentieth century: the collapse of the Soviet East European empire and the attendant end of the cold war. Many factors were responsible for that shift. But there seems little doubt that multilateral norms and institutions have helped stabilize their international consequences. (Ruggie 1993: 3)

Gaddis also points to a similar type of explanation when he hypothesises that 'linear evolution has pushed familiar cycles of war, peace, and decline into a new and wholly unfamiliar environment' (1992/3: 51–2). The peaceful transition was without precedent because the precedents are no longer relevant.

These various pairings deal with slightly different, but overlapping, sets of issues. What they have in common is that they all raise the complex question of whether the dynamics of the end of the cold war are to be located endogenously or exogenously. This relates back directly to considerations of globalization and fragmentation after the cold war. At the risk of over-simplification, it might be suggested that what lies at the heart of these various disagreements is the contention between the view of globalization as a strategy within the cold war and for bringing it to an end—as against the view that globalization was itself an attack upon the cold war from the outside, and which rendered the cold war both less relevant and less sustainable. It also facilitated the relatively peaceful manner of its passing.

To the extent that new conditions are an effect of the cold war's end, brought about by the collapse of the pre-existing order, there might intuitively be a case to be made for the radical transformation of the post-1990 world: the argument would favour discontinuity over continuity. There is a preferable alternative: to the extent that the erosion of the cold war might *itself* be accountable in terms of the impact of forces already in being, and with a capacity to be sustained in its aftermath, the argument favours a greater measure of continuity, albeit with some shift in the relative balance. Such a conceptualization allows us to escape the Manichaean starkness that is suggested by those who envisage a regression after 1990 to the instabilities of the first half of the century.

The Uncertain Debate about Security

In what ways do the two themes of globalization and fragmentation relate to the patterns of international security which began to emerge after 1990? They do so by describing the fundamental shifts as a result of which international relations were becoming an increasingly complex composite of transnational, state, and sub-state activities (see generally Buzan 1991; Booth 1991). Although the state remained central to discussions of security, its monopoly was challenged by its submergence into wider patterns of transnational activity, nowhere more apparent than in the case of international financial flows or in what some saw as the emergence of a global civil society: at the other end, fragmentation has challenged the state's capacity to manage its own domestic economic, political, and security agenda as well, whether it be in the form of separatism, regionalism, or organized crime. There was even talk of a crisis of the state itself (Dunn 1995). The argument of this chapter is that the state's role in the realm of security is increasingly ambivalent: it is both a disrupter of wider social and human patterns of order and yet, elsewhere, remains as a pocket of stability in the face of what might be regarded as destabilizing and threatening transnational forces. What is happening to security is but one manifestation of what is happening to the state in general and reflects the twin pressures exercised by both globalization and fragmentation.

Historically, international security has been conceived in interstate terms and as being predominantly concerned with military matters. In the 'international state of nature', deemed to be a potential war of all against all, the best that could be achieved was the manipulation of the balance of military power to deter aggression and to discourage any one state from seeking preponderance. Security, on this conception, was taken to mean a condition of military equilibrium or stability. This, in turn, reinforced the impression that security is negative, in so far as stability is depicted as a situation in which all states are deterred from initiating aggression: the reason for this is the external disincentives against hostile action rather than any positive incentive to cooperate.

More recent theorizing about security has attempted to shift attention away from the negative connotations of security towards a more positive aspect. This is reflected in the widely preferred terminology of common or cooperative security which emphasizes a shift away from the mere absence of violence between states and towards meeting basic human needs and rights, broadly conceived. In 1982, the Palme Commission published its report (Palme 1982) and drew attention to this new thinking: it spoke of 'joint survival' rather than 'mutual destruction', argued that states could not achieve security 'at each other's expense', and sought to go beyond 'stability' by creating 'positive processes'. Many analysts no longer see the state as the only focus of security concerns: the breakdown of the rigidly hierarchical state system, and the fact that so many international problems are currently being driven by processes of state fragmentation, require us to include the protection of minority groups, as well as of individual human beings, in any discussion of security. It is no longer valid, on this reasoning, to equate interstate stability with security for individual human beings (see International Institute for Strategic Studies 1991/2). Moreover, this attitude is reinforced by the hesitant steps of the international community in the direction of humanitarian intervention, which itself denies the sanctity of the state as the ultimate point of reference in discussions of security. It became one of the main tasks of international institutions in the 1990s to begin to create a security safety-net for minorities: this was sought to quell the proliferating demands for secession by guaranteeing some protection against governments which violated minimal standards of their own minority communities.

Equally, the search for a positive concept of security has expanded the agenda well beyond that of military security alone. Theorists of cooperative security see the attainment of genuine security as superceding negative deterrence by building upon positive interests in such areas as environmental controls, arms restraints, non-proliferation, and the spread of liberal values. The objective of security was no longer adequately represented as the deterrence of a single potential aggressor: instead, it was to build upon common interests in economic development, in environmental management, in human rights protection, in multilateral peacekeeping, in the limitation of armaments, in preventing ethnic conflict, in staunching the world's flow of refugees, and so on.[3]

Does this mean that military power became progressively redundant after the cold war? There is a strong temptation to conclude that, as other aspects of security have increased in importance, the military dimension must be devalued, and *pari passu*, the role of states as the prime wielders of military power. The argument from globalization, at this point, overlaps with the argument about the reduced military capacity of states. However, there is evidently not a secular decline of this kind. A cursory examination of the world during the 1990s reminds us that armed force remained a prominent element in international relations. It is at least as arguable that the end of the cold war reduced some of the inhibitions on resort to force inasmuch as regional actors have been liberated from former superpower constraints. While there may have been less anxiety about apocalyptic nuclear war, there remained very real concern about the effects of the end of the cold war upon nuclear proliferation as states, denied superpower umbrellas, sought to become more self-reliant: this became apparent in the case of North Korea in the early 1990s. Use of violence became widespread also in the fragmentation of states and in secessions from them: to the extent that there was an unprecedented crisis in the viability of certain state structures, resort to military means was an endemic part of this crisis, be it in Bosnia, Rwanda, or Somalia. Moreover, in a variety of intra-state conflicts and civil wars, there was recurrent use of force. The very fact that the international community itself became engaged in a wide spectrum of humanitarian, peacekeeping, and peace-making activities around the globe—almost all with an overt or latent military dimension—lent little credence to the notion that the post-cold war world was a world

[3] The role of 'new' security thinking as a transnational force in bringing the cold war to an end is discussed in Risse-Kappen (1995*b*: esp. 195–202).

less reliant upon military instruments. Indeed, commentators repeatedly pointed to the inadequacy of the military resources available for UN peacekeeping during this period (Roberts 1994, 1995/6).

The ambivalent reactions to the end of the cold war highlight this central duality of military force in contemporary international relations. No sooner did the cold war slip away than some analysts began to express nostalgia for its golden days. They did so because the cold war, if not immediately, had by its middle years taken on a degree of certainty, familiarity, and predictability. In retrospect, for all the tensions engendered by the cold war, and for all its nuclear brinkmanship, it seemed a more secure period of international history than that which unfolded in its aftermath. By way of contrast, the dangers of the post-cold war era were seen to be less apocalyptic but more pervasive and less predictable. Gaddis speculated on the irony that the 'Cold war should turn out to have been a safer and more stable era than one in which the relationship between Washington and Moscow has become "normal" ' (1992*a*: 169).

Globalization after the Cold War

This section has two principal concerns. The first is to map out and quantify the directions, and the extent, of globalization in the international system at the end of the century; and the second is to investigate the nature of the connection, if any, between these and the changes brought about by the end of the cold war. This will further develop the argument about the degree of continuity and discontinuity represented by this major international political change. Some commentators have already returned a mixed verdict on this by suggesting that the end of the cold war has eroded the globalization of security arrangements but has intensified the globalization of world economic processes (Falk 1995: 4). Is such a stark bifurcation an accurate assessment? More particularly, even if globalization is now being hastened, is this an element of continuity rather than of discontinuity, as Richard Falk has suggested?:

Of course, many of the fundamental tendencies reshaping world order were not derivative from the Cold War, especially the complex dynamics of globalisation. However, the preoccupation of the Cold War, its East–West interpretative logic, made it more difficult to appreciate the impact of globalisation . . . The immediate reaction [to the end of the cold war] was to exaggerate the discontinuity, neglecting underlying forces for change that were having a transforming impact in any event . . . The end of the Cold War definitely encourages a greater emphasis on globalisation. (Falk 1995: 1–2)

Is there more of it? How pervasive is it? And is this an *effect* of the end of the cold war or simply further evidence about what it was that destroyed the cold-war systems in the first place?

The pervasiveness of economic globalization in the 1990s can be measured both in terms of its *extensiveness* and its *intensity*. Accretions to the former seem the most obvious consequence of the end of the cold war with the gradual, and

uneven, integration of the former Soviet bloc into the world economy and financial system. Although this has not progressed as far as the high expectations of
1990, and indeed the move to market economies has faltered both economically
and politically in some countries, none the less the demise of the First
World–Second World economic divide must be accounted—in its potential—a
giant step towards a genuinely global economic system.

The significance of this is even greater when juxtaposed with the steady opening to the international market of developing country economies over the preceding decade. Under the pressures of the IMF and World Bank, the developing
world accepted a development strategy based on structural adjustment which has
further integrated the Third World into the world economy (Bretherton and
Ponton 1996: 6): these countries have abandoned hitherto national development
strategies based on import substitution and have 'more or less given up on
nationalisation' (Strange 1993: 103–4). For the developing world 'opting out, in
short, is out' (Strange 1995: 299) and much the same now applies to Russia and
eastern Europe. In this sense, there has been a surge in the extent of globalization,
even if, to be sure, the demands that the former Soviet bloc make of the international financial system might be thought to be competitive with those of the
developing world (Grant 1995: 579).

And yet it is more on the basis of the intensity of globalization in the 1990s that
the economic theorists tend to rest their case. According to the high priests of
globalization at century's end, the trends in this direction are now so entrenched,
and irreversible, that they have 'raised troubling questions about the relevance—
and effectiveness—of nation states as meaningful aggregations in terms of what
to think about, much less manage, economic activity' (Ohmae 1995: viii). Not
only is this growth of economic globalization exponential, but is claimed to follow its own technical and economic logic. Even those who offer a more balanced
account of what is happening concede that 'in the absence of a clearly defined
security agenda, economic integration has a momentum of its own' (Cable 1995:
305).

What is the evidence for such claims? Those who subscribe to them argue that
there has been such an acceleration of transnational economic activity that a
qualitatively new condition has been created, different from previous levels of
interdependence in the emergence of a 'global system of production and exchange
which is beyond the controls of any single nation-state' (Held 1995*b*: 101). Others
again proclaim that 'the nation states no longer control national economies in
Western Europe' (Wallace 1995: 67). This has been explained in various ways.
Some emphasize 'the dramatic changes in the international division of labour'
(Gill 1993: 256). Others point to the tendency towards convergence, synchro-
nization, and interpenetration of world markets (Eden and Potter 1993: 47).
Others again, relate it to the sheer availability of 'global flows of information'
(Ohmae 1995: 15).

More particularly, the manifestations of this intensification of globalization are
deemed to lie in the global mobility of capital, the growth of foreign direct investment (FDI), and the role of the multinational or transnational corporations: all

three are thought to be interconnected. The mobility of capital is not a new phenomenon and, as argued above, was regarded as itself undermining the fixed-rate foreign exchange scheme by the 1970s. However, financial deregulation in the 1980s encouraged it to develop apace and international communications saw such movements reach unprecedented levels, much of it short-term 'hot money' and speculative against currency movements: by 1989, foreign exchange dealings averaged about US$650 billion per day (Frieden 1991: 428). Even in the longer-term area, borrowings on international capital markets had increased from annual averages of $95.6 billion in 1976–80 to $536 billion by 1991 and to $818.6 billion by 1993 (Hirst and Thompson 1996: 40).

The major qualitative changes are associated with increases in FDI and in multinational corporate activity. The following gives some indication of the plethora of statistics regularly cited. FDI is regarded by some commentators as having taken over from international trade the role as the prime generator of international growth. FDI itself is estimated to have grown at an annual average rate of 34 per cent between 1983 and 1990 and to have reached a gross figure of $2 trillion by 1992 (Hirst and Thompson 1996: 54–5, 53). It was expected to double between 1988 and 1995 (Strange 1995: 293). Much of this growth is attached to the activities of corporations which numbered, according to UN statistics, some 37,000 by the early 1990s and controlled a further 170,000 offshore affiliates (Hirst and Thompson 1996: 53). Offshore production by the multinational corporations (MNCs) exceeded the volume of interstate exports by the mid-1980s (Strange 1995: 293) and their sales in 1992 amounted to some $5.5 trillion, compared with total world trade of $4 trillion (Hirst and Thompson 1996: 53; Gill 1995: 405). Impressive as these numbers might be, the significant judgements about them are that they constitute a 'threshold' opening up 'a qualitatively different set of linkages among advanced economies' (quoted in Dicken 1992: 87) and have changed 'the very nature of states and their patterns of conduct' (Strange 1995: 297). At a minimum, states have now come to embrace the MNCs, not as some putative rivals, but as welcome allies in the search for competitive advantage in a precarious international market (Eden and Potter 1993: 2).

This impression of remorselessly intensifying globalization has not, however, been allowed to go unchallenged and the extent, as well as the significance, of these developments has been questioned in some quarters. The most sustained critique of the globalization thesis is that offered by Hirst and Thompson. Their argument points out that the pre-1914 system was in many respects as open and integrated as the present; the transnationals are not genuinely transnational but depend critically on home-base markets and infrastructural supports; FDI is highly concentrated within the Triad (USA, Western Europe, and Japan), and the extent of globalization is thereby limited; and there are serious restrictions on labour migration (especially for the poor and unskilled). In sum, they reach the blunt conclusion:

The evidence . . . on the character of the world financial markets, the pattern of world trade and FDI, the number and role of MNCs, and the prospects for growth in the developing world ... all confirm that there is no strong tendency toward a globalized economy. (Hirst and Thompson 1996: 185–6)

This scepticism is shared by others who also point to the variability in the degree of globalization, more marked in financial matters than in trade and in other measures of convergence between national and regional economies (Barry Jones 1995: ch. 6 and p. 160). Full mobility is much more a feature of bond, than of equity, markets (Frieden 1991: 429). Even the notion of a global market 'is less uniform than might be assumed' and retains strong national identifications (Skolnikoff 1993: 106). 'Post-Fordist' production techniques are now able to accommodate these variations and can be organized 'around local skills and local markets' (Kaldor 1995: 79–80).[4] Above all, the notion of globalization too readily conjures up images of uniformity of economic experience and thus blithely ignores the stark reality of continuing post-cold war North–South inequalities (Grant 1995: 569) in consequence of which 'the bulk of the world's population live in closed worlds, trapped by the lottery of their birth' (Hirst and Thompson 1996: 181).[5]

The argument about the degree of globalization at the end of the century extends beyond the economic evidence alone, even if that remains the most powerful cluster of arguments within it. More generally, the processes of globalization are thought to be expressed through the changed imagery of post-cold war international relations, with the emphasis upon world order, human rights, and world ecology, all manifestations of a perceived global human condition.[6] Again, these images are not new but have evolved since they first captured public awareness in the early 1970s (Clark 1989: esp. chs. 2 and 9): however, they have intensified in many quarters since the end of the cold war. They found their highest-profile official exposition in former President George Bush's notion of the New World Order, inaugurated in 1991 but soon dispelled. Typically, it has been suggested that

the most conspicuous feature of the new international situation is the emergence of issues which transcend national frontiers . . . The limits on national autonomy imposed by the balance of terror have now been supplemented by a much subtler, more structural form of erosion caused by the processes of environmental, social and economic globalization. (Archibugi and Held 1995: 5)

More sceptically, it has been argued that there is a dissonance between 'the growing popularity of the idea of "world order" ' and the 'growing fragmentation of the world itself' (Hassner 1993: 61).

The hard evidence for a globalization of world political order is, by its nature, more difficult to come by than in the economic realm. To the extent that it can be quantified, analysts make appeal to such things as the growth of international

---

[4] It has been suggested that post-Fordist production is ambivalent in that it both 'strengthens globalizing tendencies' and is accompanied by moves to 'greater regionalism and increased geo-economic rivalry' (Bernard 1994: 222–3).

[5] On the general issue of globalization and inequality, see Hurrell and Woods (1995).

[6] For a discussion of environmental issues as a form of political globalization, see Waters (1995: 103–8).

non-governmental organizations (INGOs). By 1990, there were approximately 5,000 in existence and Eastern dissident movements, Western social movements, and sundry 'epistemic communities'—especially in the environmental sphere—were all playing important parts in a kind of international 'governance' (Risse-Kappen 1995*a*: 3–4). Many commentators claim to see the emergence of a powerful transnational civil society cutting across national borders on environmental questions (Hurrell 1995*b*: 147). More formally, the United Nations hugely expanded its peacekeeping operations in the early 1990s: some seventeen were underway in 1994, involving some 70,000 personnel (Roberts 1994: 96). But the high hopes of the UN quickly dissipated as the problems and the disillusionment set in.

Perhaps the strongest reservation about a globalized political order—just as in the case of the globalization of the economy—relates to the question of whether it is possible to speak of a single world order, or of an order fragmented on North–South lines. For all his unifying vision of a world come to rest at the end of history, Francis Fukuyama himself concedes that realist principles of international relations still apply between those countries still trapped in history and those which have moved beyond it (1992: 279). There is, then, not a single world order but a liberal democratic world order and a non-democratic world disorder. This notion is encapsulated in the thesis of the two zones:

> The real world order in the democratic part of the world will be fundamentally different from any past world order. Never in history have there been large diverse areas, containing most of the world's power, in which no country faced substantial military danger to its independence or survival . . . Unfortunately, only 15 per cent of the world's population lives in the zones of peace and democracy. Most people now live in zones of turmoil. (Singer and Wildavsky 1993: 4, 6)

This fissure touches also upon the extent of a globalized human rights order. It might have been thought that the end of the cold war ushered in conditions favourable to a new respect for universally recognized human rights, and the emphasis on such rights in the New World Order rhetoric of the early 1990s reinforced this impression. Moreover, since the superpowers had, for cold-war reasons, been supporters of regimes which notoriously violated their own citizens' rights, the removal of this structural condition appeared favourable to a general improvement in this area (Donnelly 1993: 133). The re-emergence of a determination on the part of the international community to implement war-crime trials, in association with the wars against Iraq and in the former Yugoslavia, was symptomatic of the rediscovered universalism that had first been encouraged by the Second World War. Yet further evidence of the move in this direction was the greater emphasis that came to be placed on human rights issues in North–South relations: not only was liberal democracy triumphant in the cold-war competition, but it became increasingly assertive in demanding change in political behaviour in the South. Political conditionality—the imposition of political tests of multi-party democracy and human rights performance—emerged as a major element in the financial programmes of the IMF and World Bank, and also of the multilateral aid policies of bodies such as the European Union (Hawthorn 1995: 131).

However, it is right to record some scepticism as to how pervasive—and universalist—was the new human rights regime. The wish to punish war criminals has proved stronger than the international community's ability to do so (Best 1995: 783–4). There is little to indicate that the gulf between different conceptions of human rights is narrowing and much to suggest that these conceptions have become part of the substance of international relations, a continuation of political intercourse by other means.[7] Geoffrey Best, for all his sympathies, strikes a gloomy note:

If we were in any doubt about the extent to which humanitarian and human rights law falls short of arousing universal applause and acceptance, the World Conference on Human Rights at Vienna in mid-1993 must have settled that question . . . [R]esistance to human rights progress and even a confident sort of counter attack against it have been unmistakable. In the light of these trends, the universal reign of justice, so far as human rights go, seems immeasurably remote. (Best 1995: 793)

How do these tendencies towards economic and political globalization—whatever reservations might be set against them—relate to the currents of international relations in the 1990s? Contemporary analysis is riven by deep disagreements as to the driving forces within the international political economy. For many of the supporters of economic globalization, there is a deep-rooted conviction that whatever role great powers may have played historically in establishing the political context for economic activity, there is now a sense in which economic globalization follows its own rationale: this is the notion that 'economics and politics are pulling apart' or that 'economic laws finally prevail over political power' (Hirst and Thompson 1996: 188, 14). More specifically, this is the basis for an argument that the trends towards economic globalization will continue, even without American hegemonic power to bolster them, or in the absence of a sustained American commitment to multilateralism after the cold war (Foreman-Peck 1995: 355).

As noted in the previous chapter, however, we can dissent from this sharp dichotomy between political and economic power: other commentators are right to discern both a continuing political determination of the economic framework, as well as reinforcement of structural political power from the economic realm. Thus Gill depicts a transition from a US 'national' hegemony to an as yet incomplete transnational 'post-hegemonic' order: this encapsulates the diminished role of the US in setting the framework for economic activity and reflects changes in global production, competition, and the 'quasi-autonomous structure of global finance' (1993: 277). Within this semi-autonomous economic sphere, nevertheless, he insists that US power has not been eliminated altogether and that it remains 'anchored in US political and military centrality' (Gill 1993: 246), a notion which is at once coy and difficult to pin down. Meanwhile, Susan Strange, while echoing the theme of the erosion of the power of national governments, is

---

[7] The problems are reviewed in Donnelly (1993).

equally alert to the political spillover from economic globalization: it generates greater asymmetries in national power. Thus there are two processes at work which are fully consistent with each other. There has been an increase in the 'vulnerability of the United States government to pressures coming from the market economy'—a kind of Frankenstein created by the USA but no longer controllable by it. At the same time, the USA is the beneficiary of the asymmetry of power which is structurally created by this free-market economy, for instance in the area of telecommunications (Strange 1995: 300–1).

Finally, there are those analysts who continue to adhere to the view that the international economy depends heavily upon the, often invisible, hand of politics and national governmental action. Financial globalization, it is said, is not the product of a mindless market nor of technology but has been actively sponsored by sympathetic state policies (Helleiner 1994: esp. 165–72). If anything, it has been argued in one of the strongest attacks on the globalization thesis, the role of national action has increased. This is true both in the sense that the economic order still requires military force to back it but also, more generally, in the sense that an internationalized economy requires common and coordinated policies between 'world agencies, trade blocs and major treaties' and national governments are the critical 'relay' between these (Hirst and Thompson 1996: 188, 191).

In short, general theories about the state of the international political economy are as uncertain, and contested, as the empirical reality which they attempt to portray. None the less, for a combination of the foregoing reasons, the notion of a globalizing economy now fully liberated from all forms of politics and structural control seems hardly tenable. Why then is there so much controversy about these issues? As with previous historical periods, much of this disagreement is finally traceable to profoundly differing interpretations of the role of the state itself and the extent to which changing patterns of international activity are associated with changing forms of state practice. Before returning to this core issue, however, it is first necessary to explore the opposing evidence that the 1990s heralded the onset of a new era of international fragmentation.

The End of History or the End of Post-war Integration?

The 1990s saw a resurgence of fragmentationist tendencies and a key question is whether these were simply the result of the end of the cold war or a reaction to longer-term and more fundamental processes of historical change: were they, as stated above, an effect of the end of the cold war or a symptom of the transformations which swept it away?

Has there been, since the end of the cold war, a strengthening 'of incipient counter-global trends' (Von Laue 1994: 188), and does this signify the dissipation of the favourable contextual factors which encouraged post-1945 integration? Such is a popular theme in analyses of the 1990s, and again the assertion of the dialectic between globalization and fragmentation is conspicuous at century's end. To some, there is an approximate equilibrium in which 'economic integration, driven by technological change and global competition, is counterbalanced by political disintegration' (Wallace 1995: 75–6). To others, there is the prospect of widening polarization between First and Third World orders:

given the power and interests engaged in the ever more integrated, cosmopolitan capitalist economy, the spread of chaos in the state system might lead to a two-tier international milieu, produced by the dialectic of globalisation and fragmentation: at one level, all the effective states engaged in the ups and downs, the gains and losses, of world capitalism, and at the other, a set of poor and either disintegrating or isolated societies left to fend—and feud—for themselves. (Hoffmann 1995/6: 32)

One set of arguments sees the fragmentation of the international system to be the direct consequence of the loss of cold-war structures of control and likely to issue in 'a much more unruly' world (Norton 1991: 20). In the most extreme, and ethnocentric, version of this argument it was claimed that a 'world without US primacy will be a world with more violence and disorder' (Huntington 1993: 83). As regards the Third World, the effects of this were early recognized to be ambiguous. If hitherto, superpower competition had resulted in attempts to control regional conflicts—to ensure that they would not draw in their superpower patrons—then the end of the cold war was a form of liberation (Walker 1993: 7). This new freedom came, however, at a price because the removal of the restraining hands of the cold war could be interpreted as the decline of any real interest in the Third World (David 1992/3: 131). Third World rejoicing in the end of the cold war was thus tempered by recognition that it might eventuate in a period of neglect by the rest of the world (Grant 1995: 570): while liberation might be welcome, the price might be 'disempowerment and marginalization' (MacFarlane 1991: 142–3). Thus it has been asserted that with the end of the cold war, '*Tiersmondisme* is in full retreat' and developing countries face a future of being 'a weak periphery to a strong capitalist centre' (Buzan 1994).

In short, one aspect of the new fragmentation is a renewed regionalization of international security and a disjunction between potential regional conflicts and the ordering mechanisms of the great powers (Cerny 1993: 49; MacFarlane 1991: 140). Hobsbawm regards this absence of an effective international system as one of the most salient features of the 1990s, and notes how many new states came into existence without any pretence at international tutelage (1994: 559). Such fragmentation might also affect the international economy by encouraging the formation of regional groupings, again under the influence of the reduced inhibitions of the hitherto restraining effects of the cold war (Jervis 1993: 63). However, there is less concern that regional economic groupings will lead to a repetition of the clashes of the 1930s because contemporary regionalism is more open and trade-driven, softened by the very transnationalization of finance and production (Busch and Milner 1994: 260). Current trends in regionalism are thus less threatening: 'Open regionalism means that policy is directed towards the elimination of obstacles to trade within a region,' it has been claimed, 'while at the same time doing nothing to raise external tariff barriers to the rest of the world'

(Gamble and Payne 1996: 251). Even here, a note of caution may be needed. It is possible that it was only in the unique combination of circumstances of the cold war that economic regionalism and multilateralism could reinforce each other in this way, and we should remain open-minded about the relationship between the two in the future (Wyatt-Walter 1995: 117–18).

However, it is too simplistic to regard all manifestations of fragmentation as the mere by-product of the end of the cold war, and this issue becomes particularly germane in the analysis of the apparent resurgence of ethno-nationalism and religion as powerful political forces in the international system. As the question has been posed, 'can it be explained simply as the result of the abrupt removal of a "totalitarian lid", which kept smouldering ethnic tensions in check?' (Smith 1993: 48). Certainly, the perception that questions of national and religious identity have become central in the closing stages of the twentieth century is virtually universal. Commentators speak of 'the new imperialism of parochialism' (Chipman 1993: 143) and assert that 'claims of nationality have come to dominate the last decade of the twentieth century' (Miller 1995: 1). Various states, such as Yugoslavia and Czechoslovakia, Ethiopia and the Soviet Union, have been rent asunder under its power. Why should this have been so?

One line of argument might suggest that the political fragmentation of the globe is less the consequence of the loosening of superpower security controls than the side-effect of the removal of the universalist ideological parameters which the cold war had instated. Within the confines of the cold war, the key issue of identity was with one or other of the two rival systems—and for the Third World membership of a movement which renounced both while selectively engaging with each. It is the removal of this ideological overlay which has allowed questions of national identity to 'come to the fore' (Miller 1995: 1).

Even this scarcely seems to go far enough in accounting for the phenomenon, and the arguments run more deeply into discussions of contemporary cultural formations, revolts against 'modernity', historical continuities, and a dialectical reaction against globalization itself. These positions can be briefly summarized.

The idea that the cold war would be succeeded by a period characterized by a clash of cultures or civilizations, although popularized, was advanced without any clear account of the dynamic which was bringing it to the fore, beyond some residual notion of nature's abhorrence of a threat-perception vacuum (Huntington 1994: 7). Those who have pursued the issue more fully appeal for a more thorough integration of the cultural factor into the study of international relations (Robertson 1992: 5). When this is done, the new cultural identities can be viewed as symptomatic of a more pervasive clash between society and state: in particular, the 'confrontation between these new forms of culture-based politics and the secular state' (Juergensmeyer 1993: 1–2), or as a 'revolt against the secular-modernizing state' (as quoted in Guibernau 1996: 136). The state in much of the post-colonial world had been imposed as the agency of transformation and modernization, but this had, finally, evoked a backlash against the discordance between its secular values and embedded cultural norms within the affected societies. The Iranian revolution would represent a classic instance of this dissonance and, since modernization was an agenda set by the Western developed world, it was inevitable that the revolt against the secular state would also, if only implicitly, symbolize a revolt against the West as well. The importance of such a perspective is that, chronologically, it locates the beginning of the trend towards fragmentation as early as the late 1960s or 1970s and thus stands out against any suggestion that it followed from the end of the cold war: the Third World had become disaffected long before the cold war discarded its protective mantle.

The same is true of those accounts which relate fragmentation to a more generalized crisis of modernity: cultural fragmentation is the expression of the loss of faith in post-enlightenment rationalism, its pretensions to control of the natural order, and its ability to design the social and political universe in conformity with 'universalist' aspirations. If this is the dynamic of contemporary fragmentation, then again the 'crisis' of modernity, if such there has been, was triggered at least twenty years before the end of the cold war.

An alternative account stresses historical continuity rather than discontinuity but, by attacking the argument from the opposite end, still is led to question the connection between the end of the cold war and the onset of ethno-nationalist fragmentation. Instead of regarding the dismemberment of states in the 1990s on the altar of self-determination as a new political era, it has been presented as the final working out of the logic started after the First World War. According to this historical perspective, 'the simplest way to describe the apparent explosion of separatism in 1988–92,' Hobsbawm remarked, 'is thus as the "unfinished business" of 1918–21' (1990: 165). But however appealing this reliance upon historical continuity, this scarcely serves to explain why the business should choose to have been completed at this particular juncture, and the argument hence relies, implicitly, upon other factors as well.

Finally, there is the often-repeated suggestion that cultural particularism has been reinvigorated precisely by the long post-war exposure to the attacks upon it from the homogenizing forces of cultural globalism (Bretherton and Ponton 1996: 105; Guibernau 1996: 129). On this conception, the relationship is genuinely dialectical and the long period of cultural assimilation that has been an adjunct of the cold war, modernization, and the integrating global economy is now undergoing a period of pronounced reaction that is certain to intensify heterogeneity and separatism, even if the forces of globalization are not uniformly resisted or reversed. Globalization evokes an equal but opposite reaction in the direction of fragmentation precisely because it forces cultures into mutual awareness and thereby accentuates the identity of difference (Held 1995a: 125; Huntington 1994: 9).

After the Cold War: The End of the State or the End of Globalization?

It has previously been argued that globalization is something which happens to states, and not merely to relations between them. How does such an observation pertain to international relations at the end of the twentieth century? Is globalization affecting the nature and role of states? Alternatively, what changes are taking place in states and do these provide a less congenial environment for the furtherance of globalization? Existing, and contradictory, analyses provide no easy answers to these questions.

There are two kinds of 'triumphalist' literature which have emerged in the aftermath of the cold war: both lend credence to the idea that the principal effect of the end of the cold war has been the inauguration of a new 'hegemonic' order—albeit that the nature of that order differs between the two versions. The first is that popularized by Fukuyama and already alluded to above. Its central claim is that with the failure of the socialist bloc, there disappeared the last remaining ideological rival to liberal capitalism. Although all states were not about to become democratic overnight, no other aspiration persisted with any kind of popular legitimacy. Liberal capitalism was thus entrenched as the unchallenged and hegemonic project of the late twentieth century.

An alternative version of this triumphalism is one that emphasizes the materialist and capitalist basis of this new hegemonic order. Within its terms, the 1980s witnessed the removal of the final barriers to a genuinely world system. Through the 1980s, the Third World was disciplined by the destruction of its vestigial 'national development' and 'revolutionary' projects and fully incorporated into the economic strategies set by the key capitalist institutions. Additionally, the final victory of the cold war ensured that the separate world of socialist development would also be swept away, thus leaving a single economic system and a single international division of labour. Economic homogeneity is thus to be viewed not as some incidental consequence of the end of the cold war but as an ongoing objective throughout the cold war and the primary goal sought by victory within it.[8]

There are, of course, problems to be faced by, and questions to be asked of, both these accounts. Although seemingly at odds with each other—the former emphasizing the victory of a political ideal and the latter the hegemony of an economic system—they are mutually consistent in so far as they regard the end of the cold war as a positive development within the logic of opposition, eliminating rival political programmes and economic systems: both, to this extent, have an inherent universalism in their respective analyses of the situation. What this ignores is the tension between the two doctrines and the more negative developments that might be thought to be associated with each. For instance, while Fukuyama's

---

[8] A representative account of this nature can be found in Overbeek and van der Pijl, 'Restructuring Capital and Restructuring Hegemony', in Overbeek (1993: 20–1).

account blithely runs together both the victory of democracy as political ideal, and of capitalism as economic practice (thus, implicitly, incorporating elements of the world capitalist thesis), it fails seriously to address the areas of mutual incompatibility between the two. Might it not be that universalizing capitalism constitutes a problem for democratic control and accountability?[9] Might it not be that, even more fundamentally, globalizing capitalism threatens the territorially based states in which liberal democratic values and practices are rooted? If these potential problems are accepted, then victorious democracy and victorious capitalism perhaps do not walk so comfortably hand-in-hand together.

The force of such concerns relates back to our assessment of the impact of the end of the cold war upon the nature of the state itself—or, for that matter, the role of changes in the state in bringing the cold war to an end. John Dunn notes of all three great aftermaths of war in the twentieth century—the First World War, the Second World War, and the cold war—that each 'has drastically extended the nation state as a political format and strongly reinforced it as an ideological option' (1995: 3–4), thus suggesting that the state has emerged strengthened in the 1990s. And yet as he acknowledges, and as others have testified, the situation is by no means so clear-cut, whatever the rush to establish new national states might imply. Thus it has been argued that the main consequence of the removal of the cold war was 'the exposure of the fragility of the nation-state itself' (Crockatt 1995: 368) and, elsewhere, that after the cold war 'what is now at stake is the very nature of the state' (Hoffmann 1995: 167–9). Held points to the dilemma and develops a critique of the Fukuyama thesis from a globalization perspective:

There is, accordingly, a striking paradox to note about the contemporary era: from Africa to Eastern Europe, Asia to Latin America, more and more nations and groups are championing the idea of 'the rule of the people'; but they are doing so at just that moment when the very efficacy of democracy as a national form or political organization appears open to question. As substantial areas of human activity are progressively organized on a global level, the fate of democracy, and of the independent democratic nation-state in particular, is fraught with difficulty. (Held 1995*a*: 121)

How are these varying judgements, some optimistic and others pessimistic, to be reconciled? And do they not suggest, either that globalizing capitalism is a major problem for universalizing democracy, or that both are based on the ever-more-precarious foundations of the nation-state itself?

One way of reconciling these apparently incompatible assessments of the world of the 1990s is to suggest that there are, at a general theoretical level, two ways of accounting for the role of the state and of what is happening to it. The first subordinates the state to the needs of the capitalist world system and sees no contradiction between globalizing capitalism and the transformation of the state; indeed, the latter is the handmaiden of the former. The second, and the account endorsed in this book, does recognize a tension and believes that it is

---

[9] The subject is addressed in Held (1995*a*). Ikenberry (1995: 113), notes that the victory of democracy has been accompanied by disillusionment with politics in the West.

globalization which has weakened the traditional bases of the state: the question then becomes whether the state has the capacity to strike back.

According to the first of these, state transformation occurs at the behest of the hegemonic economic system. The main characteristic of states at the capitalist core during the 1980s was the neoliberal revolution which they underwent and which was necessary to allow them to compete in the more adverse economic conditions of multiple recessions and emerging economic challengers. As a result, states were 'reduced to the role of adjusting national economies to the dynamics of an unregulated global economy' (Cox 1996*b*: 528). The neoliberal state became much less the instrument for national economic management and more 'connected' to the needs of highly mobile capital and production—'economies maximally compatible with an open world economy' (Marshall 1996: 206). Above all, in this intensely competitive environment, the state could no longer so readily afford the economic costs of national welfare programmes, and so the 1980s and 1990s were associated with the attack on the welfare state (Martin 1994: 69–70; Helleiner 1994: 173): deregulation and privatization extended the operation of the market into the provision of essential social services. This trend is recognized even by those who do not subscribe to the reified capitalist-system imagery of which it is a part, and thus Dunn, typically, draws attention to the 'central challenge of global economic liberalization' of this period 'to the Keynesian conception of the welfare state' (1995: 12). The expectation is that this challenge will intensify, with further decline in what the individual state can afford to offer its citizens. According to such claims, 'national regimes of extensive labour rights and social protection are thus obsolete', and the state can 'only provide those social and public services international capital deems essential and at the lowest possible overhead cost' (Hirst and Thompson 1996: 175–6). As part of this process, however, the national state is further eroded in its operational powers since it was by the management of the national economy, and the provision of welfare services, that it had reached the apogee of its controls in the 1950s and 1960s.

The second variety of interpretation accepts that there is a tension between post-cold war globalizing trends and the role of the state: indeed, the former has sparked off a deep underlying crisis in the capacity of the latter, and this in turn has generated problems of both expectations and accountability. In part, this is associated with the end of the cold war because the cold-war era was one which had considerably enhanced the role of states. 'The long era of global struggle, starting with World War II and continuing with the Cold War,' Ikenberry maintains, 'was a major factor in strengthening and centralising national governments' (1995: 120). This era has now come to an end and the state's capacity is weakened, including that of the most powerful state, the United States (Deudney and Ikenberry 1994: 22–3). Such an analysis confirms the earlier paradox that the cold war *both* stimulated globalization and, *at the same time*, rescued the nation-state by invigorating its economic and social functions; however, the end of the cold war has left the state weakened and fully exposed to the globalizing forces which the cold war had initially encouraged but which persisted after its end. We are now witnessing a process of 'dis-étatization or state-weakening' (Waters 1995: 99–100). Having been rescued, the state may now be in retreat (Wallace 1995: 61).

In the short term, this does create a crisis of expectations and accountability: expectations, in the sense that governments have a reduced capacity to deliver as they lose control over national economies (Ikenberry 1995: 117); accountability, in the sense of a growing divergence between those affected by decisions and those who participated in taking them (Held 1995*a*: ix). This is a problem which is by no means confined to the developed welfare state. On the contrary, its worst effects are to be anticipated in developing countries where it was precisely the role of the state as modernizer and manager of the national economy which provided its minimal legitimacy in the absence of cultural or ethnic sources of cohesion. If that is eroded, as in many cases it has been, the forces of internal disintegration will intensify. In the case of India, for instance, it has been argued that the state has traditionally been a strong intervener in, and regulator of, the national economy, but the turn to economic openness and less intervention will 'weaken those foci of national unity, undermining the functions of economic power of the central state' (Hirst and Thompson 1996: 108–9; see also Kaviras 1995: 128, who indirectly makes the same point). To that extent, the crisis of the Third World state is potentially much more serious.

And yet it is hyperbolic to think that there will be a sudden collapse of the state in the face of the new international circumstances and the corrosive effects of economic globalization. If the argument developed throughout this book has any force, then it suggests the falsity of any such crude linearity. Globalization is not a wholly autonomous force and has historically been shaped, encouraged, and thwarted by wider currents of international relations. It has also, and fundamentally, been mediated through the activities of states. States still enjoy structural powers from their economic activities and, in turn if less visibly, continue to provide the framework within which the globalized economy functions: to that extent, globalization has a persisting need for viable states and its own stake in their survival.

In the longer term, therefore, rather than envisage globalization bringing an end to the state, or the state standing Canute-like and turning back the tide of globalization, the sensible perspective is that international relations will encourage a reformulation and rebalancing of the relationship between the state and globalization. State functions have changed considerably over the century and new sources of legitimacy have been tapped by the practitioners of state power. It may well be the case, as Ikenberry believes, that there is now a secular disjunction, of historical significance, between state-building and economic modernization. 'For two hundred years,' he argues, 'the modernisation of industrial society worked in tandem [with] . . . the building of nation-states and national governments', whereas now the former erodes the latter (1995: 114–15). What this ignores, however, is the potential of political action to disturb this linear progression, and for new sources of fragmentation to contribute to the correction.

Hence it is surely more realistic to anticipate a new accommodation between state power and the forces of globalization, rather than the outright victory of the one over the other. If this analysis holds, then the most likely impact of the end of the cold war will be upon the 'construction of new forms of state power' (Kaldor 1995: 68). It is through this medium—rather than the bypassing of the state— that the new balance between globalization and fragmentation will be struck.

CONCLUSION

The themes of globalization and fragmentation lend coherence to the history of twentieth-century international relations as a whole as they draw our attention to the unique pattern created by the interaction, and oscillation, between the two: in so doing, they prompt the quest for an understanding of the tendency for both to wax and wane at different periods. Globalization has been a powerful presence throughout the century but not uniformly or inexorably so. What then promotes or retards it? Against the unidimensional views which have some currency in the globalization literature, and which present it as a self-contained and autonomous process (be it technological, economic, or cultural in nature), this work has recognized globalization as a complex, multidimensional series of developments, firmly located in the realities of international relations and changing state practices. It has often been an effect of state policies, even if not their direct or proximate goal. Such a perspective contributes to historical explanation but also introduces a note of caution into projections about the future.

This approach also offers a more judicious appreciation of the normative agenda that has attached itself to globalization: we must reject any identification of globalization with unqualified progress, while conceding that some of its aspects can have the potential for beneficial outcomes. Acceptance of the fact that globalization is, at heart, a political process—both domestically and internationally—prevents us from succumbing to notions of globalization as a technical, and hence depoliticized, trend. Globalization has been shaped and carried forward by the most powerful states and for their own ends. It is therefore a tangible expression of the inequalities of the international system. It also reflects the political bargains struck by governments as they mediate between domestic and external pressures: this determines which social sectors will carry the heavy costs globalization imposes. Nor can we accept any crude equation between fragmentation and international conflict. Certainly, states have pursued narrowly nationalist and competitive policies which have created tension and war; they have also espoused doctrines of autarchy and self-sufficiency which have undermined international stability. But equally, globalization can be destabilizing. For many, its association with former imperialism and Westernization is a source of recrimination. Its reinforcement of a hierarchy of economic winners and losers stokes bitter divisions, both domestically and internationally. And its expression in the universalization of the nation-state, especially in a 'secular modernizing' form, foments much cultural disturbance and must heavily qualify any image of the triumphal progress of liberal democracy.

The portraits of the individual phases of the twentieth century can be readily summarized as a preliminary to a final explanatory overview. The pre-1914 world was one in which starkly opposed tendencies emerged. Physically and technologically, the world became a smaller and more integrated place, an objective fact which found its political counterpart in the compression wrought by the high imperialism of the late nineteenth century. The European-based balance of power both drew new regions into its vortex and, in turn, was reshaped by the emergence of new global players. An international economy became more effectively established, even if some of the openness of the period before 1880 was thereafter under increasing pressure and threat, including its key regulatory mechanism, the gold standard. At the same time, the political temper of the period became more closely identified with competitive nationalism, expressed in the militarist and neo-mercantilist ideas which became fashionable. Above all, the dissipation of mid-nineteenth-century internationalism seemed itself to be a function of the heightened assertion of the bureaucratic and organizational powers of the modern state: caught between the highly competitive international environment and the emergence of sharp domestic political divisions, governments found that they had to pay a high political price for the maintenance of a regulated and open international system. By 1914 they were no longer willing to pay that price and sought salvation in national, rather than international, solutions.

If anything, these dilemmas were intensified, rather than resolved, by the experience of war. Ideologically, the war gave birth to a new universalism in the shape of Leninism and Wilsonianism. Their doctrines of national self-determination now established themselves as the sources of a globally legitimized fragmentation. The war itself had a substantial global impact, nowhere more so than in the mobilization of empires for the purposes of European war. Ultimately, however, the war furthered the tendency to fragmentation. The international economy disintegrated as trade and capital flows collapsed. There developed a new rhetoric of self-sufficiency which was to leave a potent legacy for the inter-war period. The collapse of empires in central and eastern Europe brought, in their wake, the dissolution of the networks of economic activity that had developed under their aegis. Above all, the change in economic balance of power that accompanied the emergence of the United States as the world's principal lender had its own disruptive impact when placed in the context of the vexed issues of reparations and allied war debts. These problems were intensified by the steps taken to meet the emergencies of war in the form of corporatism, a social compact which would reduce the scope for accommodating national to international needs in general, and for reconciling European and American wants, in particular.

This set the scene for the dynamic tension of the inter-war period. Although political internationalism was to be restored through the League and economic internationalism through a projected revival of the pre-1914 trading and exchange rate system, domestic political imperatives pulled in the opposite direction. Freedom to solve domestic political problems dictated a breaking loose from international constraints and hence self-sufficiency and autarchy became compelling ideals. Once the incipient recovery of the late 1920s had been choked off by the cessation of the international financial flows on which it depended, radical national salvationism stood unopposed. This may, in part, have been encouraged by the absence of effective international leadership during the 'hegemonic interregnum' between British and American power. More likely, however, it was the result of the inability, or unwillingness, of state leaders to pay the domestic political price which compliance with an international order, either political or economic, would exact. The alternative was to place national destiny firmly under national control, as the radical right promised. This represented a self-conscious decision to reject the globalization that had been an emerging characteristic of the pre-1914 world and which had endured, if in much-diluted form, into the 1920s. Simultaneously pursued by all states, such policies generated security and economic disasters of global proportions.

The Second World War was, without question, a *world* war that had a dramatic impact on human lives, economic systems, political philosophies, the fate of empires, and the future distribution of world power. Once again, war served as a catalyst for the globalizing of political ideas, none more so than the concept of human rights. It was itself a war between closed and open systems of political and economic order and thus directly a contest between globalization and fragmentation. Its outcome, although this was not immediately or inevitably so, dictated the future development of globalization over the next generation. Again, we have an example of a voluntaristic political act radically transforming the balance of political forces in such a way that a new set of accommodations between domestic and international needs—of a kind unrealizable in 1919—could now be reached. Assuredly, the conspicuous change lay in the dramatic accretions to American economic and political power. If hitherto, globalization had been carried on the back of Westernization, for the next three decades it was to be associated uniquely with Americanization. And yet American power by itself could not have been decisive had not the United States discovered the domestic will to exercise that power and, just as importantly, had not its post-war allies been offered an implicit bargain which nurtured their new domestic political arrangements within a sympathetic international order. Depression and then war were the necessary catalysts for national welfarism but of a type which, unlike the unilateralist policies of the 1930s, could be reconciled with an effective multilateralist economic order.

The main international facilitator of these multiple bargains was the onset of the cold war which both energized the United States to international leadership and provided a compelling strategic case for the 'West' to follow. The Marshall Plan was the key element in the construction of this new framework. If the catalyst was the geopolitical rivalry between the United States and the Soviet Union, the other dimension of the cold war, embodied in the Marshall Plan, was the development of profound patterns of integration within the Western system. It was within this economic space that post-war globalization of the economic variety was to flourish: the internationalization of production and the re-emergence of a significant international capital market were both fostered within this political context. It was also within the complex accommodations between American power and the interests of its western European allies that decolonization was to be achieved, if not quite in the form or to the timetable sought by any of its participants. But globalization was stimulated not only through the medium of new international conditions: the other prerequisite was the development of domestic polities and structures that could be harmonized with the new liberal economy and which, in turn, would have their domestic goals strengthened by that order.

The post-war international political and economic orders endured largely intact until the end of the 1960s. At that point, they became subject to two sets of challenges. The political order, which rested on unequivocal American leadership, was threatened by the restoration of a more natural distribution of power within the West itself once the anomalies of the immediate post-war period had eroded. Economically, the system which rested upon the primacy of the American dollar was subject to stresses and strains as the dollar weakened and new sources of international monetary disturbance developed. As the great post-war boom drew to a close, there took hold a pessimistic mood that the high point of liberal internationalism had passed and that recession, inflation, and unemployment were now pressing in the direction of a new phase of economic closure. There were gloomy expectations of new protectionism. The erosion of the Bretton Woods exchange system seemed symptomatic of the new instability. Whether these conditions were the effect of the passing of American hegemony, or whether the decline of American power was but one example of the passing of all state political power in the face of globalizing economic trends, was hotly contested. In fact, the choices were not so stark: while economic influences, such as capital mobility, did become much more important, there remained also a residual structural power of the states, paradoxically itself reinforced by aspects of the transnational economy.

If globalization during the cold war was a direct consequence of intra-systemic integration within the Western camp, much of the international relations of the 1970s and 1980s was preoccupied with the endeavour to find a new accommodation on the basis of which that cohesion could be preserved. However, there was also need for new domestic adjustments as the bargain between the liberal capitalist economy and the Keynesian welfare state came under stress.

And yet globalization, particularly in its economic variant, persisted and developed apace through the 1980s and 1990s. If the cold war was the necessary international context for the style of globalization which developed after 1945, then the end of the cold war might be thought a potentially momentous turning-point. Prognoses of a return to the instabilities of the first half of the twentieth century are predicated upon a direct causal link between the cold war and the patterns of integration and transnationalism that have evolved over recent decades. The expectation is that a change in this political structure will generate a new texture of international relations in which the balance will shift, once again, in favour of forms of political and economic fragmentation. However, such a sequence is by no means so clear-cut and depends on the interpretation of the dynamics of the end of the cold war. Some emphasize radical structural change, yielding a political determination less receptive to globalizing forces. If, however, globalization is itself seen to be one of the *causes* of the end of the cold war in the sense that intra-systemic integration eventually became much more important than the other aspect of the cold war—inter-systemic conflict—judgements need to become more nuanced. From this perspective, globalization becomes a point of continuity, not discontinuity, between the cold-war and post-cold-war worlds. The relatively peaceful passing of the cold-war structure may itself provide evidence for such an interpretation. If some analyses have tended to exaggerate the remorseless advance of globalization, others have made the opposite mistake of exaggerating reports of its demise.

If these are the individual parts of the history of globalization in the twentieth century, how might they be combined into some kind of explanatory whole? It is the overall argument of this book that globalization is not a pre-ordained or self-contained trend. Instead, the evidence of this century points to oscillations between globalization and fragmentation, although seldom does the one fully eclipse the other. This oscillation, in turn, is best understood as the complex interplay between attempts to construct international regulatory mechanisms (often supported by the most powerful states) and the domestic needs of the states, and state representatives, which are to be constrained by them. The states are the brokers or mediators between these international and domestic pressures and thus central to any understanding of the processes of globalization and fragmentation. If it is accepted that globalization and fragmentation are indeed salient aspects of twentieth-century international relations, it follows logically that the theoretical separation between systemic and reductionist approaches (as suggested in Waltz 1979) is wholly artificial and prevents a full understanding of these processes: globalization occurs precisely at the interstices where systemic and reductionist forces meet.

How might such a historical perspective be summarized? The following schematic presentation is much simplified but offers a rudimentary explanatory framework. The analysis follows from, and develops, the embryonic exposition found in Gilpin (1987: 132–3, as discussed in Ch. 6 above). Gilpin suggests that in the nineteenth century, international norms (gold standard, *laissez-faire*) took precedence over domestic stability. During the inter-war period, this was reversed, and international norms were abandoned in favour of unilateralist, domestic needs. After 1945, a balance was struck betwen the two and the international and the domestic reinforced each other. This explanatory model is revealing and can be extended. It might then be suggested that since 1970 there has once more been a priority given to international norms in the very specific sense of the disciplines of a highly competitive international market and a new division of international labour.

The claim that international norms are given priority over domestic needs refers solely to the brokerage role played by the state and to the distribution of political costs. During the nineteenth century, maintenance of the stable and open economic order took precedence over domestic stability (where the social costs were borne) until such time as domestic demands were channelled back into the international system. This helps explain the uneasy balance between globalization and fragmentation at the outset of the new century. During the inter-war period, states sought to regain full autonomy to pursue domestic goals by rejecting all international disciplines. In the event, they succeeded only in achieving enough freedom to all but destroy themselves. Accordingly, the urge to re-establish a viable multilateralism after 1945 was strong, but only provided it could accommodate a range of domestic needs. The great success of the period 1945–70 was that it constructed an international order that also harmoniously achieved the national goals of the managerial welfare state. These complex trade-offs were largely made possible by the cold war.

Since 1970, the political costs have again tended to be transferred to the state level, as unemployment, deregulation, and challenges to the welfare state have all been imposed as necessary adjuncts of the drive for international comparative advantage. If this analysis holds, what it suggests is not necessarily that globalization is about to be reversed but that the political costs of its continuation are now much more apparent: in the 1950s and 1960s, when growth seemed universal and permanent, globalization was politically cost free. Such a conclusion seems to fit with the evidence of state incapacity at century's end and with the increasing levels of disillusionment which this has engendered amongst citizens. In large part, the so-called contemporary crisis of the state is a product of its shouldering the political costs of globalization. This is but a reflection of the tensions between international disciplines and domestic needs and the higher political price that states are now having to pay for the levels of globalization that have already occurred.

In the circumstances, it is to be expected that fragmentationist policies will have renewed appeal amongst the motley groups and peoples who have most to lose by continuing globalization: employment sectors in the First World felt to be threatened by the 'export' of jobs to low-wage areas of globalized production; embattled politicians who see globalization eroding their own sources of power and control; traditionalist societies within the Third World disenchanted by the empty promises of development but subject none the less to its seemingly pervasive effects; ethnic identities which may seem to be the only stable anchors in the fast-moving tides of cultural change. Cox is certainly right to claim that 'the elements of opposition to the socially disruptive consequences of globalization are visible' (1996a: 515). Precisely how the balance between globalization and fragmentation will be adjusted depends on the new role that states are able to forge for themselves, and how successfully they manage to mediate between increasingly potent international pressures and the heightened levels of domestic discontent that will inevitably be brought in their wake.

ADLER, E. and CRAWFORD, B. (1991) (eds.), *Progress in Postwar International Relations* (New York).

AHMANN, R., BIRKE, A. M., and HOWARD, M. (1993) (eds.), *The Quest for Stability: Problems of West European Security 1918–1957* (Oxford).

ALDCROFT, D. H. (1993, 3rd edn.), *The European Economy 1914–1990* (London).

—— (1977), *From Versailles to Wall Street 1919–1929* (Berkeley).

AMBROSIUS, L. E. (1987), *Woodrow Wilson and the American Diplomatic Tradition* (New York).

ARCHIBUGI, D. and HELD, D. (1995) (eds.), *Cosmopolitan Democracy: An Agenda for a New World Order* (Oxford).

ARMSTRONG, J. D. (1982), *The Rise of the International Organization* (London).

ARTER, D. (1993), *The Politics of European Integration in the Twentieth Century* (Aldershot).

ARZENI, S. (1994), 'The End of Globalism?', in Clesse, Cooper, and Sakamoto (1994).

ASHWORTH, W. (1975, 3rd edn.), *A Short History of the International Economy since 1850* (London).

BARNET, R. J. (1983), *Allies: America, Europe, Japan since the War* (London).

BARRACLOUGH, G. (1967), *An Introduction to Contemporary History* (Harmondsworth).

BARRY JONES, R. J. (1995), *Globalisation and Interdependence in the International Political Economy: Rhetoric and Reality* (London).

BARTLETT, C. J. (1994, 2nd edn.), *The Global Conflict: The International Rivalry of the Great Powers 1880–1990* (London).

BECKETT, I. F. W. (1989), 'Total War', in Emsley, Marwick, and Simpson (1994).

BELL, C. (1971), *The Conventions of Crisis: A Study in Diplomatic Management* (London).

BELL, P. M. H. (1992), 'The Great War and its Impact', in Hayes (1992).

—— (1986), *The Origins of the Second World War in Europe* (London).

BERNARD, M. (1994), 'Post-Fordism, Transnational Production and the Changing Political Economy', in Stubbs and Underhill (1994).

BESCHLOSS, M. R. and TALBOTT, S. (1993), *At the Highest Levels: The Inside Story of the End of the Cold War* (Boston).

BEST, G. (1995), 'Justice, International Relations and Human Rights', *International Affairs*, 71 (4).

BETTS, R. F. (1985), *Uncertain Dimensions: Western Overseas Empires in the Twentieth Century* (Oxford).

BETTS, R. K. (1992), 'Systems for Peace or Causes of War? Collective Security, Arms Control, and the New Europe', *International Security*, 17 (1).

BIALER, S. (1986), *The Soviet Paradox: External Expansion, Internal Decline* (London).

BIANCO, L. (1971), *Origins of the Chinese Revolution, 1915–1949* (Stanford, Calif.).

BOND, B. (1984), *War and Society in Europe 1870–1970* (London).

BOOTH, K. (1991) (ed.), *New Thinking about Strategy and International Security* (London).

—— and SMITH, S. (1995) (eds.), *International Relations Theory Today* (Oxford).

BOWKER, M. and BROWN, R. (1993) (eds.), *From Cold War to Collapse: Theory and World Politics in the 1980s* (Cambridge).

—— and WILLIAMS, P. (1988), *Superpower Detente: A Reappraisal* (London).

BOZEMAN, A. (1984), 'A Multicultural World', in Bull and Watson (1984).

BRETHERTON, C. and PONTON, G. (1996) (eds.), *Global Politics: An Introduction* (Oxford).

BRETT, E. A. (1985), *The World Economy since the War: The Politics of Uneven Development* (London).

BREWIN, C. (1992), 'Research in a Global Context: A Discussion of Toynbee's Legacy', *Review of International Studies*, 18 (2).

BRIDGE, F. R. and BULLEN, R. (1980), *The Great Powers and the European States System 1815–1914* (New York).

BRITTON, A. (1983), 'World Finance and National Monetary Problems', in Freedman (1993).

BROWN, P. and CROMPTON, R. (1994) (eds.), *A New Europe? Economic Restructuring and Social Exclusion* (London).

BROWN, R. (1995), 'Globalization and the End of the National Project', in Macmillan and Linklater (1995).

BROWN, S. (1994), 'Building Order and Justice in the Emerging Global Polyarchy', in Clesse, Cooper, and Sakamoto (1994).

BUCHAN, A. (1974), *The End of the Postwar Era: A New Balance of World Power* (London).

BULL, H. and WATSON, A. (1984) (eds.), *The Expansion of International Society* (Oxford).

BUNSELMEYER, R. E. (1975), *The Cost of the War 1914–1919: British Economic War Aims and the Origins of Reparations* (Hamden, Conn.).

BURK, K. (1995), 'American Foreign Economic Policy and Lend-Lease', in Lane and Temperley (1995).

BURLEY, A.-M. (1993), 'Regulating the World: Multilateralism, International Law, and the Projection of the New Deal Regulatory State', in J. G. Ruggie (ed.), *Multilateralism Matters* (New York).

BUSCH, M. L. and MILNER, H. V. (1994), 'The Future of the International Trading System: International Firms, Regionalism, and Domestic Politics', in Stubbs and Underhill (1994).

BUZAN, B. (1994), 'The Interdependence of Security and Economic Issues in the "New World Order" ', in Stubbs and Underhill (1994).

—— (1991), *People, States and Fear: An Agenda for International Security Studies in the Post-Cold War Era* (London).

——, JONES, C., and LITTLE, R. (1993), *The Logic of Anarchy: Neorealism to Structural Realism* (New York).

—— and SEGAL, G. (1994), 'Rethinking East Asian Security', *Survival*, 36 (2).

CABLE, V. (1995), 'What is International Economic Security?', *International Affairs*, 71 (2).

CAIN, P. J. and HOPKINS, A. G. (1993), *British Imperialism: Crisis and Deconstruction 1914–1990* (London).

CALLEO, D. (1987), *Beyond American Hegemony: The Future of the Western Alliance* (Brighton).

—— (1978), *The German Problem Reconsidered: Germany and the World Order, 1870 to the Present* (Cambridge).

CARR, E. H. (1940), *The Twenty Years' Crisis* (London).

CECCO, M. de (1974), *Money and Empire: The International Gold Standard, 1890–1914* (Oxford).

CERNY, P. G. (1995), 'Globalization and the Changing Logic of Collective Action', *International Organization*, 49 (4).

—— (1993), 'Plurilateralism: Structural Differentiation and Functional Conflict in the Post-Cold War World Order', *Millennium*, 22 (1).

CHIPMAN, J. (1993), 'Managing the Politics of Parochialism', *Survival*, 35 (1).

CLARK, I. (1989), *The Hierarchy of States: Reform and Resistance in the International Order* (Cambridge).

CLESSE, A., COOPER, R., and SAKAMOTO, Y. (1994) (eds.), *The International System after the Collapse of the East–West Order* (Dordrecht).

COHEN, W. I. (1993), *America in the Age of Soviet Power 1945–1991. The Cambridge History of American Foreign Relations*, iv (Cambridge).

COKER, C. (1994), *War and the Twentieth Century: A Study of War and Modern Consciousness* (London).

COSTIGLIOLA, F. (1984), *Awkward Dominion: American Political, Economic, and Cultural Relations with Europe, 1919–1933* (Ithaca, NY).

COX, M. (1994), 'Rethinking the End of the Cold War', *Review of International Studies*, 20 (2).

COX, R. W. (1996*a*), 'Multilateralism and World Order', in *Approaches to World Order* (Cambridge).

—— (1996*b*), 'Globalization, Multilateralism, and Democracy', in *Approaches to World Order* (Cambridge).

—— (1993), 'Production and Security', in Dewitt, Haglund, and Kirton (1993).

—— (1992), 'Towards a Post-hegemonic Conceptualization of World Order', in Rosenau and Czempiel (1992).

—— (1987), *Production, Power, and World Order: Social Forces in the Making of History* (New York).

CROCKATT, R. (1995), *The Fifty Years War: The United States and the Soviet Union in World Politics, 1941–1991* (London).

CZEMPIEL, E.-O. and ROSENAU, J. N. (1989) (eds.), *Global Changes and Theoretical Challenges: Approaches to World Politics for the 1990s* (Lexington, Mass.).

DARWIN, J. (1991), *The End of the British Empire: The Historical Debate* (Oxford).

DAVID, S. R. (1992/3), 'Why the Third World Still Matters', *International Security*, 17 (3).

DEPORTE, A. W. (1979), *Europe between the Super Powers: The Enduring Balance* (New Haven, Conn.).

DEUDNEY, D. and IKENBERRY, J. G. (1994), 'After the Long War', *Foreign Policy*, 94.

DEWITT, D., HAGLUND, D., and KIRTON, J. (1993) (eds.), *Building a New Global Order: Emerging Trends in International Security* (Toronto).

DIBB, P. (1986), *The Soviet Union: The Incomplete Superpower* (London).

DICKEN, P. (1992, 2nd edn.), *Global Shift: The Internationalization of Economic Activity* (London).

DIVINE, R. A. (1967), *Second Chance: The Triumph of Internationalism in America During World War II* (New York).

DONNELLY, J. (1993), *International Human Rights* (Boulder, Colo.).

DORAN, C. F. (1991), *Systems in Crisis: New Imperatives of High Politics at Century's End* (Cambridge).

DUNN, J. (1995) (ed.), *Contemporary Crisis of the Nation State* (Oxford).

DUNNING, J. (1994), *The Globalization of Business* (London).

EDEN, L. and POTTER, E. H. (1993) (eds.), *Multinationals in the Global Political Economy* (London).

EMSLEY, C., MARWICK, A., and SIMPSON, W. (1989) (eds.), *War, Peace and Social Change in Twentieth-Century Europe* (Milton Keynes).

EVANS, P. B., RUESCHEMEYER, D., and SKOCPOL, T. (1985), 'On the Road towards a More Adequate Understanding of the State', in *Bringing the State Back In* (Cambridge).

FALK, R. (1995), 'Regionalism and World Order After the Cold War', *Australian Journal of International Affairs*, 49 (1).

FAWCETT, L. and HURRELL, A. (1995) (eds.), *Regionalism in World Politics: Regional Organization and International Order* (Oxford).

FEATHERSTONE, M. (1990) (ed.), *Global Culture: Nationalism, Globalisation and Modernity* (London).

FOREMAN-PECK, J. A. (1995, 2nd edn.; 1983, 1st edn.), *A History of the World Economy: International Economic Relations since 1850* (Brighton).

FREEDMAN, L. (1983) (ed.), *The Troubled Alliance: Atlantic Relations in the 1980s* (London).

FRIEDEN, J. A. (1991), 'Invested Interests: The Politics of National Economic Policies in a World of Global Finance', *International Organization*, 45 (4).

FUKUYAMA, F. (1992), *The End of History and the Last Man* (London).

GADDIS, J. L. (1992/3), 'International Relations Theory and the End of the Cold War', *International Security*, 17 (3).

—— (1992a), *The United States and the End of the Cold War: Implications, Reconsiderations, Provocations* (New York).

—— (1992b), 'The Cold War, the Long Peace, and the Future', in Hogan (1992).

—— (1986), 'The Corporatist Synthesis: A Skeptical View', *Diplomatic History*, 10 (4).

GAMBLE, A. and PAYNE, A. (1996) (eds.), *Regionalism and World Order* (Houndmills).

GARTHOFF, R. L. (1985), *Detente and Confrontation: American–Soviet Relations from Nixon to Reagan* (Washington DC).

GARTON ASH, T. (1994), *In Europe's Name: Germany and the Divided Continent* (London).

GIDDENS, A. (1985), *The Nation-State and Violence* (Oxford).

GILBERT, F. and LARGE, D. C. (1991, 4th edn.), *The End of the European Era: 1890 to the Present* (New York).

GILL, S. (1995), 'Globalisation, Market Civilisation, and Disciplinary Neoliberalism', *Millennium*, 24 (3).

—— (1993), 'Neo-Liberalism and the Shift Towards a US-Centred Transnational Hegemony', in Overbeek (1993).

—— and LAW, D. (1988), *The Global Political Economy: Perspectives, Problems and Policies* (Hemel Hempstead).

GILPIN, R. (1987), *The Political Economy of International Relations* (Princeton).

—— (1981), *War and Change in World Politics* (Cambridge).

—— (1971), 'The Politics of Transnational Economic Relations', in Keohane and Nye (1971).

GONG, G. W. (1984), *The Standard of 'Civilization' in International Society* (Oxford).

GOODMAN, G. K. (1991), *Japanese Cultural Policies in Southeast Asia during World War 2* (London).

GRANT, C. (1995), 'Equity in International Relations: A Third World Perspective', *International Affairs*, 71 (3).

GROOM, A. J. R. and LIGHT, M. (1994) (eds.), *Contemporary International Relations: A Guide to Theory* (London).

GROSSER, A. (1980), *The Western Alliance* (London).

GUIBERNAU, M. (1996), *Nationalisms: The Nation-State and Nationalism in the Twentieth Century* (Oxford).

HAGIHARA, N., IRIYE, A., NIVAT, G., and WINDSOR, P. (1985) (eds.), *Experiencing the Twentieth Century* (Tokyo).

HALLIDAY, F. (1994), *Rethinking International Relations* (London).

—— (1993), 'The Cold War as Inter-Systemic Conflict—Initial Theses', in Bowker and Brown (1993).

—— (1989), *Cold War, Third World: An Essay on Soviet–American Relations* (London).

—— (1986, 2nd edn.), *The Making of the Second Cold War* (London).

HARDACH, G. (1977), *The First World War, 1914–1918* (London).

HARRIS, N. (1986), *The End of the Third World: Newly Industrialising Countries and the Decline of an Ideology* (London).

HASSNER, P. (1993), 'Beyond Nationalism and Internationalism', *Survival*, 35 (2).

HAWTHORN, G. (1995), 'The Crises of Southern States', in Dunn (1995).

HAYES, P. (1992) (ed.), *Themes in Modern European History* (London).

HELD, D. (1995a), *Democracy and the Global Order: From the Modern State to Cosmopolitan Governance* (Oxford).

—— (1995b), 'Democracy and the International Order', in Archibugi and Held (1995).

HELLEINER, E. (1994), 'From Bretton Woods to Global Finance: A World Turned Upside Down', in Stubbs and Underhill (1994).

HIRST, P. (1995), *Globalisation in Question* (Political Economy Research Centre, University of Sheffield, Occasional Paper no. 11).

—— and THOMPSON, G. (1996), *Globalization in Question: The International Economy and the Possibilities of Governance* (Oxford).

HOBSBAWM, E. J. (1994), *Age of Extremes: The Short Twentieth Century 1914–1991* (London).

—— (1990), *Nations and Nationalism since 1870: Programme, Myth, Reality* (Cambridge).

—— (1987), *The Age of Empire 1875–1914* (London).

HOFFMANN, S. (1995/6), 'The Politics and Ethics of Military Intervention', *Survival*, 37 (4).

—— (1995), 'The Crisis of Liberal Internationalism', *Foreign Policy*, 95.

HOGAN, M. J. (1992) (ed.), *The End of the Cold War: Its Meaning and Implications* (Cambridge).

—— (1991), 'Corporatism', in Hogan and Paterson (eds.), *Explaining the History of American Foreign Relations* (Cambridge).

—— (1987), *The Marshall Plan: America, Britain, and the Reconstruction of Western Europe, 1947–1952* (Cambridge).

—— (1986), 'Corporatism: A Positive Appraisal', *Diplomatic History*, 10 (4).

HOLLAND, R. F. (1985), *European Decolonization 1918–1981* (London).

HOLSTI, K. J. (1991), *Peace and War: Armed Conflicts and International Order 1648–1989* (Cambridge).

HOPF, T. (1993), 'Getting the End of the Cold War Wrong', *International Security*, 18 (2).

HOWARD, M. (1978), *War and the Liberal Conscience* (London).

HUNTINGTON, S. P. (1994), 'The Clash of Civilizations?', in Clesse, Cooper, and Sakamoto (1994).

—— (1993), 'Why International Primacy Matters', *International Security*, 17 (4).

HURRELL, A. (1995a), 'Explaining the Resurgence of Regionalism in World Politics', *Review of International Studies*, 21 (4).

—— (1995b), 'A Crisis of Ecological Viability? Global Environmental Changes and the Nation State', in Dunn (1995).

—— and Woods, N. (1995), 'Globalisation and Inequality', *Millennium*, 24 (3).

IKENBERRY, J. G. (1995), 'Funk de Siecle: Impasses of Western Industrial Society at Century's End', *Millennium*, 24 (1).

International Institute for Strategic Studies (1991/2), *New Dimensions of International Security* (Adelphi Paper no. 265; London).

IRIYE, A. (1993), *The Globalizing of America 1913–1945, The Cambridge History of American Foreign Relations*, iii (Cambridge).

—— (1987), *The Origins of the Second World War in Asia and the Pacific* (London).

—— (1985), 'War as Peace, Peace as War', in Hagihara *et al.* (1985).

—— (1981), *Power and Culture* (Cambridge, Mass.).

JACKSON, R. H. (1990), *Quasi-States: Sovereignty, International Relations and the Third World* (Cambridge).

JACOBSON, J. (1983), 'Is there a New International History of the 1920s?', *American Historical Review*, 88 (3).

JERVIS, R. (1993), 'International Primacy: Is the Game Worth the Candle?', *International Security*, 17 (4).

—— (1991/2), 'The Future of World Politics: Will it Resemble the Past?', *International Security*, 16 (3).

JOHNSON, P. (1991, rev. edn.), *A History of the Modern World: From 1917 to the 1990s* (London).

JOLL, J. (1985), 'Introduction: Some Reflections on the Twentieth Century', in Hagihara *et al.* (1985).

JONES, R. E. (1993), 'Thinking Big', *Review of International Studies*, 19 (2).

JUERGENSMEYER, M. (1993), *The New Cold War? Religious Nationalism Confronts the Secular State* (Berkeley).

KALDOR, M. (1995), 'Europe, Nation-States and Nationalism', in Archibugi and Held (1995).

KAVIRAS, S. (1995), 'Crisis of the Nation State in India', in Dunn (1995).

KEDOURIE, E. (1984), 'A New International Disorder', in Bull and Watson (1984).

KEIGER, J. (1983), *France and the Origins of the First World War* (London).

KELLAS, J. G. (1991), *The Politics of Nationalism and Ethnicity* (London).

KENNEDY, P. (1993), *Preparing for the Twenty-First Century* (London).

—— (1988), *The Rise and Fall of the Great Powers* (London).

KENWOOD, A. G. and LOUGHEED, A. L. (1992, 3rd edn.), *The Growth of the International Economy 1820–1990* (London).

KEOHANE, R. O. (1989a), 'Hegemonic Leadership and US Foreign and Economic Policy in the "Long Decade" of the 1950s', in *International Institutions and State Power* (Boulder, Colo.).

—— (1989b), 'The Theory of Hegemonic Stability and Changes in International Economic Regimes 1967–77', in *International Institutions and State Power* (Boulder, Colo.).

—— (1986) (ed.), *Neorealism and its Critics* (New York).

—— (1984), *After Hegemony: Cooperation and Discord in the World Political Economy* (Princeton).

—— and Nye, J. S. (1977), *Power and Interdependence: World Politics in Transition* (Boston).

—— —— (1971) (eds.), *Transnational Relations in World Politics* (Cambridge, Mass.).

KEYLOR, W. R. (1984), *The Twentieth Century World: An International History* (New York).

KEYNES, J. M. (1919), *The Economic Consequences of the Peace* (London).

KIERNAN, V. G. (1982), *European Empires from Conquest to Collapse, 1815–1960* (London).

KINDLEBERGER, C. P. (1987), *The World in Depression 1929–1939* (Harmondsworth).

KIRBY, D. (1986), *War, Peace and Revolution: International Socialism at the Crossroads* (Aldershot).

KISSINGER, H. (1995), *Diplomacy* (New York).

KNAPTON, E. J. and DERRY, T. K. (1967), *Europe and the World since 1914* (London).

KOCH, W. W. (1984, 2nd edn.) (ed.), *The Origins of the First World War* (London).

KRASNER, S. D. (1985), *Structural Conflict: The Third World Against Global Liberalism* (Berkeley).

LAFEBER, W. (1992), 'An End to *Which* Cold War?', in Hogan (1992).

LANE, A. and TEMPERLEY, H. (1995) (eds.), *The Rise and Fall of the Grand Alliance* (London).

LANGHORNE, R. (1981), *The Collapse of the Concert of Europe: International Politics 1890–1914* (London).

LAYNE, C. (1994), 'Kant or Cant: The Myth of the Democratic Peace', *International Security*, 19 (2).

—— (1993), 'The Unipolar Illusion: Why New Powers will Rise', *International Security*, 17 (4).

—— and SCHWARZ, B. (1993), 'American Hegemony—Without an Enemy', *Foreign Policy*, 92.

LEBOW, R. N. and RISSE-KAPPEN, T. (1995) (eds.), *International Relations Theory and the End of the Cold War* (New York).

LEFFLER, M. P. (1992), *A Preponderance of Power: National Security, the Truman Administration, and the Cold War* (Stanford).

—— (1991), 'National Security', in M. J. Hogan and T. E. Paterson (eds.), *Explaining the History of American Foreign Relations* (Cambridge).

—— (1979), *The Elusive Quest: America's Pursuit of European Stability and French Security, 1919–1933* (Chapel Hill, NC).

LEVIN, N. G. (1968), *Woodrow Wilson and World Politics* (New York).

LIEVEN, D. C. B. (1983), *Russia and the Origins of the First World War* (London).

LIPSCHUTZ, R. D. (1992), 'Reconstructing World Politics: The Emergence of Global Civil Society', *Millennium*, 21 (3).

LITWAK, R. S. (1984), *Detente and the Nixon Doctrine: American Foreign Policy and the Pursuit of Stability, 1969–1976* (Cambridge).

LOWE, J. (1994), *The Great Powers, Imperialism and the German Problem, 1865–1925* (London).

MCCGWIRE, M. (1991), *Perestroika and Soviet National Security* (Brookings Institution, Washington, DC).

MACFARLANE, S. N. (1991), 'The Impact of Superpower Collaboration on the Third World', in Weiss and Kessler (1991).

MCGREW, A. G., *et al.* (1992) (eds.), *Global Politics* (Oxford).

MCKINLAY, R. D. and LITTLE, R. (1986), *Global Problems and World Order* (London).

MACMILLAN, J. and LINKLATER, A. (1995) (eds.), *Boundaries in Question: New Directions in International Relations* (London).

MCNEILL, W. H. (1983), *The Pursuit of Power* (Oxford).

MAIER, C. S. (1995), 'The Presence of the Superpowers in Europe (1947–54): An Overview', in Varsori (1995).

—— (1993), 'The Making of Pax Americana', in Ahmann, Birke, and Howard (1993).

—— (1989), 'Recasting Bourgeois Europe', in Emsley, Marwick, and Simpson (1989).

—— (1987), *In Search of Stability: Explorations in Historical Political Economy* (Cambridge).

MAIER, C. S. (1985), 'The State and Economic Organization in the Twentieth Century', in Hagihara *et al.* (1985).

MANDELBAUM, M. (1981), *The Nuclear Revolution* (Cambridge).

MANN, M. (1993), *The Sources of Social Power,* Vol. II: *The Rise of Classes and Nation-States, 1760–1914* (Cambridge).

MARKS, S. (1976), *The Illusion of Peace: International Relations in Europe 1918–1933* (London).

MARSHALL, D. D. (1996), 'Understanding Late-Twentieth Century Capitalism: Reassessing the Globalization Theme', *Government and Opposition*, 31 (2).

MARTIN, A. (1994), 'Labour, the Keynesian Welfare State, and the Changing International Political Economy', in Stubbs and Underhill (1994).

MARWICK, A. (1991, 2nd ed.), *The Deluge: British Society and the First World War* (London).

MASTNY, V. (1995), 'Europe in the Aftermath of the Second World War (1945–7): An Overview', in Varsori (1995).

—— (1994), 'The Legacy of the Old International Order' in Clesse, Cooper, and Sakamoto (1994).

MAYALL, J. (1990), *Nationalism and International Society* (Cambridge).

MAYER, A. J. (1968), *Politics and Diplomacy of Peacemaking* (London).

—— (1959), *Political Origins of the New Diplomacy* (New Haven, Conn.).

MEARSHEIMER, J. (1994/5), 'The False Promise of International Institutions', *International Security*, 19 (3).

—— (1990), 'Back to the Future: Instability in Europe After the Cold War', *International Security*, 15 (1).

MELANDRI, P. (1995), 'The United States and the Process of European Integration', in Varsori (1995).

MILLER, D. (1995), *On Nationality* (Oxford).

MILWARD, A. S. (1992), *The European Rescue of the Nation-State* (London).

—— (1984), *The Reconstruction of Western Europe, 1945–1951* (London).

—— (1977), *War, Economy and Society 1939–1945* (London).

MODELSKI, G. (1987), *Long Cycles in World Politics* (London).

MUELLER, J. (1992), 'Quiet Cataclysm: Some Afterthoughts on World War III', in Hogan (1992).

MURPHY, C. N. (1994), *International Organization and Industrial Change: Global Governance since 1850* (Oxford).

NOGEE, J. L. (1981), 'The Soviet Union in the Third World: Successes and Failures', in R. H. Donaldson (ed.), *The Soviet Union in the Third World: Successes and Failures* (Boulder, Colo.).

NORTHEDGE, F. S. (1986), *The League of Nations* (Leicester).

NORTON, A. R. (1991), 'The Security Legacy of the 1980s in the Third World' in Weiss and Kessler (1991).

NYE, J. S. (1990), *Bound to Lead: The Changing Nature of American Power* (New York).

OFFER, A. (1989), *The First World War: An Agrarian Interpretation* (Oxford).

OHMAE, K. (1995), *The End of the Nation State: The Rise of Regional Economies* (London).

OVERBEEK, H. (1993) (ed.), *Restructuring Hegemony in the Global Political Economy: The Rise of Transnational Neo-Liberalism* (London).

OVERY, R. J. (1989), 'Hitler's War and the German Economy: A Reinterpretation', in Emsley, Marwick, and Simpson (1989).

—— (1987), The Origins of the Second World War (London).

PAGE, M. E. (1987) (ed.), *Africa and the First World War* (London).

PALME, O.; Report of the Independent Commission on Disarmament and Security Issues (1982), *Common Security: A Programme for Disarmament* (London).

PANIC, M. (1988), *National Management of the International Economy* (London).

PARKINS, C. (1996), 'North–South Relations and Globalization after the Cold War', in Bretherton and Ponton (1996).

PINDER, J. (1983), 'Interdependence: Problem or Solution', in Freedman (1983).

POLLARD, S. (1993), 'Economic Interdependence and Economic Protectionism', in Ahmann, Birke and Howard (1993).

PREST, A. R. (1948), *War Economics of Primary Producing Countries* (Cambridge).

REYNOLDS, D. (1991), *Britannia Overruled: British Policy and World Power in the Twentieth Century* (London).

RISSE-KAPPEN, T. (1995a) (ed.), *Bringing Transnational Relations Back In: Non-State Actors, Domestic Structures and International Institutions* (Cambridge).

—— (1995b), 'Ideas do not Float Freely: Transnational Coalitions, Domestic Structures, and the end of the Cold War', in Lebow and Risse-Kappen (1995).

ROBERTS, A. (1995/6), 'From San Francisco to Sarajevo: the UN and the use of Force', *Survival*, 37 (4).

—— (1994), 'The Crisis in UN Peacekeeping', *Survival*, 36 (3).

ROBERTSON, R. (1992), *Globalization: Social Theory and Global Culture* (London).

ROSENAU, J. N. (1990), *Turbulence in World Politics: A Theory of Change and Continuity* (London).

—— and CZEMPIEL, E.-O. (1992) (eds.), *Governance without Government: Order and Change in World Politics* (Cambridge).

ROSENBERG, J. (1994), *The Empire of Civil Society: A Critique of the Realist Theory of International Relations* (London).

ROSS, G. (1983), *The Great Powers and the Decline of the European States System* (London).

RUGGIE, J. G. (1993), 'Multilateralism: The Anatomy of an Institution', in Ruggie (1993).

—— (1991), 'Embedded Liberalism Revisited: Institutions and Progress in International Economic Relations', in Adler and Crawford (1991).

RUIGROK, W. and VAN TULDER, R. (1995), *The Logic of International Restructuring* (London).

SAID, E. W. (1993), *Culture and Imperialism* (London).

SAURIN, J. (1995), 'The End of International Relations? The State and International Theory in the Age of Globalization', in Macmillan and Linklater (1995).

SCHOLTE, J. A. (1993), 'From Power Politics to Social Change: An Alternative Focus for International Studies', *Review of International Studies*, 19 (1).

SHARP, A. (1991), *The Versailles Settlement: Peacemaking in Paris, 1919* (Houndmills).

SHAW, M. (1994a), *Global Society and International Relations* (Oxford).

—— (1994b), 'Civil Society and Global Politics: Beyond a Social Movements Approach', *Millennium*, 23 (3).

SHONFIELD, A. (1976) (ed.), *International Economic Relations of the Western World, 1959–1971*, vol. 1: *Politics and Trade* (London).

SINGER, M. and WILDAVSKY, A. (1993), *The Real World Order: Zones of Peace/Zones of Turmoil* (Chatham, NJ).

SKOCPOL, T. (1985), 'Bringing the State Back In: Strategies of Analysis in Current Research' in Evans, Rueschemeyer, and Skocpol (eds.), *Bringing the State Back In* (Cambridge).

SKOLNIKOFF, E. B. (1993), *The Elusive Transformation: Science, Technology, and the Evolution of International Politics* (Princeton).

SMITH, A. D. (1995), *Nations and Nationalism in a Global Era* (Oxford).
—— (1993), 'The Ethnic Sources of Nationalism', *Survival*, 35 (1).
SMITH, H. L. (1986) (ed.), *War and Social Change: British Society in the Second World War* (Manchester).
SMITH, T. (1981), *The Pattern of Imperialism: The United States, Great Britain, and the Late-Industrializing World since 1815* (Cambridge).
SPYBEY, T. (1996), *Globalization and World Society* (Oxford).
STEINER, Z. (1993), 'The League of Nations', in Ahmann, Birke, and Howard (1993).
—— (1977), *Britain and the Origins of the First World War* (London).
STEVENSON, D. (1988), *The First World War and International Politics* (Oxford).
STEVENSON, J. (1986), 'Planners' Moon? The Second World War and the Planning Movement', in H. L. Smith (1986).
STEVENSON, R. W. (1985), *The Rise and Fall of Detente* (London).
STORRY, R. (1979), *Japan and the Decline of the West in Asia* (London).
STRANGE, S. (1995), 'The Limits of Politics', *Government and Opposition*, 30 (3).
—— (1993), 'Big Business and the State', in Eden and Potter (1993).
STUBBS, R. and UNDERHILL, G. R. D. (1994), (eds.), *Political Economy and the Changing Global Order* (London).
THOMAS, C. (1987), *In Search of Security: The Third World in International Relations* (Brighton).
THOMAS, S. (1995), 'The Global Resurgence of Religion and the Study of World Politics', *Millennium*, 24 (2).
THOMSON, J. E. and KRASNER, S. D. (1989), 'Global Transactions and the Consolidation of Sovereignty', in Czempiel and Rosenau (1989).
TILLY, C. (1985), 'War Making and State Making as Organized Crime', in Evans, Rueschemeyer, and Skocpol (1985).
TRACHTENBERG, M. (1980), *Reparation in World Politics* (New York).
ULAM, A. B. (1968), *Expansion and Coexistence: The History of Soviet Foreign Policy from 1917–1967* (London).
VARSORI, A. (1995) (ed.), *Europe 1945–1990s: The End of an Era?* (Macmillan, London).
VATTER, H. G. (1985), *The US Economy in World War II* (New York).
VINCENT, R. J. (1984), 'Racial Equality', in Bull and Watson (1984).
VON LAUE, T. H. (1994), 'Globalism and Counter-Globalism: Present Trends and the Future', in Clesse, Cooper, and Sakamoto (1994).
—— (1987), *The World Revolution of Westernization: The Twentieth Century in Global Perspective* (New York).
WALKER, M. (1993), *The Cold War and the Making of the Modern World* (London).
WALKER, R. B. J. (1994), 'Social Movements/World Politics', *Millennium*, 23 (3).
—— (1984) (ed.), *Culture, Ideology, and World Order* (Boulder, Colo.).
WALL, R. and WINTER, J. (1988) (eds.), *The Upheaval of War: Family, Work and Welfare in Europe, 1914–1918* (Cambridge).
WALLACE, W. (1995), 'Rescue or Retreat? The Nation State in Western Europe, 1945–93', in Dunn (1995).
WALLERSTEIN, I. (1991), *Geopolitics and Geoculture: Essays on the Changing World-System* (Cambridge).
WALTER, A. (1991), *World Power and World Money: The Role of Hegemony and International Monetary Order* (Hemel Hempstead).
WALTZ, K. (1993), 'The Emerging Structure of International Politics', *International Security*, 18 (2).

—— (1979), *Theory of International Politics* (Reading, Mass.).

WALWORTH, A. (1986), *Wilson and his Peacemakers: American Diplomacy at the Paris Peace Conference, 1919* (New York).

WATERS, M. (1995), *Globalization* (London).

WEINBERG, G. L. (1994), *A World at Arms: A Global History of World War II* (New York).

WEISS, T.G. and KESSLER, M. A. (1991) (eds.), *Third World Security in the Post-Cold War Era* (Boulder, Colo.).

WHELAN, J. G. and DIXON, M. J. (1986), *The Soviet Union in the Third World: Threat to World Peace?* (Washington, DC).

WINTER, J. (1988), 'Some Paradoxes of the First World War', in Wall and Winter (1988).

—— (1986), 'The Demographic Consequences of the War', in H. L. Smith (1996).

WOHLFORTH, W. C. (1994/5), 'Realism and the End of the Cold War', *International Security*, 19 (3).

WYATT-WALTER, A. (1995), 'Regionalism, Globalization, and World Economic Order', in Fawcett and Hurrell (1995).

YERGIN, D. (1980), *Shattered Peace: The Origins of the Cold War and the National Security State* (Harmondsworth).

INDEX